Selling Sex in the Silver Valley

A Business Doing Pleasure

Dr. Heather Branstetter

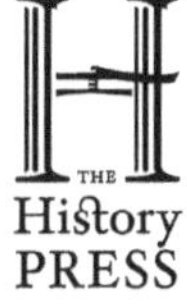

The History Press

Published by The History Press
Charleston, SC
www.historypress.net

Front cover, bottom: Wallace, Idaho, looking south along Sixth Street. *Historic Wallace Preservation Society*. *Front cover, top*: Pinup girl from 1962 Lux Rooms/Plaza Rooms calendar. *Oasis Bordello Museum display; photo by Heather Branstetter*. *Back cover, top*: Madam Effie Rogan in 1906 and madam Connie Foss in 1908. *Barnard-Stockbridge Collection, University of Idaho Library Special Collections and Archives*. *Back cover, bottom*: Pinup girl from 1957 Lux calendar. *Oasis Bordello Museum display; photo by Heather Branstetter.*

First published 2017

Manufactured in the United States

ISBN 9781467136563

Library of Congress Control Number: 2016961715

For Joann Branstetter and Mom and Dad.

In memory of Ken Branstetter.

To the women and men of Wallace, Idaho, past, present and future. I am thankful for the opportunity to serve this community.

Contents

Preface

The goal of this book is to relate the way the Silver Valley valued and validated its historic traditions of prostitution, drinking and gambling in accordance with hardrock miners' "work hard, play hard" approach to life. Much of our community's past has been preserved in memories and stories passed on through oral history tradition, but if these stories are not written down, our history fades when memory keepers pass away. I have tried to honor the multiple perspectives I encountered during my research.

Sex work in Wallace, Idaho, was decriminalized, socially acceptable and even embraced by community members from 1884 to 1991. It was also an equilibrium that balanced complex power relationships among madams, sex workers, town leaders, citizens and clients. The women who worked in the Silver Valley's rooms provided a valued service by offering sex, companionship and discretion to rough mining towns in need of stability.

In what follows, I offer a variety of viewpoints to show how our collective memories include negotiated values and culture created through myths, oral histories and official written records. I incorporated information from published sources, archival materials and interviews with a range of people. The book organized itself according to chronology and research materials: the first part is written more like a traditional history while the second two parts feature more primary sources with less interpretive analysis. I tried to balance the personal privacy of those who lived this history with my feeling that we should preserve their stories and knowledge for future generations. Since sex work is still a stigmatized issue, thirty-eight of ninety-nine oral history research participants requested anonymity. I recorded most of the interviews for quotation accuracy but only name participants according to their personal preference.

For those who want content warnings, I should mention what may or may not be obvious: this book discusses sex in some detail, especially parts two and three. Drug use, violence and sexual assault are also a part of the narrative at times. Certain classes of people will consider some of the language in this book "inappropriate for polite conversation." Reader discretion is advised.

Versions of the information presented here have been published in *Rhetoric Society Quarterly* and *Peitho*. I have also shared this research on the public radio show *With Good Reason* and my website, abusinessdoingpleasure.com, where you can read more.

Acknowledgments

There are many people who contributed to this project in a huge way. Mitch Alexander, John Amonson, Rich Asher, Dick Caron, Kristi Gnaedinger, Dee Greer, Tom Harman, Jack Johnson, Richard Magnuson, Jim and Peggy McReynolds, Bill Mooney, Cathleen Ryan and Chase Sanborn really helped make this book happen. I am also grateful to Tammy Copelan at the Wallace District Mining Museum; Shauna Hillman at the Northern Pacific Depot Museum; Eva Truean, Linda Harbuckle and Zach Darrah at the Oasis Bordello Museum; Bernie Ludwick and Annette Kologi at the Wallace Public Library; Marla Anson and Debbie Ruggles at the District Court; Joanne Jaggard and Penny Michael at Wallace City Hall; Marilyn Hinsz in the Shoshone County Assessor's Office; Janice Shiner in County Records; Don Hoffman and Mark Burmeister at City Limits Pub; and Mike Murray and Karen Mooney at Rossi Insurance. I often wrote at the 1313 Club and was grateful for their delicious coffee and breakfast. The Dayrock offered a nice place to work in the evenings. Everyone at Wallace Brewing Company supported this project in more ways than they know! Marcy Hayman and Callie Hegbloom, thanks for your encouragement. Artie Crisp, Julie Foster and Julia Turner at The History Press, I appreciate your interest, attentive reading and guidance. I can't thank you all enough.

I acknowledge research participants by name in the bibliography if they have chosen to be "on the record," but there were also many people helping me "off the record." Some of their words are quoted anonymously in this book. There were also many people I did not quote directly, but they influenced my thinking, offered important insights or helped me with the research. Here is a list of those who are not otherwise acknowledged in the record of citations: Mike and Sam Achord; David Albertini; Clyde Albright; Hollis Anderson; John Andrasco; Nichole and Tom Baumann; Carole and Doug Bell; Eileen Bieber; Cheri Breidt; Jerome Bunde; Bill Carlson; Bobby Christian; Dick and Antje Cripe; Dave DeRoos; Norma Douglas; Bob Dunsmore; Rob Fairweather; Barbara and Wray Featherstone; Robert Field; Doris Fleming; Nick Fluge; Anita Garcia; Gian Ghigleri; Fred and Gordon Gibler; Denny Gravely; Wayne Greenfield; Sano Haldi; Tommy Hayes; Phil and LouElla Hodges; Archie Hulsizer; Dan Hussey; Steve Jemmings; Wayne Jurkovich; Jerry Keane; Troy Lambert; Mike Lavigne; Paul Levitch; Jim Lieschner; Dick Lilienkamp; Leigh, Lori and Lynn Lutich; Elmer and Corki Mattila; Dan McGee; Ken McKinnon; Marty McNamee; Shirley Messerly; Dottie Mitchell; Ted Nickelby; Brian Nixon; Bruce Nyman; Patti Pennington; Loren and Kay Pitt; Roy Reel; Severin Robinson; Betty Scott; Ted Sproles; Bryan Stepro; Dylan Stiegemeier; Scott Stranger; Randy Thatcher; Ellie Thompson; Amy Tosh; and Jeri and Susan Walker.

I am grateful for the teachers who taught me how to think and write: Janet Adams, Dan Anderson, Bill Balthrop, David Barber, Kim Barnes, Carole Blair, Jane Danielewicz, Tom Drake, Rick Fehrenbacher, Gregg Flaxman, Karen Frank, Nick Gier, Karen Hegbloom, Jordynn Jack, Jason Johnstone-Yellin, Douglas Lind, Erika Lindemann, Chris Lundberg, John McGowan, Kerry McKeever, BP Morton, Michael O'Rourke, Joy Passanante and Todd Taylor. Thank you for your influence on my life. My women's writing group at VMI also provided friendship and feedback—thank you Julie Brown, Valentina Dimitrova-Grajzl, Deidre Garriott, Jennifer Gerow, Meagan Herald and Rose Mary Sheldon. The Wallace District Mining Musuem provided material support, funding and guidance for this project. Thank you Gordon Ball, Rob McDonald and Emily Miller for helping me secure funding for this project, which was also supported by a research grant from the Virginia Military Institute. Thank you to Deborah Vigil at the North Idaho College Library. The University of Idaho Library Special Collections and Archives provided crucial research materials: thank you Julie Monroe, Garth Reese and, especially, Amy Thompson and Erin Stoddard.

Mike and Nancy Branstetter, I appreciate your constant support and love; Joann Branstetter, thank you for sharing your wisdom; Katie and Joe Bauer, it's so nice to be able to live close to you and the nieces; Sam Branstetter, you are one of my biggest inspirations. I am also so grateful to have supportive friends: Sara Agre, Jocelyn and Mathias Bachman, Kelly Bezio, Katie

Comer, Siobhan Curet, Jameela Dallis, Michael Faris, Sara Hamann, Coye Heard, Josh Iddings, Tara Kearns, Jessica Kee and family, Kristen Lacefield, Amanda Henry Lind, Judith Madera, John McNally, Aimee Mepham, Mary and Dave Platz, Nicolaas Rupke, Ryan Shirey and Aina and Naomichi Sawada. I appreciate your continued presence in my life. Risa Applegarth, Erin Branch, Sarah Hallenbeck, Chelsea Redeker and Lindsay Rose Russell, thank you so much not only for being good friends but also for reading and responding to my writing in thorough and thoughtful ways. I am so lucky to know you.

Introduction

"I thought all towns had whorehouses," Kristi Gnaedinger told me in 2010 when I interviewed her for this project. She grew up in the small silver mining community of Wallace, where her father was one of the doctors who examined the women who worked in the houses. Gnaedinger herself worked as a maid in a brothel called the U&I Rooms during the mid-1970s. "I didn't know [Wallace] was different until I got to be a teenager. I just thought that was the way it was," she told me. Many locals reiterate Gnaedinger's point, including Patti Houchin, who used to give the women rides into and out of town: "Everyone just thought it was normal.... You grew up with it, didn't really know any different." Or, as former miner Bill Mooney explained, "it was just common, normal here, the gambling and the prostitution. Only later you look back and see that it was unusual, only after perspective from the outside."

Since the town's founding, professional prostitution had been the norm in Wallace, and it continued to be accepted by the majority of residents, despite its illicit nature. To this day, many residents "wish we had the houses again" and add that the community was "never ashamed of them, you know: they were there for a purpose."[1] The "houses," as the brothels are often called, adapted to and endured major reform periods during which other restricted districts shut down. Across the United States, most cities had abolished designated zones for prostitution by 1920, but in the Silver Valley, the sex industry flourished openly through the late 1980s, with one house continuing to operate until 1991. The brothels were not legal, yet they were accepted by most of the residents.

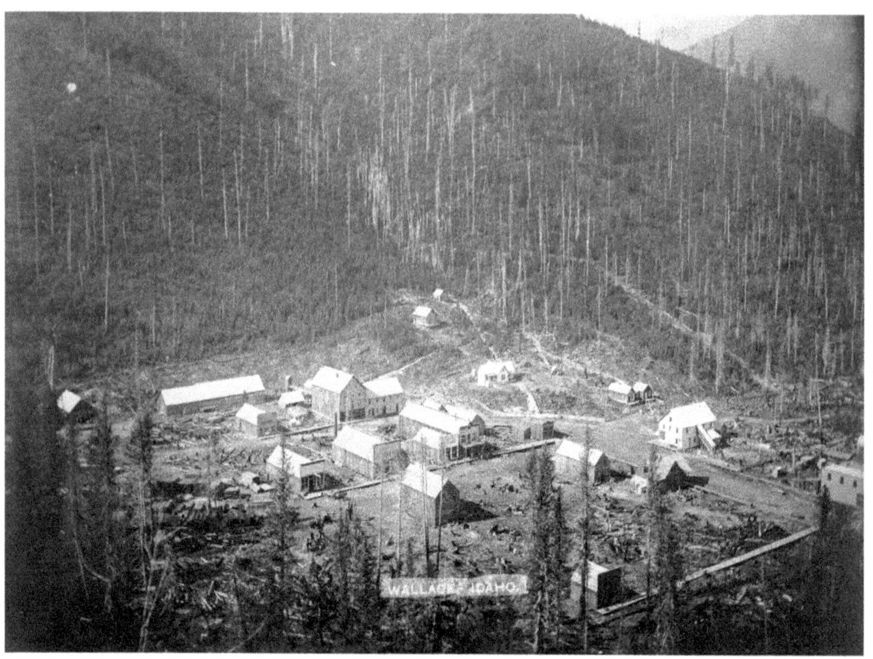

The beginning of the town of Wallace in 1886. This picture was taken from the hill northeast of town, looking southwest. *Historic Wallace Preservation Society.*

For more than a century, Wallace's underground economy, built on Wild West–style brothels, hard drinking and illegal gambling, functioned much as it had during the early days beginning in 1884, before Idaho became a state. As historians Patricia Hart and Ivar Nelson observed in 1984, the town's rowdy mining camp heritage was apparent "in its attitudes toward public vice. That heritage and Wallace's isolation in the mountains led to an unabashed and unrepentant acceptance of drinking, gambling, and whoring, seen as commonplace elements of town life."[2] Most community members believed—and continue to believe—that places like Wallace, full of single miners, require an outlet for sexual release provided by professionals. Maurice Pellissier, who was Wallace's mayor during the period when the houses closed, put it this way: "I'm eighty; the houses have been here my whole life. What would this place have been like if they weren't here? There was a *need* for this sort of thing." Mining towns in the American West simply accepted prostitution as an integral part of the culture, as inseparable from mining as gambling and drinking.

Located in northern Idaho along Interstate 90 midway between Missoula, Montana, and Spokane, Washington, the Silver Valley is geographically isolated within the Bitterroot Range of the Rocky Mountains. The area once produced more silver than anywhere on earth, but as of this writing, only two mines remain in production. The town of Wallace has now shifted toward tourism, marketing its history and outdoor recreation. Even though there are fewer than one thousand residents year-round, Wallace has three museums that highlight its history. The Wallace District Mining Museum educates visitors about the mining industry, the Depot Museum offers information about the influence of the railroad and tourists who are curious about the long-lived sex industry can tour one of the town's historic brothels at the Oasis Bordello Museum. Although the main floor may appear to be a tourist trap, the guided tour of the rooms upstairs often surprises those who visit. This journey into the not-so-distant past begins at the base of a long, narrow staircase, winds by an old jukebox where men paid for drinks to sneak around liquor licenses, continues down a narrow hallway and enables a peek into tiny rooms preserved since the last women to work there abandoned the establishment in early 1988. Several women who used to work in the Oasis have even returned to take the tour themselves, pausing to grab cash hidden beneath the base of a statue on the bedside stand. All of this according to one version of the story, that is.

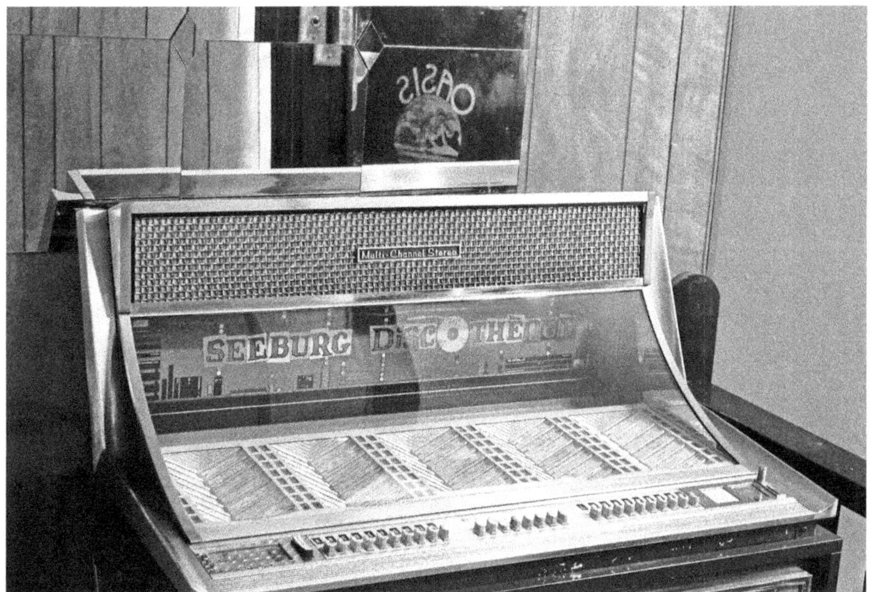

Oasis jukebox. *Oasis Bordello Museum display; photo by Heather Branstetter.*

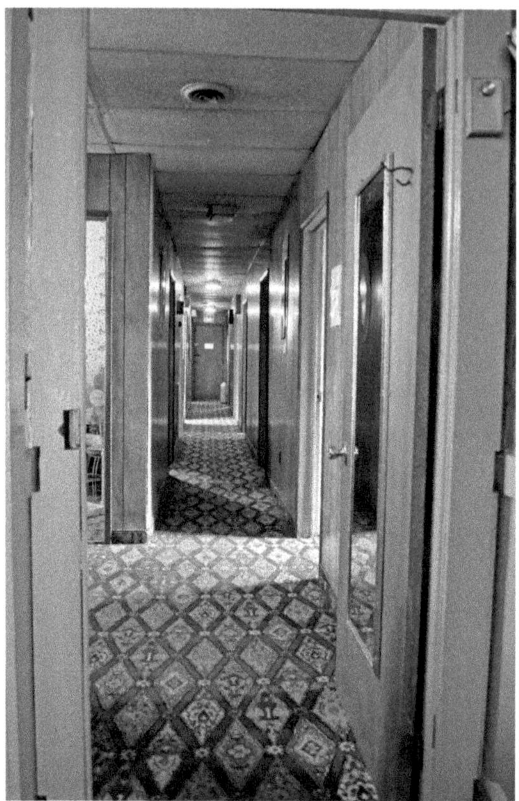

Left: Oasis hallway from madam's room. *Oasis Bordello Museum display; photo by Heather Branstetter.*

Below: Pegasus statue and scarf one of the women knitted for Paul, a regular client. *Oasis Bordello Museum display; photo by Heather Branstetter.*

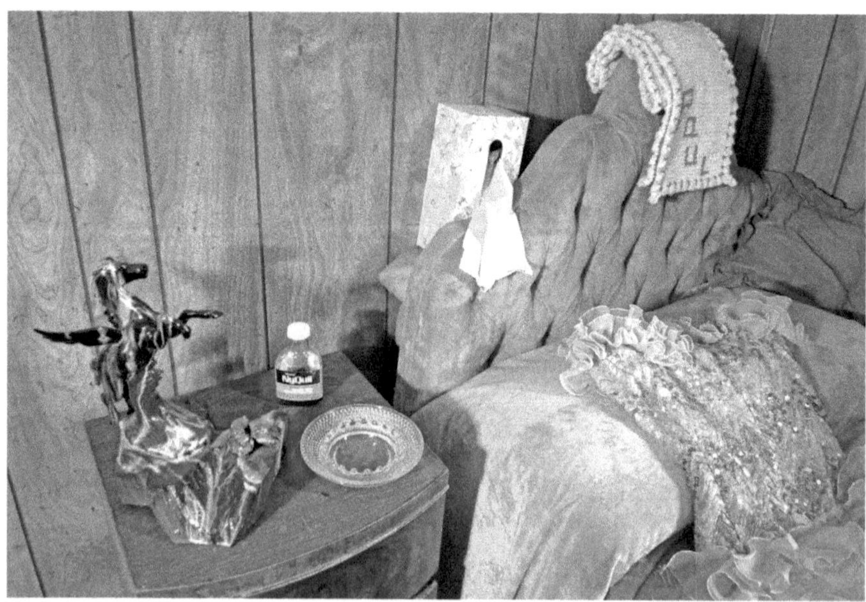

The last remaining house, the U&I Rooms, which had operated continuously since the 1890s (if not earlier), finally closed its doors only weeks before 150 FBI agents raided the area in "the biggest single Federal law-enforcement raid ever in the Rocky Mountain region," according to *New York Times* columnist Timothy Egan.[3] Locals deny that the investigation ended sex work in the region, however, citing a struggling economy, AIDS and brothel management transition for the closure of the houses. According to another interpretation, the goal of the raid was to prosecute the sheriff for racketeering, and such a charge required the investigation to target both gambling and prostitution. While it does seem clear that federal intervention was not primarily responsible for the closure of Wallace's whorehouses, the FBI raid ultimately coincided with and probably catalyzed the end of the Silver Valley's regulated sex work industry.

Throughout the twentieth century, Wallace was seduced by the women in its upstairs rooms because their presence provided a tangible connection with the libertarian Wild West ethos of its past: the red-light district offered evidence that the town continued to inhabit a rebellious space outside the law, a place where people said "live and let live." Single miners, high school boys and sexually frustrated married men could visit discreet professionals without worrying about social consequence, and most women in town accepted the houses in exchange for the perception of increased personal safety. History professor Katherine Aiken suggested to me that the presence of tolerated prostitution also gave the "upright" members of the community an excuse to whisper about otherwise taboo topics. Historically, brothels provided "respectable" people with "an affirmation of their own morality"; as long as "prostitutes are at once tolerated and stigmatized they can serve as social safety valves offering those services while indicating the activities' inherent deviance."[4]

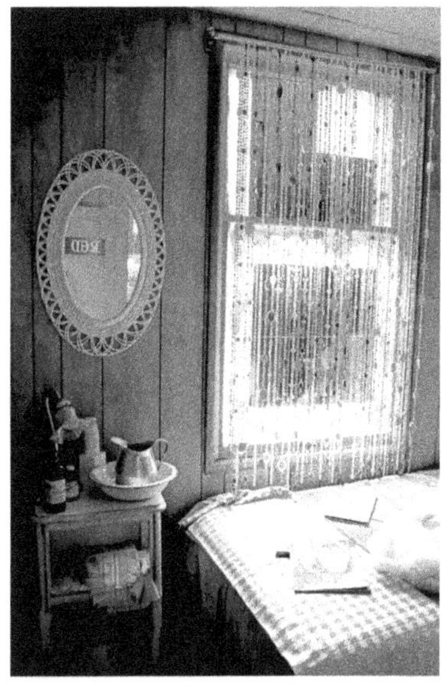
Oasis Red Room. *Oasis Bordello Museum display; photo by Heather Branstetter.*

Like human nature itself, Wallace's cathouses—the word perhaps most often used by locals in reference to the houses—

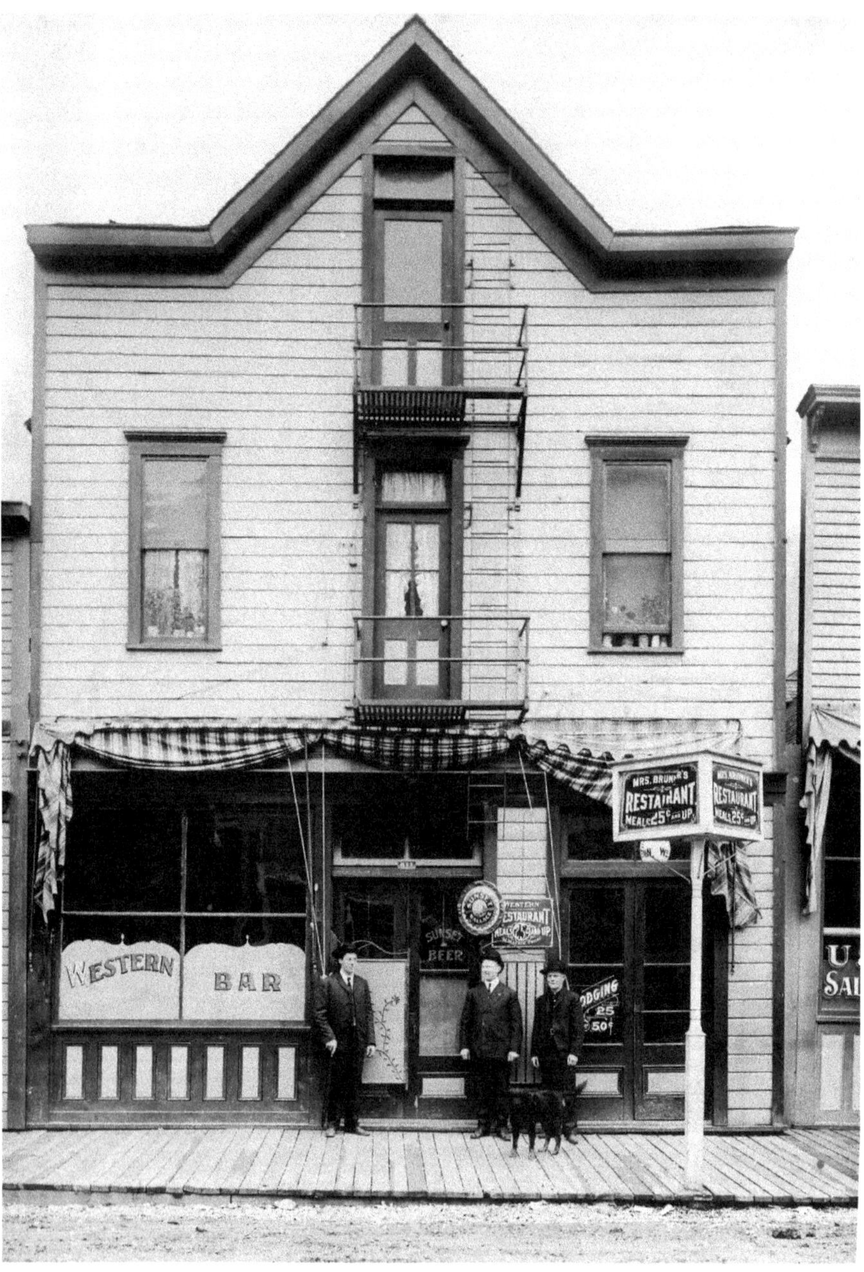

At 611 Cedar Street in the 1890s, the Western Bar featured beer brewed locally at Sunset Brewery. Pictured to the right is the U&I Saloon. The U&I brothel operated continuously from this time until 1991. *Historic Wallace Preservation Society.*

offer a messy tangle of contradictions wrapped up in a complex package oriented toward efficiency and survival: they were famous and secret, commonplace and exotic, classy and trashy, operating without regard for the law but in accordance with a strict code of conduct. Part of the appeal surrounding the presence of prostitution in Wallace was comfort in knowing that commercial sex exchange happened in a designated space according to specific "rules." It was an orderly business, and that was no accident. The madams emphasized the way in which they served the community through donations to support children and families in need. As former judge Richard Magnuson put it, "Dolores thought she was in public service."[5] Magnuson was referring to Wallace's most famous madam, who also argued that the houses were instrumental in saving marriages and bringing money into town. "It was a fact of life that was the best-known secret ever kept in this area," another research participant said.[6] According to local residents, the sex industry kept the residential streets safe at night, attracted truckers and college kids throughout the region and was even internationally known, drawing visitors from Montreal and recognition in London.

As times changed, the Silver Valley's communities could point to the brothels and know the area hadn't abandoned its mining camp roots—and accompanying libertarian values—which created a kind of shared identity. Local storytelling and word of mouth continues to connect sex work in Wallace to the town's sense of itself as a mining town. Wallace's brothel managers appealed to regional values and preferences to ensure their profession was integral to the area's understanding of its history and purpose as a mining camp. Madams catered to residents' perception of community need as they promoted a positive image that emphasized service, civic duty, discretion and a sense of humor. The idea that there was a reciprocal relationship between the town and its brothels provided a solid foundation for the long-lasting underground vice economy in Wallace, which continues on as the town transitions to a tourism economy.

This book provides an overview of sex work in Wallace, focusing on the town's decriminalized brothels and accompanying vice economies. I highlight the ways local culture enabled the acceptance of illicit activities. The story of selling sex in the Silver Valley was influenced by prostitution's historic story nationally: the area was affected by the sex trafficking panic that the FBI invoked to justify its first major expansion during the early 1900s, and Wallace's first steps toward regulating the bodies of sex workers coincided with the War Department's social and moral hygiene propaganda campaign. By World War II, however, decriminalized brothel-based sex

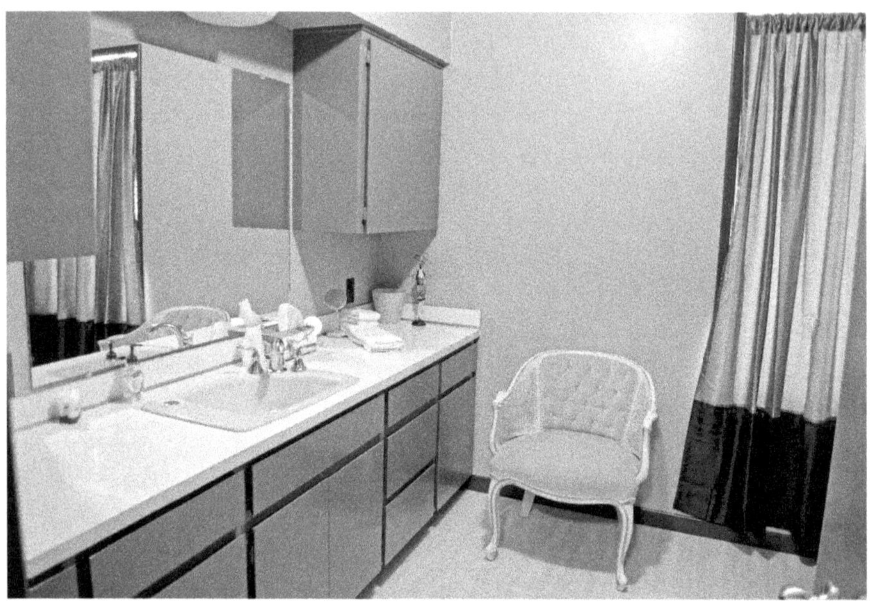

Above: The "madam's suite" at the recently remodeled Lux Rooms, which is now a historic inn. *Photo by Heather Branstetter.*

Below, left: Remodeled Lux Rooms featuring a pink bathtub left from the days when madam Dolores Arnold managed it. *Photo by Heather Branstetter.*

Below, right: Remodeled Lux Rooms with one of the gold-veined mirrors preserved. *Photo by Heather Branstetter.*

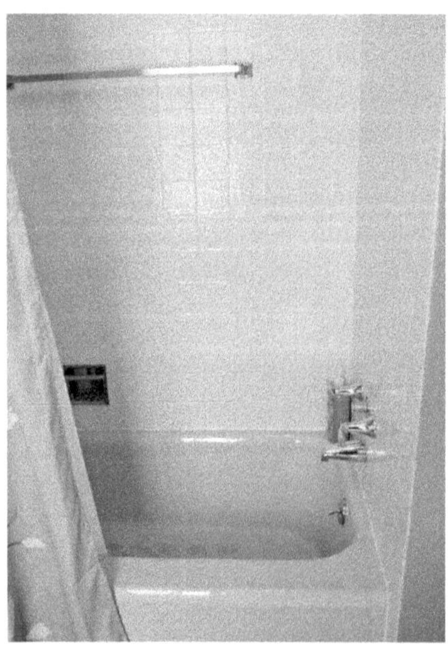

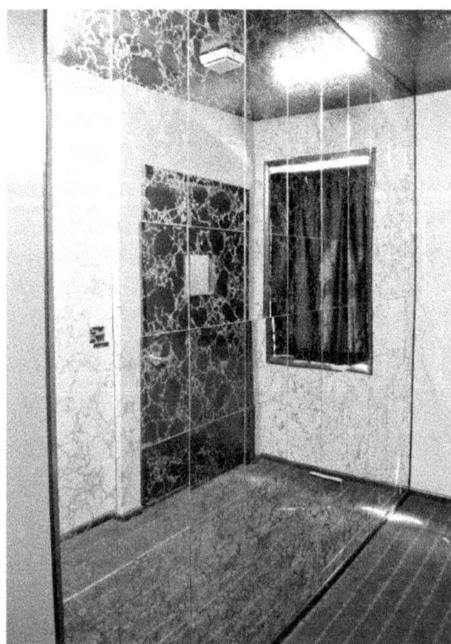

work had become rare throughout the rest of the country, although some other towns also chose to monitor or regulate illegal sex work. The houses in Wallace were unique because of their regional notoriety and notable for the way they were integrated into a community narrative that framed prostitution as an acceptable open secret, providing a service that offered economic and social benefits.

Part I

"A Mining Town Needs Brothels":

The Early Days

1

Mining Camp Lifestyle and the Politics of the Restricted District

Wallace emerged as a mining boomtown and operated according to a code of frontier justice in the early days. The large population of single men and lack of women led the first residents to accept sex work as necessary. Men and women alike thought commercialized sex was a natural part of mining camp life—a requirement, even, if the town wanted to meet the needs of the miners. From 1884 until 1903, women owned and operated brothels throughout Wallace without much restriction. On average, there were at least a dozen houses of prostitution operating during any given year. Before 1903, the majority were located on Pine Street between Fifth and Sixth Streets, with a few on the southwestern corner of Fifth and Pine and one large brothel on the corner of Seventh and Cedar, where the Samuels Hotel would stand by 1908.

By 1905, most of the women had been forced to migrate to an official restricted district on Block 23, the triangular patch of land where the Depot Museum is located today, between Sixth Street, Cedar Street and the south fork of the Coeur d'Alene River. The city built housing for the women along Avenue A, the alley in this block, after President Theodore Roosevelt visited town in 1903. Migration to the restricted district segregated the sex workers from the residential area of town, and it made the women's bodies and business easier to control. During the early years, prostitution worked in symbiosis with saloons, but after sex workers moved, their workspaces evolved to include dance halls, "disreputable saloons" and variety theaters. Women lost ownership and control over the industry as "saloon men's

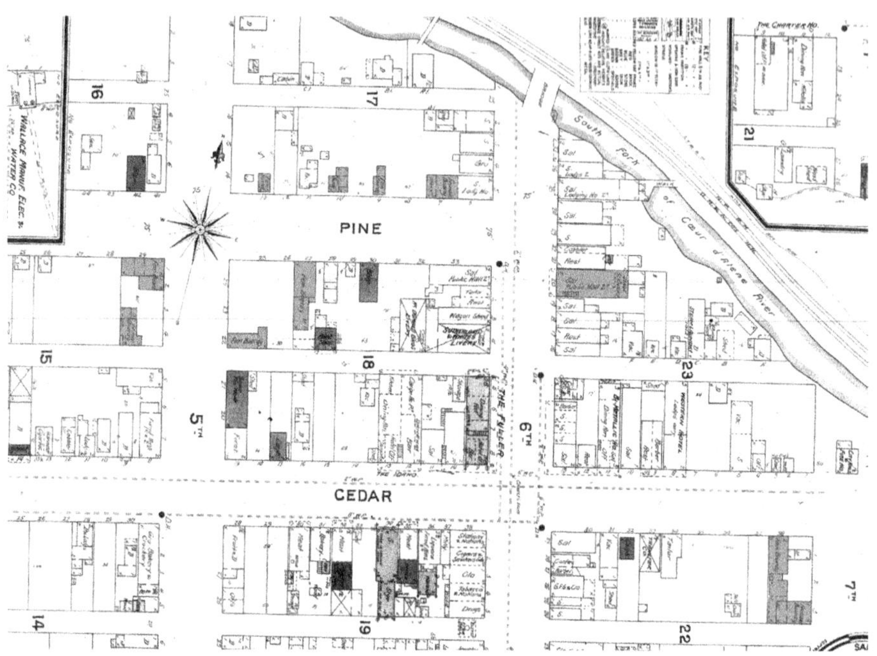

A map of Wallace brothels in 1896. *Adapted from Sanborn Fire Insurance Maps.*

affiliations with prostitution grew more parasitic."[7] From 1910 to 1917, as the town developed into a longer-term mining community and calls for moral reform swept the nation, the city opted to regulate commercial sex work by requiring the women submit to health department inspections and pay licensing fees. In 1913, tax revenues from prostitution, gambling and the sale of liquor enabled Wallace to pave its streets and fund a general infrastructure upgrade, beginning with the section of town that housed the saloons and red-light district.[8]

Table 1: Brothels, Locations and Proprietors, 1891–1916

Brothel or Dance Hall Name	Location & Dates	Madams or Proprietors	Associated Saloon Men, Landlords or Investors
The Star	Fifth and Pine, 1891–1904	Gracie Edwards	Jerome B. Smith, D.C. McKissick and L. Oppenheimer

BROTHEL OR DANCE HALL NAME	LOCATION & DATES	MADAMS OR PROPRIETORS	ASSOCIATED SALOON MEN, LANDLORDS OR INVESTORS
Miner's Home	215 Sixth Street, 1911	Jennie Girardi	Joe Girardi
Palm Garden & Surprise Theater	307½ Avenue A, 1906–11	Jennie Girardi	Emil Vaucamp and John J. Wourms
The Reliance	510 Pine Street, 1891–1904	Effie Rogan	
Unknown Name	Avenue A, possibly 305½	Effie Rogan	
The Trilby	624 Cedar Street and 408 Seventh Street, 1891–96; Sixth and Cedar, 1896–1901	Carrie Young	
Wigwam Theater	1900	Emma Whitney	Carl James and P. Nugent
U&I Rooms	613½ Cedar Street, 1890s–1991	Josie Morin/ Moore, from 1914 into the 1920s	Koski, Makinen and Palosari
The Montana	615½ Cedar Street after 1905		Lieb brothers
The Western	611½ Cedar Street		Stolberg and Anderson
The Arcade	215 Sixth Street, 1900–11		Dan McInnis and Bob Gillett
Chicago Club	Sixth and Pine, 1895		Joseph Camia
"Blue Front Bldg"	Block 23, 1914	Mrs. J.P. Ryan	
Coliseum Variety Show & Rooms	301 Sixth Street, 1900–08		Richard Daxon
Unknown	306½ Sixth Street, 1900–08		
Unknown	"1st house above Bank St. bridge"	Irene Thornton	

Brothel or Dance Hall Name	Location & Dates	Madams or Proprietors	Associated Saloon Men, Landlords or Investors
Unknown	Avenue A, 1910	Mary Bessette	
Unknown	Avenue A, 1906–10	Connie Foss	
Unknown	Avenue A, 1910	Hellen Temple	
Unknown	826 Bank Street	Mrs. M. Vinas, Mrs. Della Mount	
The Comet	Cedar Street		McGowan and Greer
Unknown	Avenue A, early 1890s	Ella Tolson	
El Rey	Sixth Street		Basil Rizzonelli and James McGinnis
Jameson Hotel	304 Sixth Street		Theodore Jameson
The Klondyke	605 Cedar Street		Holst and Limacher
Unknown	1889–91	Broncho Liz Skeels	
Unknown		Mamie Stephens	
The Butte			K. Skipstad
Unknown		Bonnie Earl	
Unknown		Jessie Stuart	
Unknown	411 Cedar Street		
Unknown	409 Cedar Street		
Unknown	Avenue A		Sunset Brewing Company
Unknown	Pine Street		Joe Bertilacchi and G. Rossi
Unknown	Pine Street		Oscar Mattson
Unknown		Blanche Burnard	
Unknown	Avenue A	May Brown	

Brothel or Dance Hall Name	Location & Dates	Madams or Proprietors	Associated Saloon Men, Landlords or Investors
Unknown	Pine Street		Caro Caludio and Simon Bartolomeo
Unknown	Avenue A	Irene Rogers	
Unknown	Avenue A	Sadie Williams	
Unknown		Lizzie Williams	
Unknown	Avenue A	Dollie Morgan	

"A Miner's Sort of an Independent Person"

The labor battles of the 1890s, baked into the Silver Valley's origin story and sense of collective identity, illustrate the initial conditions that would lay the groundwork for the brothels' longevity in Wallace. There were two notable conflicts in the "Rocky Mountain Revolution," as Stewart Holbrook describes it. Mine owners hired Pinkerton Agency mercenaries as spies and strikebreakers in an attempt to stifle miners' attempts to organize, leading to a series of battles that were among "the most violent labor-versus-capital confrontations in American history."[9] Miners fought back with political advantage and sabotage, eventually resorting to Winchester rifles and dynamite. After the first deadly series of events in 1892, when the unions fought the mine owners' association—blowing up the Frisco mill and causing sixteen to eighteen casualties and $20,000 worth of damage—the governor proclaimed martial law and dispatched federal troops to the area, declaring Shoshone County to be "in a state of rebellion."[10]

The second major conflict took place in 1899. Known locally as the "Dynamite Express" incident, it was inspiring from conception through execution. Union miners hijacked a train, loading it with four hundred pounds of powder stolen from the mill blown up in the previous battle, and rolled slowly through the Silver Valley amid the cheers of townspeople, picking up nearly one thousand miners along the way as they headed toward the nonunion Bunker Hill and Sullivan mill. Then, "with the discipline and

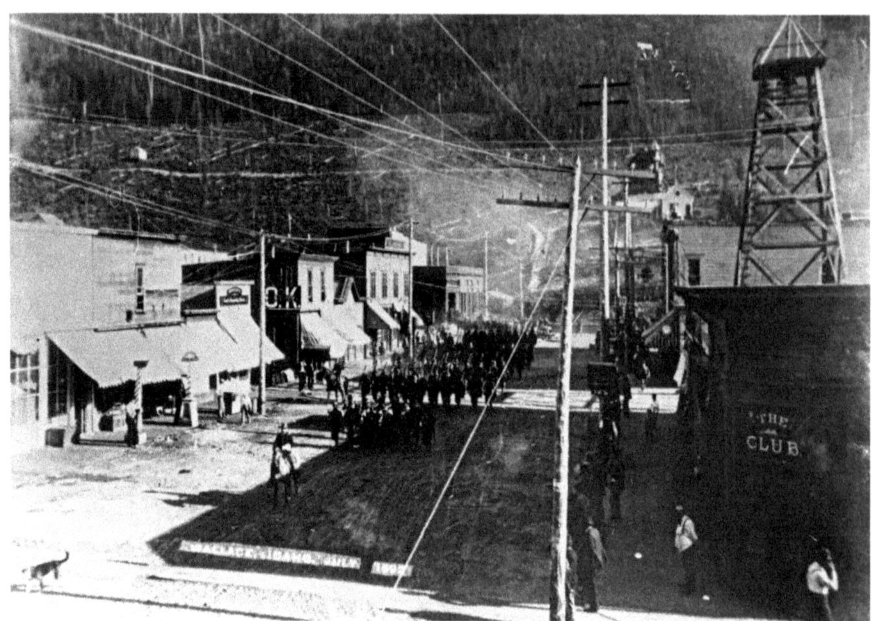

Troops marching on Sixth Street in 1892. *Barnard-Stockbridge Collection, University of Idaho Library Special Collections and Archives.*

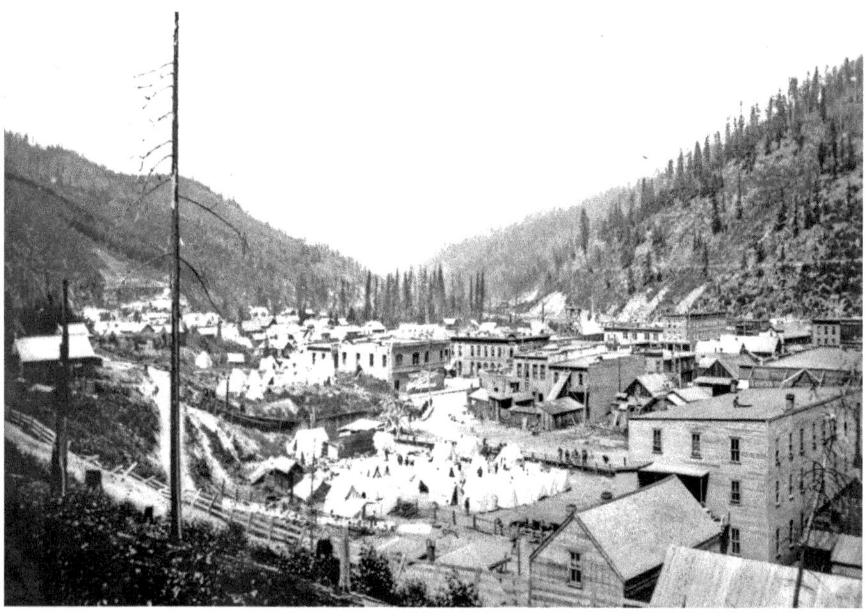

The "bull pen" on Hotel Street where men were held without regard to *habeas corpus*, 1892. *Historic Wallace Preservation Society.*

precision of a perfectly trained military organization," the miners blasted "one of the largest concentrators in the world, costing the company the enormous sum of $250,000," which would work out to about $7.5 million in contemporary currency.[11] Idaho governor Frank Stuenenberg declared martial law, and federal troops were again brought in to quell the unrest.[12]

During this time, the "law-and-order element," a phrase used pejoratively by the miners' union leaders, was associated with the army troops brought in "to suppress insurrection" as they rounded up union supporters by the hundreds and incarcerated them in military prison or concentration camp–style bull pens without regard to *habeas corpus*.[13] This was the first of many instances when federal or state authorities would selectively intervene in the governance of the Silver Valley while suspending respect for basic civil rights. Written laws, especially those imposed by outsiders, came to be seen as unnecessary, oppressive and inconsistent with the pioneers' understanding of human liberty that organized Wallace's anarchic sense of order. There arose a perceptual gap between "justice" and "the law," a distinction between an unwritten code of conduct and the official written rules. For example, in a series of oral histories initiated by David Barton in 1979, Silver Valley miner Maidell Clemets tells a story about a gambler making moonshine during Prohibition. When agents destroyed his operation, he explained, the gambler did not get a jury of his peers or receive a fair trial because it was a federal offense, which meant he was not tried locally:

> *He said he knew that if he'd been tried in Wallace, Idaho, they'd turn him loose. He said he'd got* justice *in Wallace, but in Coeur d'Alene, all he got was* law. *And ah, that was the attitude oft times. Some of the district here...that attitude is still, more or less, predominant.... They don't like to have people from the outside tell 'em what to do. A miner's sort of an independent person.*[14]

Independence—including from the necessity of following laws written and imposed by outsiders—became a key value that manifested in discourse about the brothels. The town developed a reputation for being "wide open," which meant that a person could easily find an avenue for any variety of illicit activities, especially gambling and prostitution. According to local historian John Amonson, wide open also implied "no real respect for the more technical aspects of the law as long as everybody was satisfied."[15] Wallace's leadership filtered national and state laws through the lens of unofficial local rules, in accordance with community custom. When asked whether prostitution has

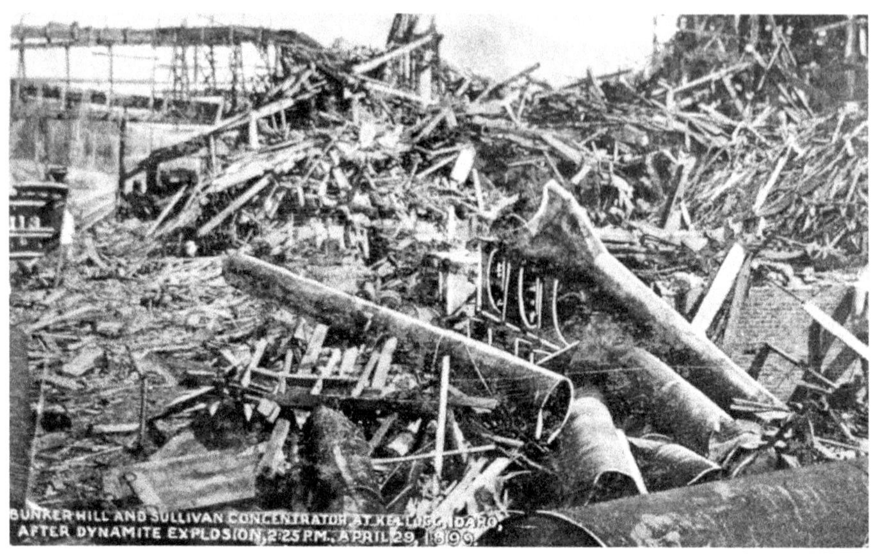

Bunker and Sullivan Concentrator destroyed in "Dynamite Express" episode of the Silver Valley's labor wars, April 29, 1899. *Historic Wallace Preservation Society.*

been legal or quasi-legal in Wallace, for example, another one of Barton's research participants responded, "I don't know. I really don't know. I think the law enforcement people—your leadership in the community, has, has, might say, tolerated, under certain restrictions—with certain restrictions, the existence of them."[16] In other words, city leaders and politicians historically felt it was appropriate to enforce a local code of conduct in lieu of state or national law.

Wide-Open Wallace

Some historians have made the argument that prostitution was initially tolerated as a part of mining enterprises because it was central to the economic system. That is, commercial sex kept the miners mining.[17] This sentiment provides useful context, but there is also the more obviously pragmatic justification for the initial presence of sex work in historic mining towns like Wallace: "In the reality of the American mining West, a combination of demography and geography brought the moral and immoral cheek to cheek. In early mining camps women were a minority, and frequently the first and most numerous female migrants were prostitutes."[18] Hundreds of women cycled through the Silver Valley's houses, and turnover rates in the area were high. Most of the women stayed in one town for only six months or less, and of the 105 prostitutes working in Wallace and Wardner during 1908, for example, only 25 were still working there by 1910, even though there were still around 94 total verified sex workers during this time.[19]

Although mining towns have earned a reputation for being particularly *laissez faire* in their approach to sex work, most city councils passed ordinances prohibiting prostitution and gambling.[20] Because attempts to control vice elements in frontier western communities usually failed, however, city leaders focused their efforts on regulation, control and taxation instead of prohibition.[21] Wallace's city council minutes from 1895 reveal that early citizens preferred the houses "be removed to some less conspicuous locality" rather than removed entirely, so town leaders introduced an ordinance to license dance halls. Reform would not begin to affect the town seriously until 1903, when a series of articles appearing in the regional newspapers

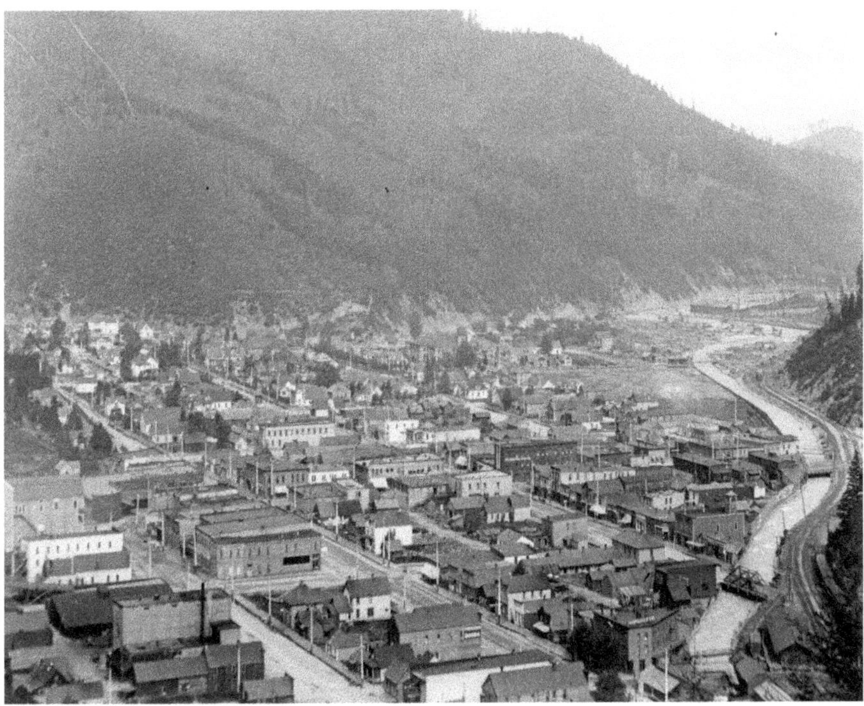

Bird's-eye view of Wallace before the 1910 fire, year unknown. The Pacific Hotel is pictured in the lower right. *Historic Wallace Preservation Society*.

reveal how President Theodore Roosevelt's visit coincided with a temporary shutdown of the sex industry initiated by Mayor Connor.[22]

During the early days, saloonkeepers served as prostitution directories, providing newcomers with services, prices and insider information, such as quality ratings. Much of the available written information about the early mining camp days comes from newspaper sources, but reporters often wrote libelous and wildly exaggerated material, especially when covering prostitutes. In fact, nearly "the only coverage working women received in western newspapers involved accounts of prostitutes' attempted suicides, arrests, fights, or other escapades."[23] An article appearing in the *Wallace Free Press* on October 10, 1890, offers a striking example of such sensationalism, reporting an argument between two "angels of the night": Lulu Dumont stabbed Frankie Dunbar seven times with her stiletto. Dunbar was critically wounded but survived the attack. The fight was over money and happened in the street near Fifth and Pine after a night of working in a parlor house called the Star, one of the city's most "high-class" establishments.

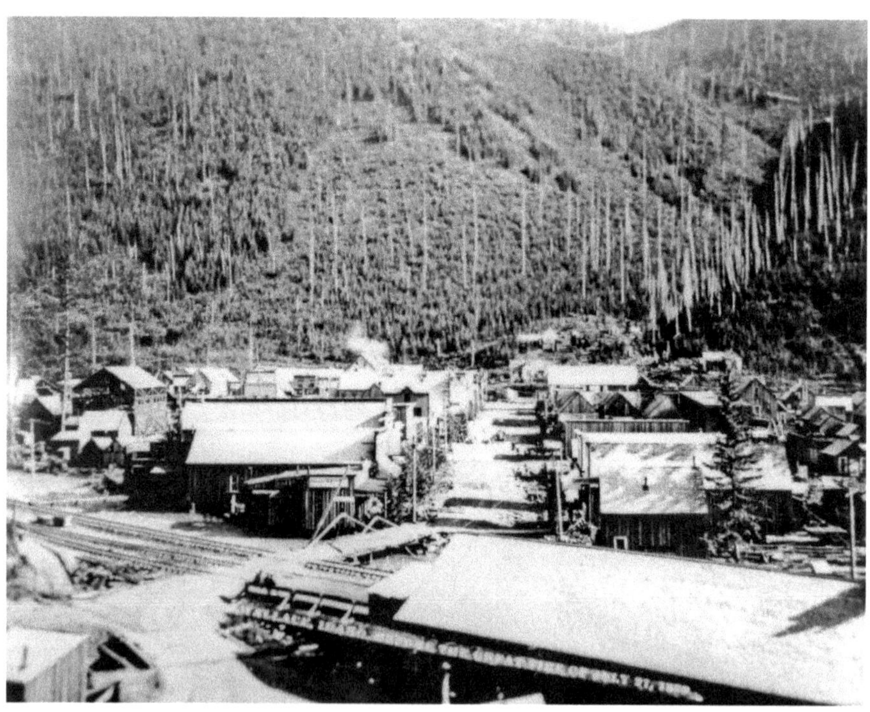

Looking south along Sixth Street before the fire of 1890. *Historic Wallace Preservation Society.*

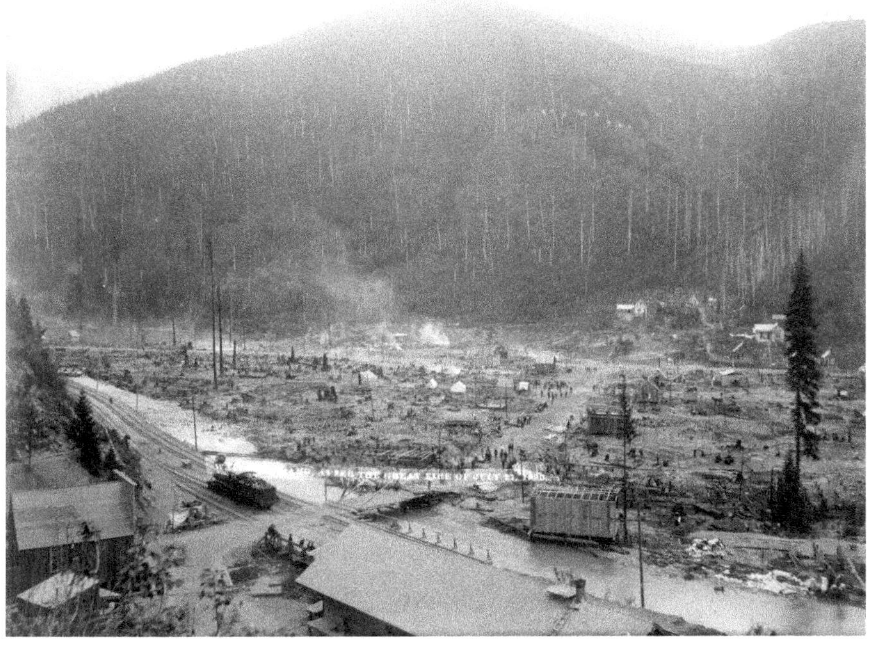

Looking southeast along Sixth Street after the fire in 1890. The south fork of the Coeur d'Alene River is in the foreground. *Historic Wallace Preservation Society.*

The Star was owned and operated by Gracie Edwards and Jerome B. Smith. They also operated houses in Wardner, which was home to a thriving red-light district at this time. Cynthia Powell, who documented a thorough history of prostitution in the Silver Valley during the early years, wrote:

> *The Star catered to a more elite clientele and Edwards emulated larger city parlor houses by furnishing the brothel with lavish fixtures. Her "girls" entertained customers in an environment of relaxed luxury. After-midnight dinners, wine from crystal goblets, and satin spreads and pillow shams on the beds indicated that Edwards knew from experience the ambiance upper-class brothel patrons required.*[24]

Powell reported that Edwards probably left Wallace around 1903 rather than relocate to the restricted district, where she would have been subject to control by saloon men. Despite this decision, Edwards "knew the value of maintaining discrete [sic] alliances with the powerful men in the district,

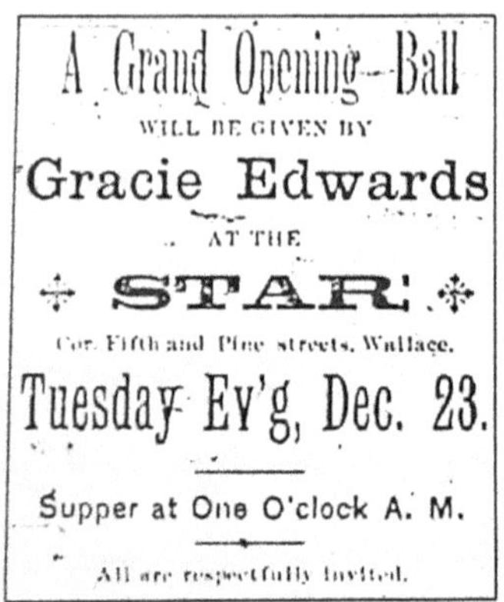

Newspaper ad for Gracie Edwards's high-class parlor house at the corner of Fifth and Pine Streets. *From the* Wallace Press, *December 20, 1890.*

especially liquor dealers," as evidenced by the fact that she "raised over twelve hundred dollars within a year" by mortgaging her property to expand operations.[25]

Despite the voyeuristic and sometimes tragic tales that appeared in the local papers, the sex industry offered some women economic opportunity and political influence during the boomtown phase of Wallace's development. During this time, women who owned or operated brothels were "central figures in the economic life of many early mining towns," controlling much of the local real estate and using their profits to invest in local business interests and mining operations.[26] Revenues to the city and its officials were also significant. On March 18, 1905, the *Idaho Press* reported a case in which a city judge sued the city of Wallace because he was not paid his three-dollar fee for his share of a monthly fine against whores. The judge counted 352 cases for which he was not paid his fee between June 20, 1904, and March 13, 1905, for an average of about forty women per month.

Another sensational newspaper account reported that Ione Skeels, also known as "Broncho Liz," shot her husband, Charles, after she heard he was spending the night with a variety actress. According to stories that appeared in the *Wallace Free Press* on December 21 and 28, 1889, "Mrs. Skeels armed herself with a pistol and proceeding to the building, enticed her husband from the room by sending word by a messenger boy that he was wanted at his place of business. Skeels when he saw his wife struck her and she put three bullets into him." It was "a pretty strong case of justifiable homicide," and Ione was not punished for the murder because the evidence revealed "the deceased was a bad and dangerous man in the community." An "unusually high percentage" of sex workers in these days had likely turned to prostitution because their family of origin had been "severely disturbed" economically—they "came from families that were not originally destitute; rather, certain conditions had disrupted the entire family's means of survival."[27] Women like Skeels did what was necessary to make a living, and mining communities were violent, rough places where stabbings and shootings were commonplace.

Some women in Avenue A did not live in the rooms where they worked, behind the saloons that opened up onto the north side of Cedar Street. Instead, they rented from bar owners on a daily or weekly basis. The rooms they worked out of were called "cribs." Richard Magnuson related the situation to me in this way:

> *There are remnants from the old cribs in the alley behind what used to be the U&I, around the back and to the east of where the Oasis Bordello Museum is now. Back there, you can see a small door-window-door-window, which was how the cribs were structured—they were little one-room places with just a door, a window and a bed. That whole alley used to be lined with cribs, and the women would pay their rent by the day or week to the saloonkeeps. That alley had a gate across it, which you can see in old pictures taken looking east. My father and his brother used to sell newspapers and would fight for who got to sell on the corner by that gate, because the tips were the best there. Back in those days, there were all sorts of newspapers, including ethnic ones, from all countries, like Sweden. The cribs are now in disrepair, but one might still have a doorbell if you look closely.*[28]

Two men who handled the Avenue A rental process were the Lieb brothers, who ran the Montana Bar.[29] The son of one of the Lieb brothers later became the newspaper editor Wes Lieb, who ran the *Wallace Press-Times*.[30] Dan McInnis, who owned the Lobby Bar in the Arment Building on the corner of Sixth and Cedar, likely profited from a primitive crib rental arrangement as well; he requested that a partition be built around the rear entrance to his building, which opened up onto Avenue A.[31] Through the years, McInnis was associated with several disreputable rooming houses or dance halls, both in Wallace and in Burke, including the Arcade and the Owl. Some of the women who rented rooms in the alley lived in places like the Sweets Hotel. Magnuson told me the story of reading a letter written from the Sweets Hotel back in these early days. One of the sex workers had written to her boyfriend, "Business is so good!" but the madam had warned her, "Slow down, you haven't seen anything yet; just wait until payday."

Newspapers reported several black women who were madams or sex workers as well. Even though race relations in the area were intolerant, African American women in Wallace lived in red-light districts, where they often operated laundry facilities and sometimes worked as sex workers as well, Powell explained, adding that "there existed an indisputable demand

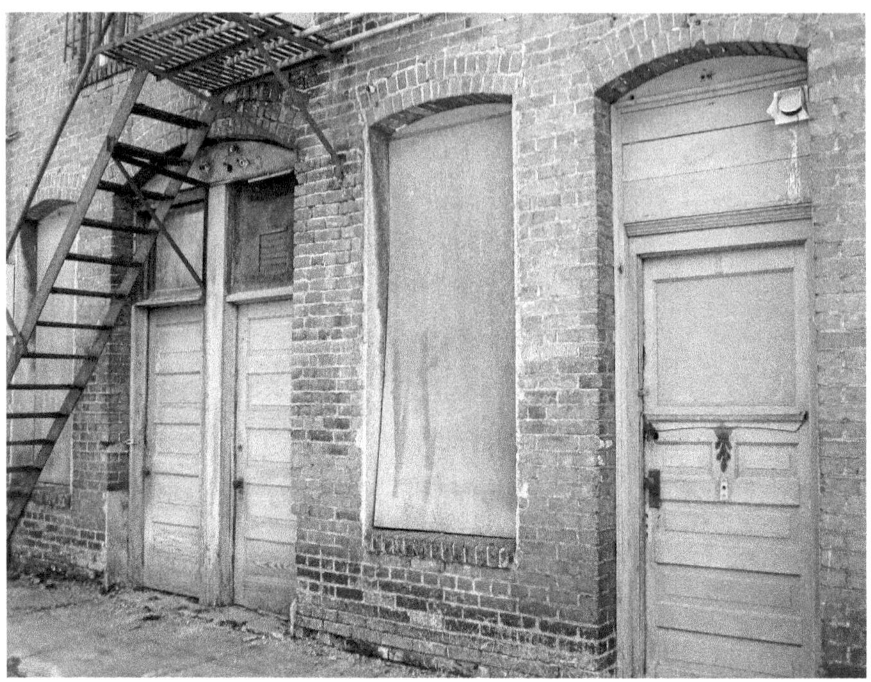

Obsolete doors in Avenue A. *Photo by Heather Branstetter.*

for black prostitutes during the labor war of 1899, when a black regiment was brought in to quell labor tensions."[32] According to Magnuson, the government chose black soldiers in particular because they were seen as less likely to befriend or sympathize with the miners. Like the white women, black sex workers appeared in the paper most often because of violence or crime. Ella Tolson, "who lived over the Troy Laundry in Wallace's Pine Street sector," was reported to have shot Howard B. Johnson, who was "described as 'the most widely known colored man in Wallace.'"[33] Irene Thornton owned a laundry business and the land it occupied in Wardner before moving to Wallace, where she was arrested for "conducting a disorderly house."[34] On March 25, 1893, the *Coeur d'Alene Miner* reported that "'a colored woman who live[d] on the opposite side of the street,' from the disreputable Montana Saloon, witnessed a brutal beating. Her vantage point, according to the newspaper's description of her Wallace location, was an 'Avenue A' crib."[35] In the Silver Valley, black men and women seem to have inhabited roles that were relegated to Chinese immigrants in other western mining communities.

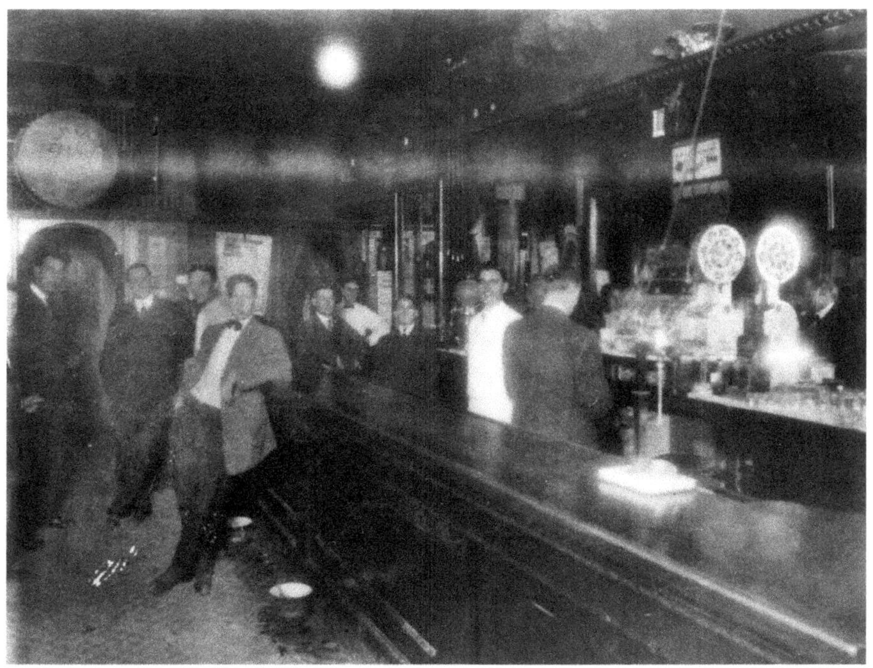

Inside the Montana Bar, 615 Cedar Street, during the 1890s. *Historic Wallace Preservation Society.*

After Wallace passed the ordinance requiring dance hall licensing in 1895, madams were increasingly subject to arrests and routine fines for failing to obtain a permit for a dance show. Variety shows and disreputable theaters became more popular. Between 1893 and 1904, "Wallace madams arrested for keeping houses of prostitution included Blanche Burnard, who was arrested four times, Effie Rogan who was arrested five times, and Jessie Stuart who had just one arrest."[36] The women arrested were exceptional cases, though; police dealt informally with most sex workers. It would have appeared hypocritical to enforce the rules strictly when the city and so many of its leaders, such as Theodore Jameson, profited from prostitution.[37]

City leaders overlooked the licensing requirement for many dance halls and disreputable theaters, despite citizens' dismay. The Coliseum, for example, featured a carousel stage and enabled men to watch burlesque entertainment from a horseshoe-shaped gallery.[38] It was the largest of the theaters in town and could probably hold about one hundred people, with rooms available for prostitution.[39] Powell explains how early town leaders allowed sex work even when it crossed lines of acceptability:

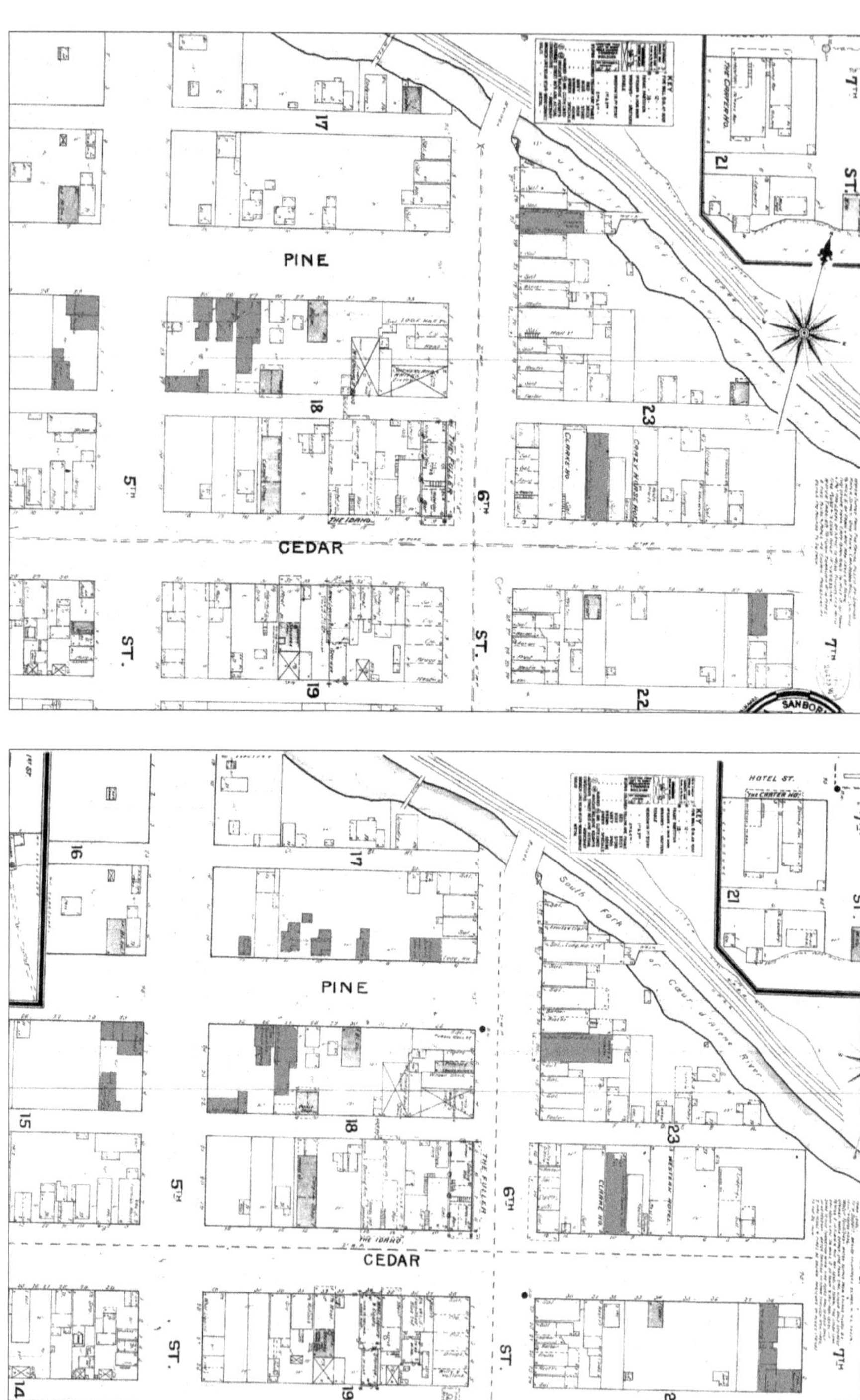
PINE
CEDAR
5TH ST.
6TH ST.
7TH ST.
THE IDAHO
THE FULLER
CLARKE HO.
CRAZY HORSE HOTEL
THE CARTER HO.
KEY
SANBORN
PINE
CEDAR
5TH ST.
6TH ST.
7TH ST.
HOTEL ST.
South Fork of Cœur d'Alene River
THE IDAHO
THE FULLER
CLARKE HO.
WESTERN HOTEL
THE CARTER HO.
KEY

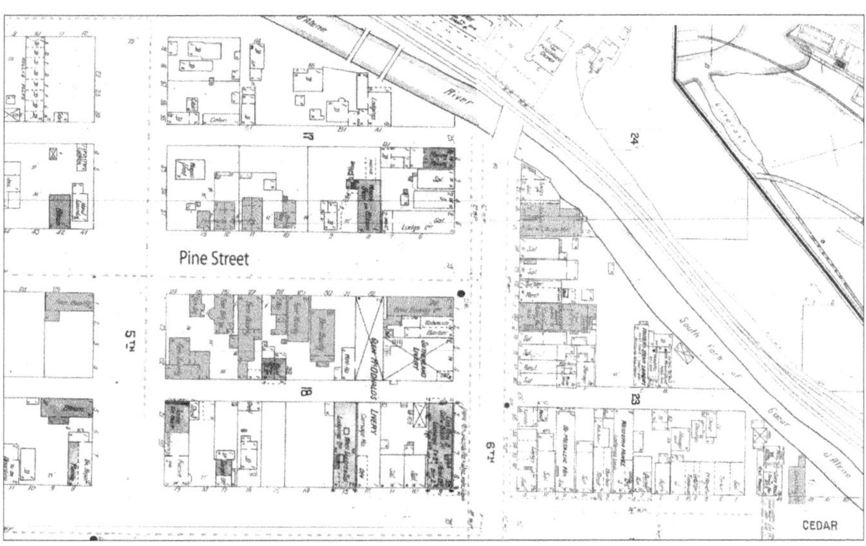

Above: A map of Wallace brothels in 1901. Houses started to consolidate around Pine Street, with a disreputable dance hall and variety theater in the area that would soon become the official restricted district. *Adapted from Sanborn Fire Insurance Maps.*

Opposite, top: A map of Wallace brothels in 1891, showing where variety shows began to appear. *Adapted from Sanborn Fire Insurance Maps.*

Opposite, bottom: A map of Wallace brothels in 1892. *Adapted from Sanborn Fire Insurance Maps.*

> *When the community railed against the reports of "outrageous activities" at Richard Daxon's "Coliseum Theater,"* [Mayor] *Rossi appeased the community by appearing "tough" on Daxon. He slyly excused Daxon from the Coliseum's status of being a combination of a dance hall and theater, while demanding Daxon pay prostitute fines for the women who worked for him. The net result for the city was probably the same amount of money, yet he could maintain that the dance hall portion of Daxon's business was closed down.*[40]

The licensing ordinance was thus selectively enforced, depending on the political connections of the dance hall managers and the actions of those who worked in or patronized the establishments. A flexible interpretation of the law was applied in accordance with local customs and preferences.

Between 1893 and 1904, Powell reported, "four disreputable saloons or dance halls on Sixth Street housed prostitutes on their second floors. 'The Trilby,' 'the Wigwam,' 'the Arcade,' and 'the Show Shop,' were the major disreputable theaters during this era."[41] Variety-show life appears to have been difficult, as evidenced by the many suicide attempts among the women who worked in these theaters and dance halls. Edna Ferrell, the *Idaho State Tribune* reported, "attempted suicide by swallowing a vial of carbolic acid.… While she had a close call, it is believed she will recover."[42] Drinking carbolic acid appears to have been a common method for suicide attempts during this time.[43] These attempts were often unsuccessful, however. The *Idaho Press* reported that variety-theater actress Georgia Ross tried three times to kill herself.[44] In 1907, the *Times* reported that Kitty Gregg, "one of the inmates of the 'Show Shop' on Sixth Street drank a vial of carbolic acid early yesterday morning and as a result is lying seriously ill at Providence hospital."[45]

The Arcade, located on the northeast section of Sixth Street near the river, was a combination bawdy theater and dance hall run by Dan McInnis. It was the only dance hall left in Wallace by 1909 and closed in 1911: "With the closing of the bars in the Arcade Theater today," the *Spokesman-Review* reported, "one of the last of the west's notorious dance halls passed into history.… Like the dance halls which have gone before it, the Arcade was a combination of women, wine and song. It consisted of its bars, its dance floor and stage and its curtained boxes."[46] The dance halls were too rowdy to last beyond the widespread calls for reform between 1910 and 1917 that shut down brothel-based prostitution in most cities across the country.

Migration to Block 23

Restricting sex workers to dance halls, variety shows, disreputable saloons and bawdy theaters in an official restricted district would enable the rise of liquor men in the business and political life of the city.[47] It appears that President Roosevelt's visit in 1903 was an important catalyst for the eventual geographical relocation of the houses to a restricted district in the northeastern corner of town. There was also a general movement toward a more grounded and less transient lifestyle in Wallace during this time. A large number of brothels lined Pine Street between Fifth and Sixth, but churches and schools began moving into nearby areas on Pine Street near Fifth Street. As early as November 1900, "a deliberate attempt to alter the location of prostitution was evident in the city council records," prompted by a petition signed by over one hundred residents and presented by Reverend Brown.[48] Powell observed that this petition was likely the result of churches

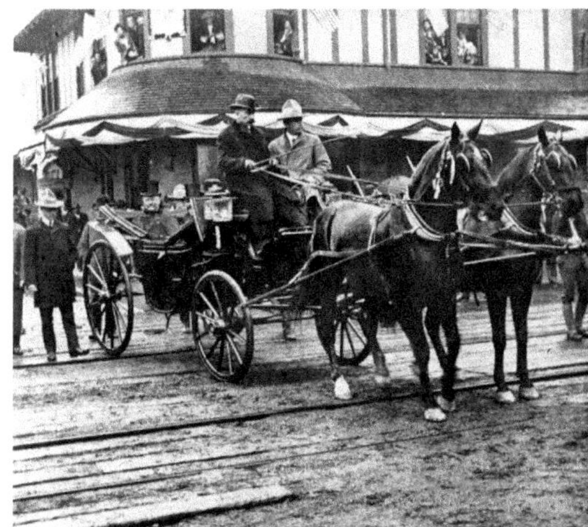

Left: "President Theodore Roosevelt Leaves Depot in 1903." His visit was part of the reason why the houses moved to an official red-light district. *Barnard-Stockbridge Collection, University of Idaho Library Special Collections and Archives.*

Below: Wallace showed off its prosperity by "cleaning up" the town in preparation for President Roosevelt's 1903 visit. Here, flags line Sixth Street. *Barnard-Stockbridge Collection, University of Idaho Library Special Collections and Archives.*

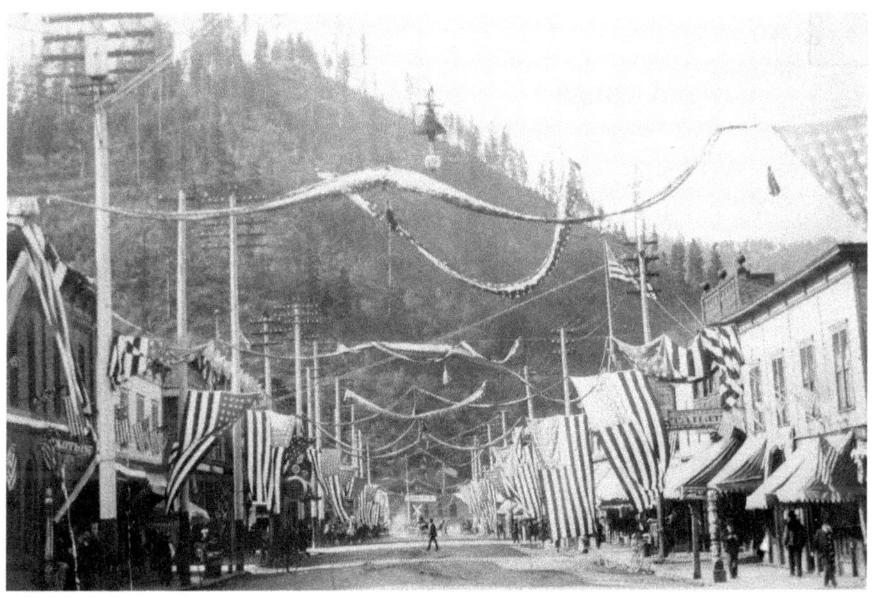

and schools "finding the brothels and cabins frequented by prostitutes intolerable."[49] The council tabled the petition until the residents' protests lost momentum. Petitions appeared before the city council repeatedly during this time, but it appears that Roosevelt's visit may have been needed before the leaders finally found the political will to act.

The *Spokesman-Review* reveals movement toward reform in May 1903. Around the beginning of the month, Mayor Connor gave "orders to run out of the city all the women of questionable character."[50] This announcement garnered praise from a woman "of a refined character" in Missoula, who named the mayor alongside Carrie Nation (called "the smasher" in the subheadline) as the two people in the world with whom she'd most like to shake hands. The newspaper's tone here seems to be amusement. The following day, the paper announced a "moral wave which is sweeping over Wallace" and declared one of Wallace's dance halls closed, adding that the "girls" would "no longer have the privilege of the license scheme" they previously enjoyed. According to Hart and Nelson, however, the mayor's example of "turning the slot machine at his cigar store to the wall" was only meant to put on a good show because "off the record," he "accused various officials of attempting to make a Sunday school out of Wallace."[51] Several days later, the paper implied that Wallace was cracking down on vice because of the president's visit, featuring an article about a Wallace man found guilty for playing blackjack alongside an article about the city cleaning up for Roosevelt's stay.[52]

By the following week, an article in the *Spokesman* melodramatically proclaimed:

> *The "fairies" of scarlet color and deep shame have but one day more to reside in Wallace. Then Pine Street redlight district will be no more. The danger signal lights which hang out in front of the houses will be turned off; red curtains will be torn down; carousing, drunken men will be no longer heard in this portion of the town, which has long been filled with the lowest kind of life. All will be silence and darkness.*[53]

The headline and opening paragraph of this article suggest the complete eradication of prostitution from the city, but a careful reader from those days would likely have noticed the emphasis on the particular section of town. The final paragraph added, "The latest rumor, and it is believed to be true, is that the city officials wish to only change the redlight district to another section of the city," mentioning Block 23 as the future location. The article ends by saying that because the city leaders don't want to be in the business of determining who is allowed to live in Wallace and who isn't, "it is generally believed they are willing to allow these women who ply their trade to establish in a new district." The paper appears to be making a "live and let live" argument to the reading public.

Finally, a May 22 article more explicitly connects vice district reformation to Roosevelt's visit, giving the impression that the houses would shut down temporarily. Most of the girls were apparently instructed to leave town with

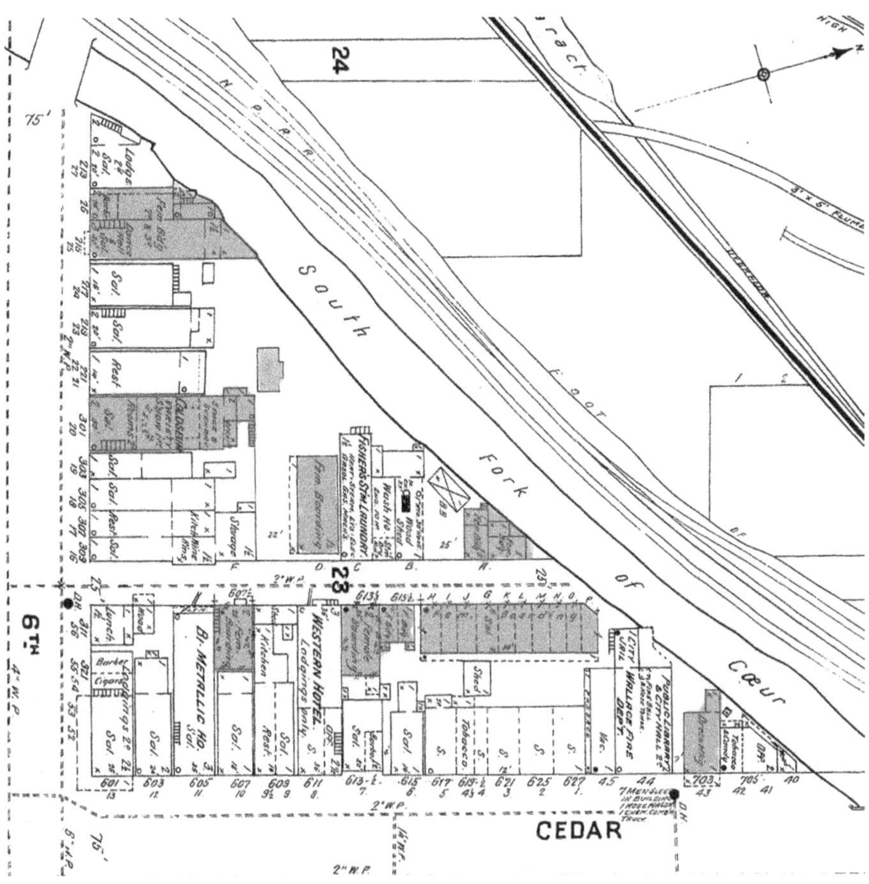

A map of Wallace brothels in 1905 after the women were forced to move to Block 23, along the northeast of Sixth and Cedar Streets. *Adapted from Sanborn Fire Insurance Maps.*

the understanding that construction for housing would begin along the river east of Sixth Street, "immediately after the reception of the president next Tuesday," adding that the "landladies say they will willingly move to another section if lodging apartments are provided." Confinement within Block 23 would not be complete for at least another year, however. Even though there was movement toward establishing the new red-light district along the river and in "Avenue A," the alley just north of Cedar Street, there were still stragglers in other parts of the city. When Herman J. Rossi was elected mayor in 1904, he mandated that "all lewd women" would be confined "absolutely" to Avenue A, and he began to enforce the kind of segregation that some had wanted.[54]

By 1905, Mayor Rossi declared to the city council that prostitution was "a necessary evil and productive of holding virtue in the highest esteem" but must be limited "to its present quarters with a strong hand."[55] He meant that it was important to permit prostitution while limiting its spatial boundaries—rather than outlaw it altogether—because regulated sex work would prevent "respectable" women from being raped. This Victorian-era understanding of male sexuality as an uncontrollable, explosive appetite reverberated through the years. The commercial sex industry was seen as necessary to protect women from the abundance of single "tramp miners" (referring to transient production miners who specialized in a particular kind of work and traveled from town to town based on where their skills were valued more). In 1982, a *Seattle Times* reporter quoted a madam: "Running a house of prostitution in Wallace, she said, keeps young girls from being raped."[56] Wallace mayor Dick Vester told me in 2010, "I'm positive it's already been said that there were no sex crimes when we had the houses." He was correct, although I have not been able to verify whether or not prostitution in Wallace actually prevented rape.

The belief that prostitution prevented rape was common in mining communities. Marion Goldman's study of the Comstock Lode in Nevada puts it this way: the miners "had money to spend and tensions to dissipate, but the release patrons found with prostitutes" was "*socially* defined."[57] Local scholar Ron Roizen has offered his insight along similar lines: the presence of regulated sex work probably made rape less socially acceptable than it otherwise might have been.[58] Contemporary research supports the idea that the availability of commercial sex may correlate with lower rates of rape. Two recent studies, for example, show a statistically significant decrease in sexual assault and sexually transmitted infections in areas where prostitution has been decriminalized. A 2014 paper found that when lawmakers decriminalized indoor prostitution in Rhode Island from 2003 to 2009, rates of gonorrhea and rape dropped significantly.[59] In 2015, researchers looking at the effects of decriminalization in the Netherlands also found dramatic decreases in rates of sexual assault.[60] In Wallace, the written record is ambivalent on this point—there is not enough evidence to draw conclusions either way.

Reference to spatial restriction is often noted in conjunction with the idea that sex work was required to protect the modest women of Wallace. Henry Kottkey, a local forest service officer featured in a 1979 oral history, argued that the city "deserved a lot of credit for their management of the prostitution set up.... It has been very much controlled...pretty much confined all the way through, to a certain part of town."[61] Many people today echo Kottkey by pointing out that the men "knew where to go" to get their needs met, so young girls in town could walk the streets without fear. For example, one woman explained, "You knew you were safe leaving work at two, three, four in the morning. You didn't have to worry because these guys had their choice up there."[62] Such words echo Mary Murphy's findings in nearby Butte, Montana. One woman "expressed the common opinion that Butte streets were safe for women despite the presence of so many rough men" because they "knew where to get their pleasures."[63] Helena, Montana historian

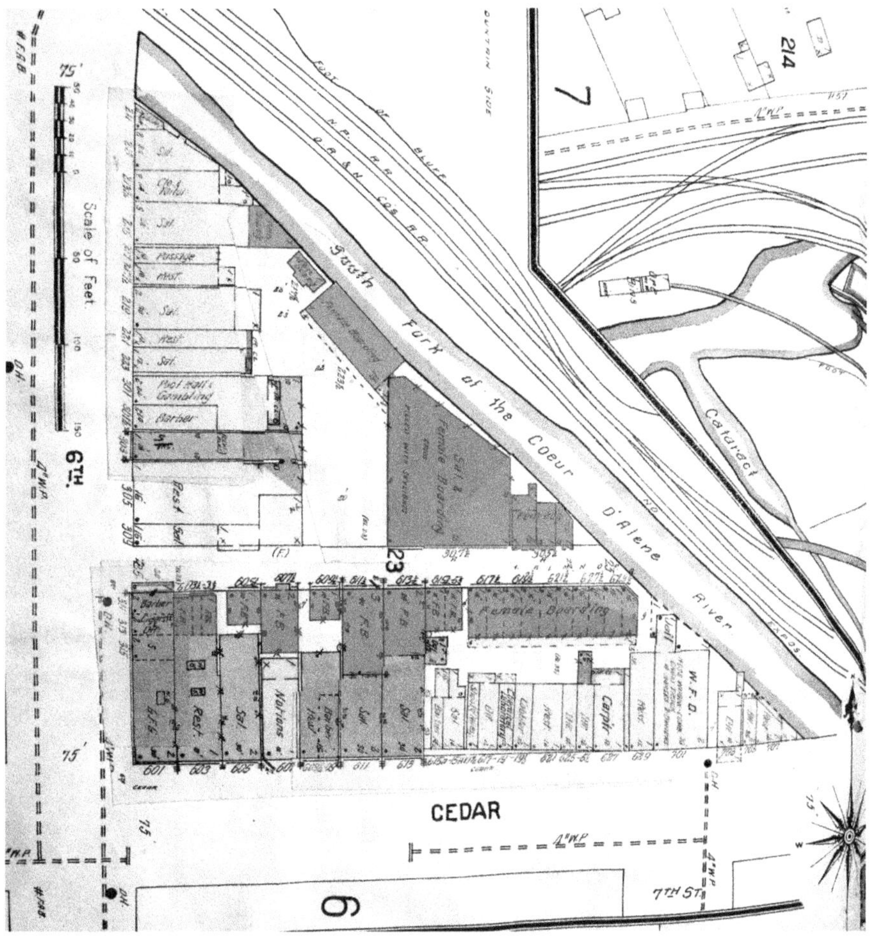

A map of Wallace brothels from 1908 to 1912 after reforms pushed the women farther back from public view. Eventually, a gate or fence would span this alley to solidify the perception of discretion. *Adapted from Sanborn Fire Insurance Maps.*

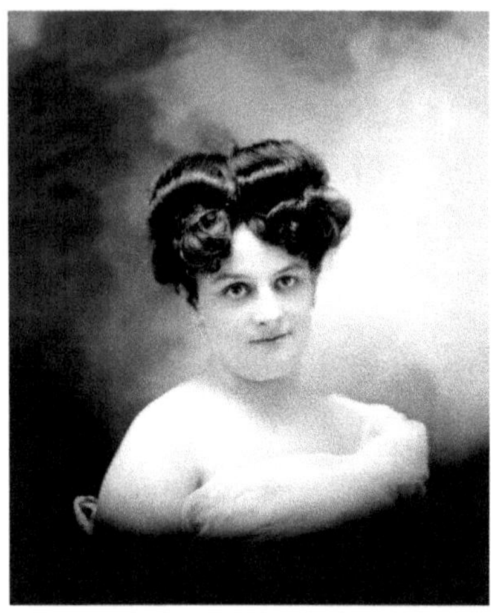

Madam Connie Foss in 1908. We know little about the life of this woman, who lived on Block 23 with two other women. *Barnard-Stockbridge Collection, University of Idaho Library Special Collections and Archives.*

Paula Petrik has argued that confining prostitution within a set location "removed the threat of male sexuality" and rewrote gendered social space such that "respectable women profited" from other women's willingness to provide sexual services.[64] Ultimately, though, the relocation of prostitution into an official restricted district in Wallace was not positive for the women who sold sex because it limited their ability to work independently: they would now rent from saloon men instead of owning and managing their own establishments.[65] Sex workers' mobility was reframed socially and spatially as their economic freedom diminished.

To emphasize the perception of segregation, Rossi recommended "a sectional high fence permitting the passage of teams, be erected in the alley landing east from Sixth below Cedar Street," and the overseer of streets was told to "construct said fence at once."[66] Such a fence, obscuring the sex work industry from the rest of the town, would also create the perception of moral distance. Residents who disapproved could find solace in a literal barrier between the morally pure and impure. Impartial Wallace citizens could see the fence as a move to reinforce the idea of discretion: commercial sex, if necessary for a mining community, might at least be out of sight, out of mind. There is no map-based evidence for a fence across the alley, but its existence, possibly as a gate, has been independently asserted by a historian who wrote about the early days of the Silver Valley, a woman who wrote about her experiences growing up in Wallace during this time and two nonagenarian community members.[67]

In her history of prostitution in the area, Cynthia Powell develops a grim snapshot of sex work in Wallace at the end of the nineteenth century, especially after the women were made to move to the restricted district, where they lost control of their industry. They would not regain the ability to own and manage their businesses again until around the time of the Second World War. Powell concludes that city leaders and the greater community profited from prostitution even as the sex workers themselves were isolated and "treated as a commodity."[68] There was little to redeem the situation for these women, who endured social stigma and primitive working conditions even as they supposedly "protected community women from the lustful natures of a predominantly male population," funded the city government and schools, "helped stabilize the region's economy" and "made the liquor fraternity a powerful player in business and politics."[69] The Silver Valley's eventual development into the silver capital of the world would have been impossible without the presence of prostitution and a group of women whose significance has gone largely unacknowledged. As long as the complexity and depth of historic sex workers' "lives, stories, and historical significance" remains overlooked, Powell argues, the history of the region remains incomplete, because these women "established a dynamic social institution which remained an integral part of the region's economic, political, social and even cultural life for over a century."[70]

2

Sex Trafficking Panic and the Effect of War

A prostitution reform movement swept through Wallace between 1905 and 1920. During this time, major waves of reform washed over the rest of the country as well, and most official vice districts shut down as a result. There were two phases of argument against prostitution during this time: the first grew out of religious concern about morality and the worry that most sex workers were actually sex slaves or victims of trafficking; the second was initiated by the War Department, prompted by anxiety about sexually transmitted infections preventing military men from fighting. The rhetoric of both phases aligned with the language of Progressive-era arguments about nationalism, industry efficiency and temperance. City leaders were primarily interested in reforming sex work enough to protect the commercial interests of the town by improving Wallace's reputation. It had, after all, been declared "about the widest open, most flagrantly and shamelessly wicked city for its size in America."[71] From the early mining camp days through World War I, there were on average between thirty and sixty women working in Wallace's sex industry at any given time.

At the federal level, calls for reform led to the passage of the Mann Act in 1910. This law prohibited the transportation of women across state lines "for the purpose of prostitution or debauchery, or for any other immoral purpose, or with the intent and purpose to induce, entice, or compel such woman or girl to become a prostitute or give herself up to debauchery, or to engage in any other immoral practice."[72] Such sweeping and vague language was oriented toward eradicating what was known at the time as "white slavery," or the procurement and confinement of women for the purpose of coercive or nonconsensual sex. Sex trafficking and slavery were problems, but reformers' rhetoric and fear mongering were likely out of proportion to the reality. This legislation was driven by moral panic about prostitution and anxiety about immigrants. The Mann Act's passage ultimately led to the development and growth of the FBI, which began as a niche investigative branch of the Department of Justice. Before the passage of this act, the FBI was a boutique agency, but the need to police the interstate transportation of women demanded more employees, increased funding and, of course, a larger bureaucracy.[73]

Steps Toward Reform: The Sex Trafficking Panic

The Silver Valley remained relatively immune to nationwide pressures to reform prostitution until conditions in the dance halls, variety shows and disreputable theaters finally prompted community members to take action. The suicide of one young man in connection with Dan McInnis's Arcade Theater led some Wallace residents to urge the eradication of sex work. Despite the many instances of women's suicide in the papers, it took the suicide of a man before people began to care enough to try to change things. For the first time in the city's history, "moral concerns rather than business interests were emphasized," and this moral argument "could only align itself with a prohibitionist position."[74] The reformers argued that "young men are, and have been, debauched, even into suicide," and that "young women are being imported for immoral purposes," suggesting that the women were simultaneously seducers and victims.[75]

The Arcade would outlast the other dance halls, however, probably because of McInnis's connections or standing in the business community. Instead, the city targeted Emil VauCamp and Jennie Girardi, who ran the Surprise Theater and Palm Garden. After being denied a liquor license in 1909, VauCamp ignored the city and operated the combination brothel and bawdy theater without a license.[76] City police seized "obscene films" and slot machines when they arrested VauCamp and Girardi, who were raided several more times before they finally came under scrutiny for procurement.[77] In front of a federal court in Moscow, Lillie Dubois, a French immigrant, testified against the VauCamps through an interpreter,

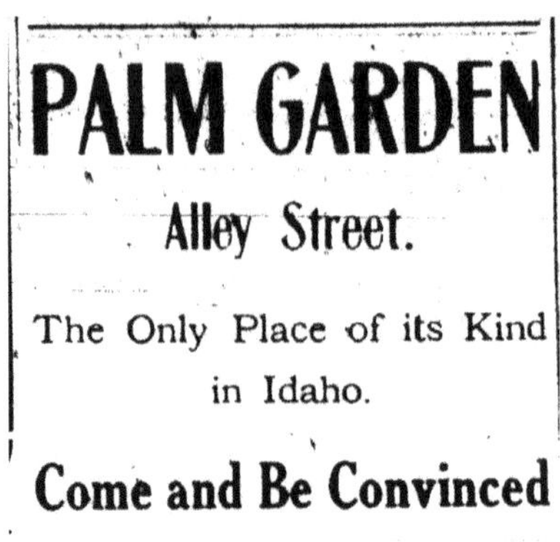

Newspaper ad for the Palm Garden, one of the last bawdy theaters in Wallace. *From the* Daily Times, *July 16, 1908.*

claiming that she had been kept a prisoner against her will, not allowed to leave the premises and not allowed to keep her earnings.[78] The girl explained that "at all times her clothes had been taken from her and they had refused to let her leave the house unless under some sort of guardianship or unless accompanied by one or other of the two defendants or their satellites."[79] VauCamp and Girardi did not serve time, but they continued to be targeted by police and eventually left town.[80]

The story of Dubois was similar to a common narrative about sex work at this time. Across the country, a trend of literature detailed the procurements of young women by those trafficking in sex slavery, and it made the middle-class and elite populations nervous about the welfare of their daughters. According to the mostly sensational stories about this time, it's unclear whether the women were trafficked or wanted an exit from sex work that wouldn't leave them branded as prostitutes. Of course, many prostitution prohibitionists who encouraged the printing and distribution of these stories had self-serving agendas. They passed around exaggerated stories meant to invoke pity and generate political influence. But there were also those who genuinely felt called by God or their conscience to be a voice for others. They believed prostituted women could not speak for themselves or choose otherwise because they were essentially pressured into sex slavery by con artists who took advantage of vulnerable women. These men, who we might now refer to as pimps, were then called "procurers," "peddlers," "undesirables" or "secretaries." The Mann Act targeted the men and labeled the women who were "inmates of bawdy houses" victims, effectively absolving them of moral responsibility and reframing them as rescued or saved.

Local papers fanned the flames by reprinting stories of sex slavery across the country, publishing tales of sex trafficking in Pittsburgh or nearby Butte.[81] For example, the *Wallace Press-Times* featured this story of a San Francisco woman on trial for murdering her former peddler with a hatchet before proceeding "for more than 24 hours to dismember his body and hide the evidence of her crime":

> *"Weinstein was a fiend," she sobbed. "He followed me here from the east and threatened to ruin my home by exposing my former actions unless I again became his slave. Monday evening he went down town with my husband, but quickly returned home. He demanded that I leave my husband and go with him, or that he would show my husband letters. When I refused, he intimated we would begin the old life then. He advanced toward me, partly dressed. I can see his fiendish glare now. Oh it was horrible.*
>
> *"Possibly it was because of the fear of losing my husband's love that I struck him over the forehead with the hatchet. I must have been partly demented. It seems now that it was like a dream."*[82]

Even though the fears and rhetoric surrounding sex trafficking were overblown, as journalistic and popular reports around the country produced literature sensationalizing the seduction and procurement of women by predatory men, "a careful review of the evidence" does document "a real traffic in women: a historical fact and experience that must be integrated into the record."[83] Many vulnerable women who ran into financial insecurity were indeed coerced into prostitution and felt unable to leave even when not physically constrained, because they felt degraded and believed they would bear the stigma of immorality.

Procurers and madams lured women with promises of marriage or jobs like dressmaking, met them at train stations and then manipulated the women until they felt too demoralized or "ruined" to leave. Once a woman had been procured, her street clothes were taken away and replaced with "flimsy transparent gowns" to prevent her from entering the street until she was properly "broken in," usually by being drugged and raped by customers until she felt disgraced and intimidated.[84] Some men staged mock marriages that had no legal status, deliberately attempted to "entangle a woman in financial debt or emotional dependency" or took advantage of foreign immigrant girls who had no immediate family ties or could not speak English.[85] Other women were told they would have to "work off" their train tickets, and then they entered into what amounted to indentured servitude, unable to pay the original debt as well as the constantly accruing room and board debt.

In Wallace, few people were actually convicted under the Mann Act, but several were arrested. In most of these cases, the evidence was determined insufficient, or there were problems with the witnesses. But in the case of a madam named Effie Rogan, the charges stuck. Rogan ran a house called the Reliance from 1895

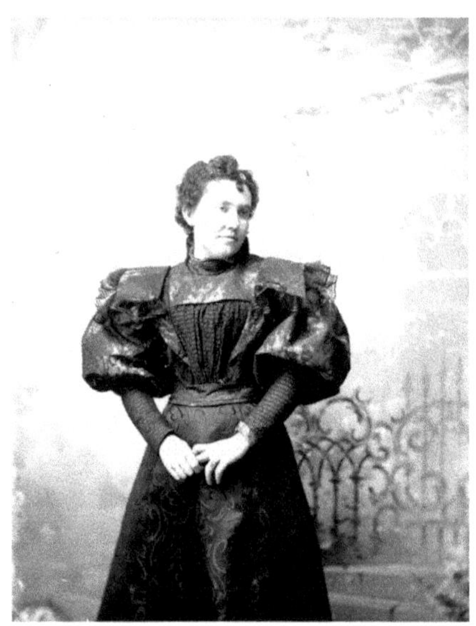

Wallace madam Effie Rogan in 1906, later convicted under the Mann Act. *Barnard-Stockbridge Collection, University of Idaho Library Special Collections and Archives.*

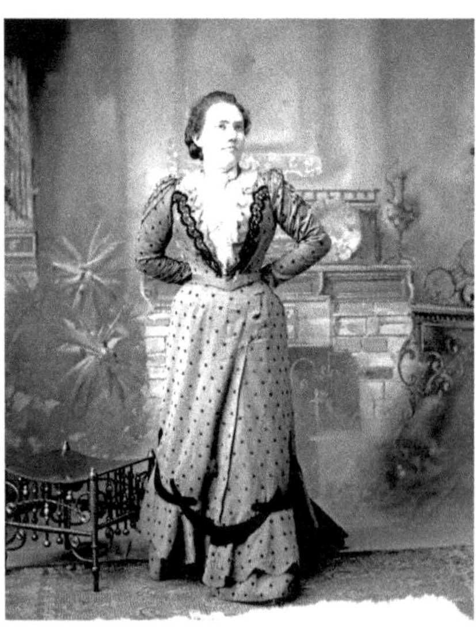

Effie Rogan, madam of the Reliance, pictured here in 1906. *Barnard-Stockbridge Collection, University of Idaho Library Special Collections and Archives.*

to 1911. Her brothel was located at 510 Pine Street from 1891 to 1904, at which point she moved to the triangle-shaped patch of land by the river, where she lived with two other women on the alley.[86] Like many women who were selling sex in those days, her housemates' occupations were listed as "dressmaker" or "hairdresser" during the 1910 census. Within a year, Rogan was in court on charges of keeping a house for the purpose of prostitution.[87] Rogan ran into further trouble in 1912 when the district court convicted her on a charge of "white slavery" under the Mann Act.[88] The details of these cases are missing from the files, but we do know Rogan ended up serving time in prison and paid a $1,000 fine.[89]

In the cases where the charges were dropped, the offending parties were supposedly run out of town. In 1915, William Fanrick (or Fanrich—his name is spelled both ways) ended up in court for "being fighting drunk," and upon further investigation, "it was found that he is in the class termed as 'undesirables.'"[90] Two days later, however, the newspaper claimed that the evidence against him "was submitted and pronounced insufficient to warrant a prosecution," so the man promised the judge he "would mend his ways and leave the state of Idaho at once if he were turned loose."[91] The charges for disorderly conduct were dropped, and the article concluded he left town.

District court records also reveal one case against Charles Dereanzio, who apparently paid for a woman to travel across state lines under the false pretense of marrying him. The arrest warrant reveals that Dereanzio

> *did furnish to a certain woman, namely Pearl Ray, transportation on the railroad from the City of Spokane, State of Washington, to the City of Wallace, State of Idaho, and by such transportation and by letters and divers methods did induce, entice and procure the said Pearl Ray to come into this state for immoral purpose, to wit—for the purpose of prostitution; contrary to the form, force and effect of the Statute in such cases made as provided and against the peace and dignity of the State of Idaho.*[92]

Witnesses on behalf of the state included Mrs. Harley Lamb, who ran the rooming house by the Northern Pacific Roundhouse where Dereanzio rented a room. Dereanzio admitted to buying Pearl Ray's train ticket. Ray testified that she did housework as a domestic girl in Spokane, and she claimed to have known Dereanzio for about one and a half years, writing back and forth until he asked her to come to Wallace. Supposedly, they would be married as soon as she came to Wallace. They lived together in Mrs. Lamb's rooming house until Ray decided he'd "told a lot of stories that wasn't true and I just picked up and left him."[93]

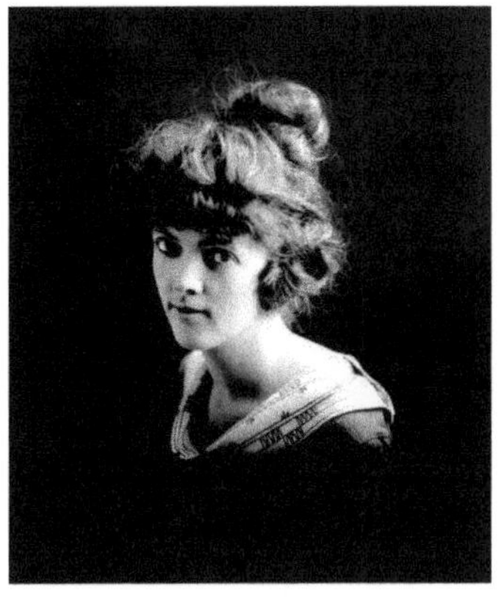

Mrs. Lamb, who ran a boardinghouse involved in a 1916 sex trafficking case. She is pictured here in 1918. *Barnard-Stockbridge Collection, University of Idaho Library Special Collections and Archives.*

Dereanzio's lawyer, A.H. Featherstone, implied that she had been a "streetwalker" in Spokane before moving to Wallace and that she had requested Dereanzio bring her to town. Dereanzio therefore shouldn't be prosecuted under the Mann Act, irrespective of the statute's vague language, which might have justified the charge. A copy of the letter Pearl wrote is in the file (errors as in original):

> *My Dearest Husband*
>
> *Your most kind and loveing letter recived and was very glad to here from my dear say sweetheart be sure and send for me right away. That if you want*

your wife I am so lossome I don't know what to do now if you want me to come send right away say dharling I want you to have me up there befor wensday now be sure and wire me the ticket right away

love and kisses from your wife
address Pearl Ray
Gen Del
Spokane
write soon
and send for me[94]

Ray claimed that she wrote it according to Dereanzio's instruction. She does appear to have been naïve and desperate. It's obvious that her position was vulnerable, and it would have been easy for someone to take advantage of her by promising marriage. The case was eventually dismissed on June 24, 1916, by prosecuting attorney H.J. Hull, "due to the witnesses taking off."[95]

During this time, according to Richard Magnuson, there was a series of attempts to eradicate gambling and pass "blue laws" as the reformist attitude spread.[96] Sweet, W.A. Simons and the Sweet Hotel Company were charged with "willfully, unlawfully and knowingly" permitting "the games of poker and pangingy [panguingue]," but the case was dismissed by a grand jury in 1914.[97] Stories about raids on poker games and bars having to close on Sundays appear in the *Wallace Press-Times* on December 17, 1915, and December 29, 1915. Most of the arrests appear to have been for show, and little was actually done to stem drinking, gambling or prostitution. Within individual cities in the Silver Valley, the women became less visible and less mobile, but in the greater region, they became increasingly mobile and began to move from city to city, facilitated by improvements in rail transportation.[98] In later days, this would come to be called "the circuit." Women frequently revised their names when they moved or changed working houses.[99] Jessie Morin, also known as Josie Morin and Josie Moore, for example, ran several houses in Wardner and Wallace before settling in as a madam at the U&I Rooms in 1914.

Instead of attempting to eliminate sex work in town, city leaders chose to generate income for the city, in the form of both fees and fines. According to a *Wallace Press-Times* article, there were thirty-four women working in the red-light district in January 1912, and "the only effort" the town had made "to deal with the evil" was to charge them with "vagrancy, made in the police court once each month, where a fixed and nominal fine" was

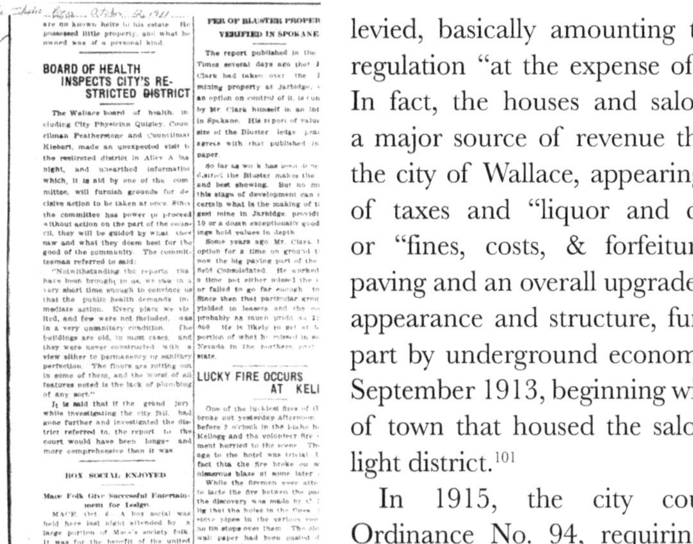
are no known heirs to his estate. He possessed little property, and what he owned was of a personal kind.

BOARD OF HEALTH INSPECTS CITY'S RESTRICTED DISTRICT

The Wallace board of health, including City Physician Quigley, Councilman Featherstone and Councilman Kiebert, made an unexpected visit to the restricted district in Alley A last night, and unearthed information which, it is said by one of the committee, will furnish grounds for decisive action to be taken at once. Since the committee has power to proceed without action on the part of the council, they will be guided by what they saw and what they deem best for the good of the community. The committeeman referred to said:

"Notwithstanding the reports that have been brought to us, we saw in a very short time enough to convince us that the public health demands immediate action. Every place we visited, and few were not included, was in a very unsanitary condition. The buildings are old, in most cases, and they were never constructed with a view either to permanency or sanitary perfection. The floors are rotting out in some of them, and the worst of all features noted is the lack of plumbing of any sort."

It is said that if the grand jury while investigating the city jail had gone further and investigated the district referred to, the report to the court would have been longer and more comprehensive than it was.

BOX SOCIAL ENJOYED

Mace Folk Give Successful Entertainment for Lodges

MACE, Oct. 6.—A box social was held here last night attended by a large portion of Mace's society folk. It was for the benefit of the united secret societies and at the end it was seen that $47 had been received from the sales of the boxes.

LUCKY FIRE OCCURS AT KELL

Newspaper article about the Wallace Board of Health's Inspection of Avenue A, around the time the city chose to regulate the houses rather than eradicate the district. *From the* Idaho Press, *1911.*

levied, basically amounting to authorized regulation "at the expense of the county." In fact, the houses and saloons provided a major source of revenue that came into the city of Wallace, appearing in the form of taxes and "liquor and city licenses," or "fines, costs, & forfeitures."[100] Street paving and an overall upgrade in the town's appearance and structure, funded in large part by underground economies, began in September 1913, beginning with the section of town that housed the saloons and red-light district.[101]

In 1915, the city council passed Ordinance No. 94, requiring that hotels and lodging houses keep publicly available registers of occupants and visitors, with a fine of twenty-five dollars or a fifteen-day jail sentence as penalty. Every owner, proprietor or manager was instructed to record true names, not "false or fictitious," and keep said register "open for the inspection of all persons at all times."[102] With large numbers of people moving into and out of town, this move appears to have been oriented toward improving records at ordinary hotels and lodging houses, but the ordinance would also provide the perception that the city would be better able to investigate sex slavery cases and regulate the women working in the houses.

War and Social Hygiene

By 1917, it had become apparent that the United States would intervene in the war ravaging Europe. Everyone was expected to support the war effort—newspapers published articles encouraging people to buy bonds, conserve resources and help keep morale high. The government singled out restricted districts as a special part of the preparations, with the War Department and the attorney general launching a massive campaign that they called a "war on prostitution." Even in communities like Wallace, where people generally feared what they called "scatteration"—the idea that the women would scatter throughout the community if they were not contained within red-light districts—government officials recognized the power of citizens' support, so they drove home arguments equating moral cleanliness with healthy soldiers and patriotism. Propaganda distributed to businesses recruited community members to pressure their local law enforcement officials: residents' "eternal vigilance" would be needed to ensure a "morally clean city," the materials urged. These pamphlets explained that "flimsy arguments in favor of segregation as the only alternative to 'scatteration'" would not only "separate the soldier from his two dollars" but also "infect him with syphilis or gonorrhea" and "keep him out of the trenches."[103] The government literature linked prostitution to bootlegging and other so-called vice industries. This line of argument reasoned that there was a powerful web of mutual economic interests at stake, an alliance of people who had been "loud in their denunciations of the enforcement of laws against prostitution."

In Wallace, during an address at the Methodist church, a U.S. Army lieutenant pleaded with the citizens to understand that soldiers would be "useless if debilitated by venereal disease," citing "the fall of Rome as an example of what Wallace could expect if it let prostitution thrive in its midst."[104] This hyperbolic language was not unusual during this era, and it took its toll. While a great number of community members continued to be in support of keeping the brothels, they did begin to worry about health and sanitation consequences. The government's propaganda campaign emphasized the values of efficiency as well as moral and social hygiene. The men from town had just been drafted and were preparing to leave for training, which suddenly made the need for reform seem more urgent. This development, coupled with the economic symbiosis of the brothels and local government, would lead to increased anxieties about cleanliness. Ultimately, the result would be more regulation for the women working in the houses.

Brown Manufacturing Company and the American Social Hygiene Association teamed up with the War Department to distribute propaganda meant to educate potential soldiers about the dangers of succumbing to the temptations of women of ill repute. But the bigger-picture strategy was more complex and paternalistic: federal authorities targeted restricted districts and the women within them by rallying employers and community members as the enforcers, calling on everyone to do their part to "protect" the soldiers from these women, who were framed as morally degenerate

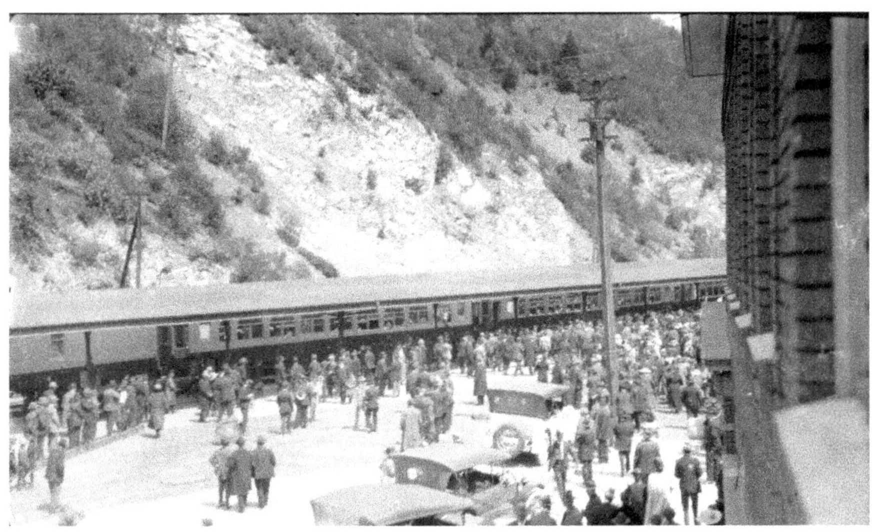

Young men boarding a train to go to Camp Lewis, Washington, during World War I. This photo was taken from the Idaho Building on the corner of Seventh and Cedar Streets, looking east. *Barnard-Stockbridge Collection, University of Idaho Library Special Collections and Archives.*

and disease-ridden. Federal officials discussed women who worked in red-light districts as though they were pests on par with mosquitoes, spreading contagion wherever they were found. This "war on prostitution" was more of an ideological battle than it was a matter of sniffing out and arresting offenders. As one government authority put it: "To drain a red-light district and destroy thereby a breeding place of syphilis and gonorrhea is as logical as it is to drain a swamp and destroy thereby a breeding place of malaria and yellow fever."[105] If soldiers were infected with venereal diseases, the rhetoric went, they would not be "fit to fight," which was the slogan that the military pushed as it advocated the closure of brothels across the nation. Such language invoked old stereotypes of women's bodies as mysterious and dank incubators capable of unleashing disease and destruction. One pamphlet, *Keeping Fit to Fight*, warned:

> *A venereal disease contracted after deliberate exposure through intercourse with a prostitute is as much of a disgrace as showing the white feather.*
>
> *A soldier in the hospital with venereal disease is a slacker.*
>
> *His medicine and care cost money that could be otherwise used to win the war.*

> *He has lost the self-respect which is the backbone of every true soldier.*
> *If you go with a prostitute, you endanger your country because you risk your health, and perhaps your life. You lessen the man-power of your company and throw extra burdens on your comrades. You are a moral shirker.*
> *WOMEN WHO SOLICIT SOLDIERS FOR IMMORAL PURPOSES ARE USUALLY DISEASE SPREADERS AND FRIENDS OF THE ENEMY.*
> *No matter how thirsty or hungry you were, you wouldn't eat or drink anything that you knew in advance would weaken your vitality, poison your blood, cripple your limbs, rot your flesh, blind you, and destroy your brain. Then why take the same chance with a prostitute?*

The War Department sent these materials to regional places of employment in order to "attack the problem through industrial channels—reach the men before they are called," distributing pamphlets, posters, lecture notes and pay stub enclosures that warned against the dangers of disease. As they explained, "There is no magic formula, which, when adopted, will insure a morally clean city. There is no royal road to cleanliness any more than there is to learning. Eternal vigilance is just as much the price of municipal cleanliness as it is of liberty."[106]

The pamphlets and flyers repeatedly claimed that 70 to 90 percent of "professional prostitutes" were infected with gonorrhea or syphilis "all the time." *Keeping Fit to Fight* urged, "That kind of girl is likely to lie," so the soldiers were instructed to "just remember this—all loose women are dirty. Therefore, any man who joins his body with the body of a prostitute or loose girl runs the risk of catching one of these terrible diseases." *Your Job and Your Future* advises all men to prevent the spread of syphilis and gonorrheal "germs" in the following way: "You've got to keep away from the kind of women who are willing to 'give you a good time,' whether they want money for it or not. Don't forget it: Keep away from prostitutes, whores, hookers, chippies and so-called 'private snaps.'" Employers near military training camps were asked to help fight businesses profiting from vice interests. These pamphlets included instructions for leading educational workshops, instructional syllabus and tips for teaching. One War Department propaganda poster features huge red letters, announcing, "BEWARE! Keep Away from Prostitutes," associating venereal disease with prostitution, adding that 70 percent of all "loose women" have both clap and syphilis.[107] The government expected employers to educate their workers and recruit friends and family members to the cause. These packets also contained model laws to be written

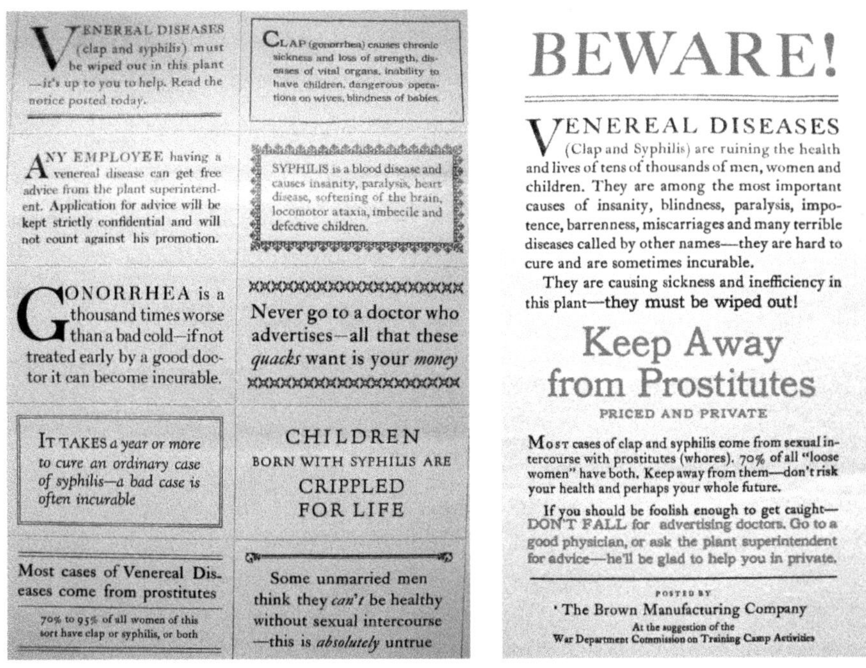

Left: Government anti-prostitution propaganda, 1917. *Potlatch Forests Papers, University of Idaho Library Special Collections and Archives.*

Right: "Beware Prostitutes" flier, 1917. *Potlatch Forests Papers, University of Idaho Library Special Collections and Archives.*

into city ordinances, with templates leaving blanks for the town name, and license applications for proprietors from boardinghouses.

The U.S. War Department targeted Wallace and surrounding area because of its proximity to the large military camps. On October 19, 1917, an article appeared in the *Spokesman-Review* reporting that the War Department had ordered the closure of the Wallace red-light district. The article associated the brothels with bootlegging and petty robbery, claiming that during the year, there had been one hundred or more women operating in the town. As evidence of the need for this closure, the reporter explained, "Married women have complained that their husbands were neglecting their families and squandering their money buying whiskey."[108] Despite the paper's announcement, local operations continued, insulated by the decision in Wallace to regulate instead. The resilience of this decision is apparent in former mayor Moe Pellissier's 2014 explanation: "If you shut down the upstairs, it just moves to the bars and the streets. You can regulate venereal diseases if you regulate prostitution." The idea was not to legislate against behavior that would continue anyway in a riskier form.

In reality, prostitution and the government—especially the military—have been interdependent throughout American history. Wallace's sex industry faced this moment of existential crisis that closed many other red-light districts as city officials acknowledged the full extent to which their economic interest was invested in the brothels; symbiosis between the brothels and local government actually intensified after the War Department's social and moral hygiene campaign. Rather than acquiesce to pressure, the town doubled down on prostitution. City officials struck a quiet compromise: for the first time in history, Wallace would officially require its sex workers to undergo health examinations, and this tradition of medical regulation would continue up until the closure of the houses. On September 10, the city council initiated a discussion about the "conditions in Alley A."[109] The actual discussion was not recorded, but considering the pressure exerted by the War Department with regard to concerns over venereal disease, it's likely that a large part of the debate concerned the need for doctors to examine the working girls living in and operating out of the Alley. The madams probably didn't attempt to oppose this regulation because they understood that the exams would help ensure the men's continued patronage, despite the fear mongering.

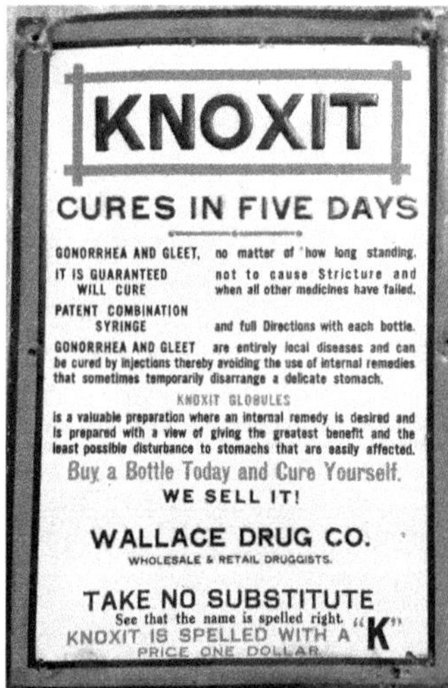

Knoxit tin, advertising a compound made locally, meant to treat sexually transmitted infections in the days before penicillin. *Richard Asher Collection; photo by Heather Branstetter.*

From a social hygiene perspective, it does seem to be the case that venereal disease was quite rampant and a rather serious public health issue during this pre-penicillin era. The health exams also served another important social function—they helped to placate the concerns of local community members and they provided an improved image, which was needed in order to effectively counter the government's public relations campaign, which would soon amplify, both in terms of scale and intensity. In the face of the War Department's negative publicity campaign, the madams understood that the exams would help ensure the men's continued patronage, and indeed, brothel managers would continue to emphasize cleanliness and medical regulation in both rhetoric and ritualized practice from this time onward.

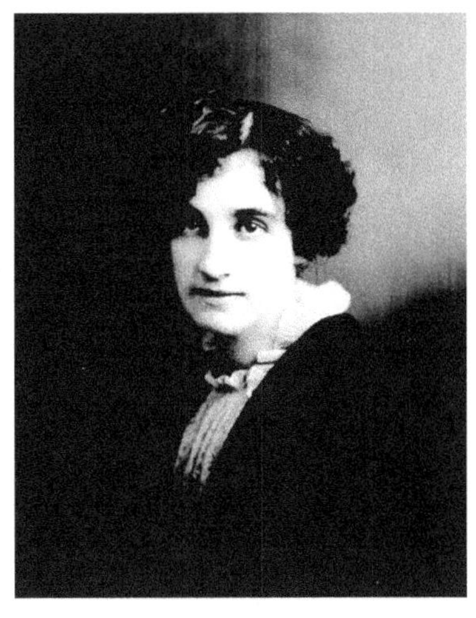

Josie Morin, pictured here in 1914. *Barnard-Stockbridge Collection, University of Idaho Library Special Collections and Archives.*

By January 1918, amid declarations that the war against prostitution had been successful, the federal government acknowledged that simply closing down the red-light districts had not worked to eliminate prostitution. One official conceded, "I do not think we will ever absolutely eliminate the prostitute, but we do want to make it impossible for the prostitute to flaunt herself in the face of men on the streets when they are not thinking about her."[110] The War Department's efforts did shut down the majority of restricted districts across the country. In Wallace, however, the campaign reinforced a convincing anti-reform argument: if prostitutes were not segregated and thus easy to identify, it would be impossible to enforce health regulations. It soon became clear that prostitution in the Silver Valley had not run its course. The approaching war ensured that mining activities would continue to flourish, which in turn ensured a large population of single men who would provide ongoing economic demand for women who would sell sex. Long-term mining camp communities like Wallace adopted a pragmatic acceptance of prostitution. Wallace residents would continue to prefer a decriminalized model rather than a prohibitionist stance so sex workers could be regulated rather than spread informally throughout residential areas, where sexually modest girls might be lured into the profession. As local historian John Amonson described it, "The community felt better leaving that particular element in that particular place rather than having it be pervasive all over."[111]

Madams and sex workers supported the war effort, too, despite the War Department's anti-prostitution campaign. During World War I, for example, Josie Morin, madam of the U&I Rooms, donated $25 for a Red Cross fundraiser. That amount of money would be worth about $585 in contemporary currency. Mary White Gordon described the incident in her 2001 autobiographical narrative about growing up in Wallace:

I rang the bell and a very nice lady asked me to come in. Her living room had pink shaded lights and a lot of shiny satin pillows, and she seemed very friendly and very pretty.... I told about my lucky afternoon at dinner that night, my father said he knew her. She was a very generous lady. She gave money and other helpful things when needed.... Jessie Moran, a very well known madam who had a booming business in Wallace and the Coeur d'Alenes definitely knew my father. He wasn't ashamed of that and I doubt very much that he was one of her customers, but he had the Victorian belief that women shouldn't know about those things—certainly not his sweet little daughter.[112]

3

Prohibition, North Idaho's "Threefold Conspiracy" and Depression

During the Prohibition era, sex workers remained in the restricted district above the drinking establishments, which constructed fronts as pool halls or cigar shops, but some women also worked out of hotels and taxis. Most maintained alliances with liquor dealers, selling alcohol to their clients, and some women were bootleggers themselves. Several prominent madams were arrested in an event referred to as "the north Idaho whiskey rebellion," when federal investigators arrested around two hundred Shoshone County residents in 1929 for bootleg liquor production, distribution, gambling and prostitution activities. We don't know as much about the women who sold sex in the Silver Valley during the Great Depression, but oral histories reveal the trade continued until the Second World War, when the profession began to flourish again.

Prohibition Era

Public opinion in Shoshone County wavered back and forth on the Prohibition issue, which also affected the townspeople's perspective regarding the two major interests that remained intertwined with saloon culture: gambling and prostitution. Much of the rhetoric against prostitution focused on protecting families and innocent young girls as well as soldiers. New anxieties about gender had already begun to crop up as Americans began to worry about the entry of women into speakeasies and the resulting possibility that more women would be vulnerable to becoming prostitutes.[113] Those in favor of reforms connected crime to underground liquor activities, prostitution, moral degradation and, ultimately, the demise of traditional families. Prohibition changed the traditional drinking patterns: before this time, it was uncommon to see women in drinking establishments. Any woman who drank in a saloon was assumed to be a prostitute or, at the very least, a "bad" woman, but during Prohibition, new social spaces created for drinking encouraged women to join the men at speakeasies.[114] For moral traditionalists, increased freedom for women led to concerns about sexual promiscuity. Mothers worried their daughters would choose frivolity or prostitution instead of marriage and children while men were concerned about women invading formerly male-only venues.[115]

TABLE 2: BROTHELS, LOCATIONS, AND PROPRIETORS 1917–1947

BROTHEL NAME	LOCATION & DATES	MADAMS OR PROPRIETORS	ASSOCIATED SALOON MEN, LANDLORDS OR INVESTORS
Arment Rooms	601½ Cedar Street	Grace Beatty (prior to 1928), M.A. Davidson	Charles Keating, Herman J. Rossi
Merle's Rooms	212½ Sixth Street (Kelly's Alley)	Marie Lindsay, Helen Scott	Tony Armani, Matt Jurkovich, Fred and Cora Kelly, Mary Albertini
The Comet	Cedar Street		R.A. Greer
Oasis Rooms (Possibly called the Club Rooms during the 1940s)	605½ Cedar Street	Helen Rose, Ruth Poska (1940s)	George Austin, E.C. Florine and Joseph F. Whelan
The Metropolitan	411 Cedar Street	Mrs. Anna Watson (1917–20s)	
U&I Rooms	613½ Cedar Street	Josie Morin/ Moore (1914–20s)	

Brothel Name	Location & Dates	Madams or Proprietors	Associated Saloon Men, Landlords or Investors
The Montana Club	615½ Cedar Street	Jackie Hansen	Lieb brothers
Unknown	Avenue A (behind and east of the Oasis)	Anna Brass, aka Mrs. Julius Brass (1922–37)	
Western Rooms	611½ Cedar Street		"Mutt" Ralls
St. Frances Hotel	1920–31	"Big Nell" Reed	
Unknown	Rooms above Sixth and Pine	Bertha Lee (1920s)	
Unknown	1928	Dolly Summers	
Pastime Cigars			Matt Jurkovich, Nick Pavelich, Tom Franrich
Unknown	1922–29	Babe Kelly	
Unknown		Mary Norman	
The Lodge			
Unknown	1920s	Ethel Bay	
Unknown	1920s	Mrs. William Clough	
Unknown	1920s	Jeanette Martin	
Unknown	1930s	Katherine Mautz	
Unknown	1930s	Anna Bernardi/ Bernardy	
Unknown	1929	Mona McDonald	
Unknown		Jimmie Ryan and Bertha Strom	

In Idaho, Prohibition began when the state legislature voted to become officially dry on January 1, 1916, in a move that was received with some ambivalence in Shoshone County. As Barton put it the summary of his 1979 study interviewing old-timers in the area, "Many loggers and miners took their pleasures very seriously. The transcripts are loaded with stories about men in search of gambling, bootleg alcohol, and ladies of the night."[116] Prostitution was "entwined with other entertainments that were sacred to miners, which meant that any potential attack on prostitution could be construed as an attack on these other entertainments as well" and vice versa.[117] Those who were in support of alcohol reform, on the other hand, praised the decision's potential to increase worker efficiency and bring greater stability to family life. City leaders worried they would be unable to run the town if their revenues were seriously depleted. According to Donna Krulitz Smith, city officials in the Silver Valley began to face a dilemma as the mining camps grew into mature and long-term communities and business leaders recognized how an unruly wide-open town reputation could tarnish the kind of wholesome small-town image that attracts stable middle-class families.[118] Could the town find a balance between economic interests and residents' desires?

In the wake of the new dry laws, which went into effect on January 1, 1916, many Wallace buildings remodeled in order to better facilitate continued liquor sales. Most of the saloons turned into "soft drink establishments" or "cigar stores," while the Samuels and Sweets made plans to run as billiard parlors. Other bars called themselves confectionaries or fruit stands. The *Press-Times* reported on December 30, 1915, that R.A. Greer would be closing the Comet as a saloon but would open again the very next day as a "soft drink establishment and as a lobby for the rooming house on the second floor"—that is, liquor would be available downstairs and a brothel would continue upstairs. Even though the laws changed, old behavior would be tolerated locally as long as the liquor proprietors kept things quiet enough to evade potential state or federal enforcers. Each "soda shop" had a receiving area with a lookout and double doors blocking the visibility of the area inside, so if a federal agent walked in, the bouncer could push a button connected to a trapdoor that opened underneath the well liquor bottles, which would drop down to the basement, where they would crash and break.[119] If anyone looked inside the bar, they wouldn't find any alcohol, and if they went downstairs, they would only find broken glass and a wet floor. The bars had rooms in the back or partly upstairs where the gambling took

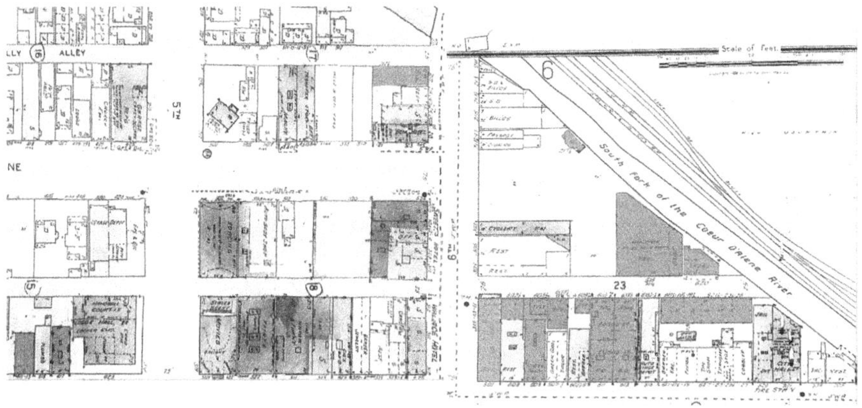

A map of Wallace brothels in 1927—the saloons are labeled more discreetly, with sex for sale in locations indicated by solid gray. *Adapted from Sanborn Fire Insurance Maps.*

place—not exactly out in the open, but not really hidden either. In the Club Bar below the Oasis brothel, for example, there was a small balcony area up a set of stairs, which is still visible in the northwestern corner of the Oasis Bordello Museum.[120]

A sex worker named Bertha Lee was the first person arrested under the new Prohibition laws. She was arrested only two weeks after the laws went into effect, caught with a man and a partially filled flask of whiskey in a room above a former saloon at the corner of Sixth and Pine. According to the story reported in the *Press-Times*, Lee claimed that "some man brought the liquor to her room and left it on the table. She told this story when she was first arrested and, if she has information regarding bootlegging, she is not giving it to the authorities."[121] The article's title calls her a "Woman Bootlegger," but she was also selling sex (as a man pretending to be Mr. Lee explained, without explicitly naming the woman's profession).[122] Donna Smith's thesis detailing the north Idaho whiskey rebellion describes the situation for sex workers during Prohibition:

> *Bawdy houses offered trays of drinks in the front parlors (some filled with tap water) for 25 cents a glass; if poured carefully, six glassfuls could be squeezed out of one bottle of beer. Prostitutes in cribs sold beer for a dollar a bottle, while paying the supplying saloon twenty-five cents. If, as in the early days of prohibition, finding a supplier proved difficult, other means could be found. Juanita Wilson, who admitted to planning to "lay over in Mullan until after the payday season," was apprehended with a suitcase*

full of alcoholic beverages when she stepped off the train from Missoula. Prohibition simply added another risk for prostitutes already employed in a business fraught with pitfalls.[123]

Gambling and alcohol distribution would remain interconnected with sex work. In November 1916, the *Wallace Press-Times* editorial page describes a "little clique [that] has subsisted among the gamblers, the liquor dealers, and the shame of the community [sex workers]."[124] Women sold alcohol out of the rooms where they sold sex, and liquor dealers directed customers to their businesses accordingly. Wallace townspeople not directly invested in the underground operations had begun to speak out more openly, and by December 1916, the City of Wallace passed an ordinance making gambling illegal. This decision followed complaints from the wives of the town that "persistent carrying on of gambling" had been depriving them and their families of the "necessities of life" as "the husband's income was lost over gambling tables."[125] The ordinance made sure to note that it was the women of the town who had been the driving force behind the ordinance, but the motivation was actually more nuanced: the wording also reflected the city's desire to keep pace with reforms taking place across the nation. There was not really much opposition to the council's decision. The mayor claimed to have consulted with the business owners, who were "willing to cooperate in bringing about the elimination of gambling," in the interest of "the welfare of the community."

In reality, the mayor appears to have communicated to the business owners that they would merely have to function under the radar. Wallace wasn't alone in continuing with operations—throughout north Idaho and Shoshone County, towns reached similar arrangements, most likely because they knew the decreased revenue from alcohol licensing fees would dramatically affect the economy. Silver Valley towns made up for the missing income by instituting an unofficial taxation system. The money didn't go into personal pockets, though; it went back into the community.[126] By "licensing the bootleggers, gamblers and sporting houses," the Mullan mayor would later explain, the city was able to raise money without having to levy taxes on the rest of the townspeople.[127] It would have been illogical for Wallace to close down gambling and other vice interests if Kellogg, Mullan and other adjoining towns didn't do the same. Wallace officials also considered the city's "desperate need of improvements in bridges and a viaduct to the homes on the steep southern slope of town."[128] Problems were often worked out through extra-legal means. In many instances, the violators were arrested and charged but never prosecuted, as was the case with Anna Watson, who was selling sex and liquor out of the Metropolitan Hotel, which was located on the north side of Cedar Street between Fourth and Fifth Streets.[129]

Despite the anti-gambling ordinance, then, speakeasies continued to feature a wide array of choices, with games ranging from penny ante poker to high-stakes card games. Firsthand accounts from men who were alive during this time reveal that during this era, the low-stakes card game panguingue (pronounced "pan-ghee-nee," often simply called "pan") became one of the most popular games around.[130] As one miner put it: "Panguingue was invented to keep the tinhorns and pimps off the streets. And ah, as a result of that they had a class of people in town…there always was, in a mining camp there always were just as many people who tried to mine the miners."[131]

NORTH IDAHO'S "THREEFOLD CONSPIRACY"

The Silver Valley, with its abandoned mines and rugged mountain terrain, was a moonshiner's paradise. Eventually, it would be impossible for federal authorities to ignore the area's blatant disregard for the law. The resulting conflict would culminate in an episode called the "north Idaho whiskey rebellion." There are few oral histories about this significant event, which seems to have been forgotten by contemporary Silver Valley residents. The federal government sent in an undercover agent pretending to be a bootlegger looking to get into business. A local bartender told the agent whom to contact for supplies, advised him to "check with the police chief and sheriff when ready to open" and then displayed his wares, which included "bonded Canadian whiskey, moonshine, and Heidelberg beer."[132] One year later, in 1929, federal agents raided and attempted to prove a countywide conspiracy, resulting in a series of eighty-seven grand jury indictments against "soft drink proprietors, prostitutes," city officials and law enforcement from Wallace, Mullan and Kellogg.[133] An article appearing in the *Spokesman-Review* called Wallace a "modern Sodom," and the *Wallace Press-Times* answered that those were "fighting words," featuring a resolution asserting that more than one hundred businessmen would stop subscribing to Spokane papers and boycott the Spokane businesses that supported them.[134] It wasn't the first time the mining district had been upset with Spokane and its newspapers. During the mining labor wars in 1899, for example, the *Mullan Mirror* wrote that money from the Silver Valley's mining district had "made Spokane what it is. Yet the people and prose of that hobo town are ungrateful enough to smite the hand that feeds them."[135]

The *Wallace Press-Times* described a few of the defendants as "visibly affected" when they were brought into the commissioner's office, but the majority apparently "laughed and chatted.... Most jovial of all was fur-coated [sex worker] Babe Kelly, who draped herself in a chair, lit a cigarette, and began 'kidding' the officers and telling jokes."[136] Silver Valley residents and their lawyers were confident throughout the trial, which revealed the extent to which local government and law enforcement had institutionalized sex work, liquor distribution and gambling. Wallace mayor Herman Rossi unapologetically told the *Seattle Star* he would take his case all the way to the Supreme Court, because, "Wallace residents 'knew that the miners demanded a certain amount of license, and they knew that certain conditions would exist, even if they did close their eyes. So they left their eyes open.'"[137] During the trial, it was revealed that Mayor Rossi owned a quarter share of the Arment Rooms, as did Wallace city treasurer Charles Keating, who testified that Grace Beatty and later M.A. Davidson "managed the sixteen upper-floor 'lodging rooms' for the 'very reasonable' sum of $110 a month."[138]

Many of those arrested were convicted for their role in what was called a "threefold conspiracy" to fund city operations through the "licensing of gambling, prostitution, and bootlegging," but the judge went relatively easy on the sex workers, sentencing most of them to two months of incarceration in local jails.[139] On January 1, 1930, the *Spokesman-Review* reported that Babe Kelly received a four-month sentence in a Kootenai County jail but did not pay a fine; the judge told her, "Too much of your money has been taken away from you for the support of the government already."[140] Judge Webster believed that the women involved were victims of circumstance and chafed at the defense's claim that there was not a moral issue at the heart of the case. He preached:

> *There is nothing in the scale of society that is more loathsome or despicable in the form of a human being than a man who will knowingly accept in whole or in part or live off the earnings of a fallen woman.... And how does accepting the earnings of a prostitute on the part of an individual become decent when it is practiced as a means of supporting a municipality? ...Instead of being willing to share their gain, it ought to be the impulse of every decent man to remove the crown of thorns from their brow. God knows they are hard enough off without taking the money that they degrade their persons and forfeit their souls to get, and surely the time has not come*

in this great country of ours where a municipality can openly live and exist upon money so filthy as that.... Surely, gentlemen, surely it has not yet come to pass that whole organized municipalities can accept money from these sources and do so brazenly in the name of the welfare of the city and expect any enlightened court to approve it? The welfare of the city! Yes, but what of its moral welfare?[141]

The judge argued that in the case of Wallace and Mullan, city officials were essentially pimps profiting from sex workers' wages in the name of community welfare. Webster shamed the chief of police for making "regular rounds in the houses of prostitution" to collect the "bloody spoils" from "the pitiable women whose fate has brought them there."[142] As he sentenced sex worker Mona McDonald, the judge speculated that she "ought to know what the seamy side of life means and what it leads to and the degradation and the grief that it entails," urging her to

find a place in society that will be worthy of you. I would rather be the wife of a respectable miner than to be the bedecked and bejeweled mistress of the finest bedazzled bawdy house in the world, and you will find in it more happiness and certainly more self-respect.[143]

Ultimately, however, the Ninth Circuit court disagreed with the jury and Judge Webster, reversing most of the original verdicts and ordering new trials for the defendants who appealed their cases. The circuit court called the case "an interesting chapter in the history of vice and crime" because the defendants "without doubt" should have been guilty, but the convictions couldn't be sustained because there was "not a particle of evidence in the record tending even remotely to establish or prove any such conspiracy."[144] The trials ended up demonstrating that "Shoshone County law enforcement was graft-free, allowing them to maintain control and respect of the citizenry" despite the fact that they were ignoring the law.[145] Madam Dolly Summers, for example, asserted that she willingly paid the fee for police protection in case "anybody started a rough house in her place," and city clerk L.L. Leighty testified that "there was no graft and no secrecy involved, as the collections were a matter of public record."[146] In other words, because county residents trusted they were not taking payoffs and pocketing bribes in an obviously corrupt manner, the unofficial fee system for regulating vice enabled Shoshone County officials to more effectively enforce local preferences about legal and community priorities.

Depression Era

The Depression affected the mines and all of the industries associated with them, including prostitution. During this era, "it was very difficult. Very, very difficult," miner Maidell Clemets lamented during a 1979 oral history interview, noting that even though books were written about how the Depression affected rich people and those who had invested in Wall Street, those books

> *never told of the troubles and misfortunes of the mining camps, and the common ordinary small communities.... The bubble broke all right. It was about in the latter part of October, around the 29th* [of 1929].... *They came down and laid off all the single men. Those with families, they kept.*[147]

Residents of Wallace did what they could to get by in the rugged landscape, using the old logs that had been burned in the 1910 fire for warming their houses.[148] Prostitution in Wallace and Wardner continued to "run at a very orderly fashion," with the women having to get a license at city hall, pay a fee each month and submit to "medical inspection every week." Wallace "had a lot of prostitution there. That's right. It was wide open. Even held on through the '30s there were prostitutes in the community," Clemets explained.[149]

According to Mary White Gordon's unpublished autobiographical narrative, Wallace was a very condensed town of about 2,800 people in those years. Gordon knew everyone, except in one district, which had a high fence around some of the buildings. This section of town was quiet and unnoticed, she explained: "I don't remember at all how I eventually found out that this was a thriving red-light district and had steady business, but when it was payday at the mines the place was really jumping."[150] One madam used to walk by Gordon's house on sunny afternoons

> *wearing beautiful clothes and big willow plumes in her hat. Jack and I thought she was lovely, but she never came to our house or to any of the houses of our friends. She was very pleasant and friendly and we would try to say something to make her smile, because she had a beautiful diamond flashing in her front tooth.*[151]

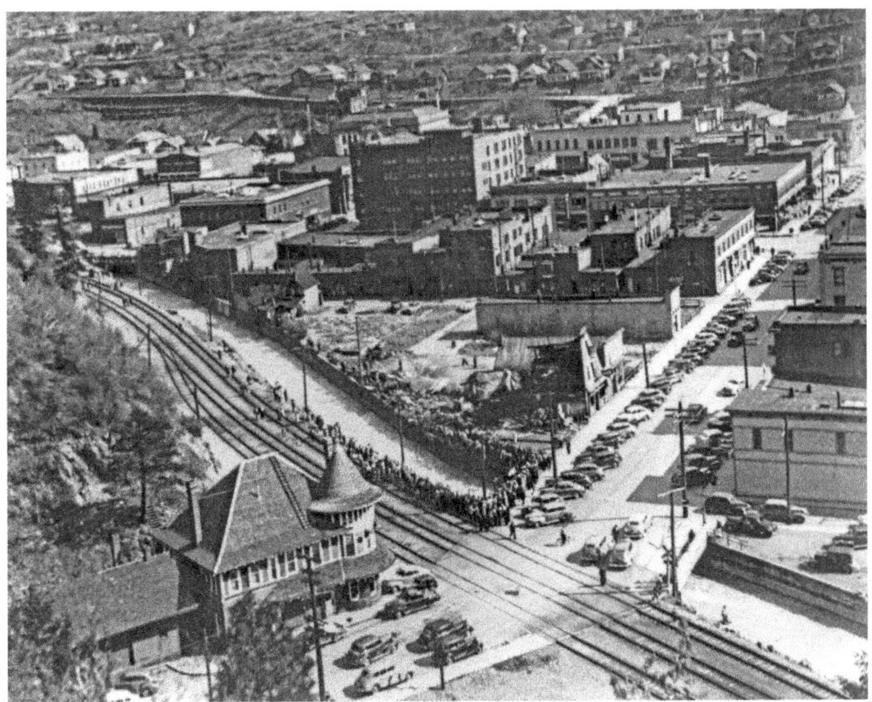

Lead Creek Derby, around 1940, from the hill northwest of town, looking southeast. The restricted district was to the right of the river and left of the line of cars. Many houses had been demolished by this time. *Historic Wallace Preservation Society.*

One of the madams at the Oasis, which was possibly called the Club Rooms during this time, was named Helen Rose. It was said that people driving in from out of town would mistake the brothel for a legitimate place to stay because of the "Rooms" sign. When this happened, "Rose supposedly took pity on a few of them and would send them to the café next door and spring for a meal."[152]

During this time, the brothels were partially under the purview of the health officer and the Street and Alley Committee. Many of the businesses in the restricted district became dilapidated, and a number of them were torn down at the recommendation of the Health and Sanitation Committee. In August 1931, for example, the committee, along with the fire chief and chief of police, recommended to the city council that the brick building on Avenue A owned by Madam Anna Brass, alias Mrs. Julius Brass, should be torn down.[153] The committee explained that the property "is so dilapidated and/or is in such condition so as to menace the public health and/or safety

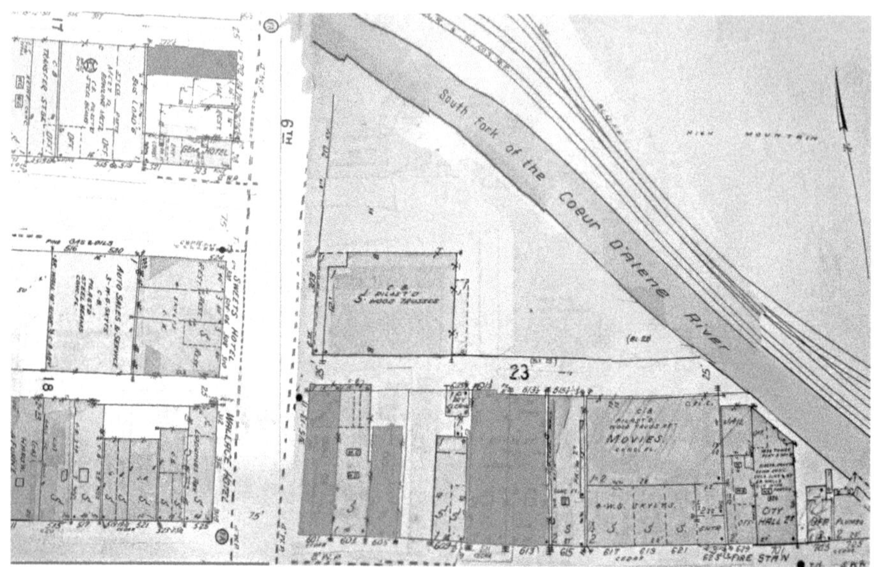

A map of the brothels still standing by the end of the Depression era. *Adapted from Sanborn Fire Insurance Maps.*

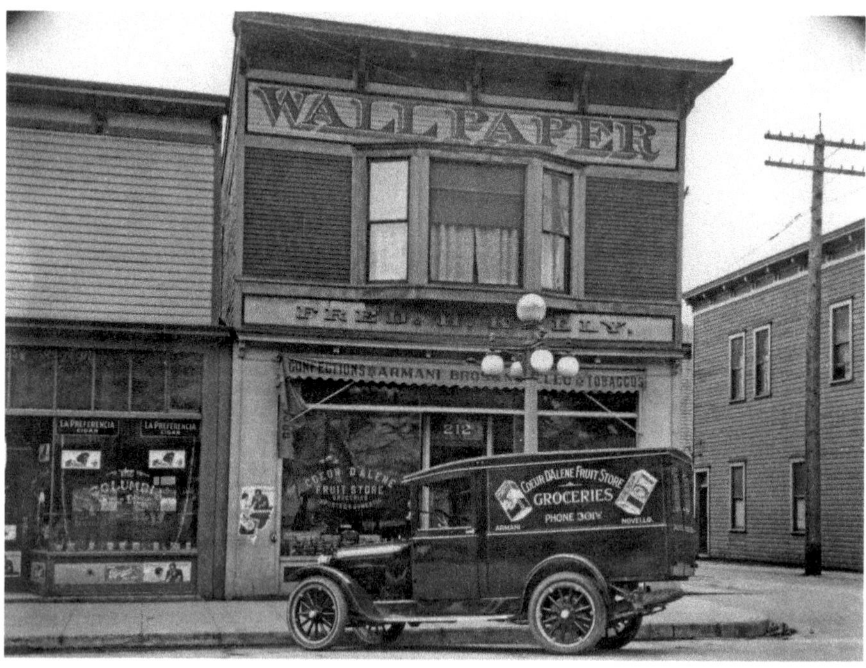

Kelly Building—the original Lux Rooms was on the second floor, with the entrance in "Kelly's Alley." *Historic Wallace Preservation Society.*

of persons and/or property on account of increased fire hazard and/or otherwise." The council ordered Anna Brass to have the building removed within ten days, or else the city would demolish it for her and tax her for the cost. The city drew the same conclusions regarding the "Frank Flood Estate," which was also on Avenue A and appears to have been a brothel.

After 1933, when the town's taverns were once again able to operate openly, bar owners and madams were required to buy bonds at $250.00 apiece, along with a fee of $6.25, for the privilege of selling beer again.[154] Slot machines appeared in about the 1930s, which was when "people really went to gambling."[155] Taxing prostitution, gambling and liquor continued to be a major source of municipal revenue. Fire insurance maps reveal the shifts in the restricted district during this time, when prostitution consolidated into five brothels.

Part II

SEX WORK IN WALLACE DURING AND AFTER WORLD WAR II

4
The Madam Next Door

During World War II, women finally regained control over the commercial sex industry in the Silver Valley, funded in large part by men at nearby military bases. The economy was thriving once again, and the invention of penicillin meant that most sexually transmitted infections could be treated with a course of antibiotics. These events led to a renaissance of sorts in the business; the houses did very well after the war ended, and so this time was more or less the post–pioneer era heyday for sex work in Wallace. Even though the town was officially off-limits to the military during the war, sailors from Farragut Naval Base and airmen from Fairchild Air Force Base found clever ways to sneak around the rules. The prohibition against visiting Wallace during leave continued through the years, and men who were in the military during the 1960s and '70s explained how the list of cities military men were not allowed to visit backfired in one key way: "They were telling us exactly where we could go to have fun."[156]

Women came to work in the Silver Valley's houses seeking wages comparable to what they'd made working in wartime industries. They rotated into and out of town from mining and logging towns in Nevada, Montana, California, Oregon, Utah and Washington. Women who called themselves Dolores Arnold and Loma Delmonte came to Wallace during this time, and together with Ginger Murphy, who arrived around 1963, they brought the image of "class" to Wallace's brothels, despite Loma's reputation for chewing out misbehaving customers and teenage-boy pranksters with a stunning array of expletives.[157] It was said that these madams "ran a tight ship," and they cultivated a reputation for discretion and civic contribution.

TABLE 3: BROTHELS, LOCATIONS AND PROPRIETORS, 1947–91

BROTHEL NAME	LOCATION	MADAMS OR OWNERS & PROPRIETORS	TIMEFRAME
Arment Rooms	601½ Cedar Street	Fay Wilson	
		Sandy Allen	mid-1950s
		Vicki Turner	late 1960s
		Peggy Arnette	
		Ginger Murphy	assumed ownership in 1966
		Tammy	early 1970s
		Barb	closed in 1977
Lux Rooms	212½ Sixth Street (Access from Kelly's Alley)	Dolores Arnold	until 1977
	Moved to 601½ Cedar Street	Managed in part by Ginnie Freeman	1977–86 or 1987
Oasis Rooms	605½ Cedar Street	Zonia Martain	
		Nancy Parson	
		W.J. Emacio	
		Dorathy Smith	1940s
		Shirley Jackson	1940s
		Ruth Poska	1944–49
		Ginger Murphy	1963–January 1988
Western Rooms	611½ Cedar Street		until 1952
Jade Rooms	611½ Cedar Street	Loma Delmonte	1953–67
Luxette Rooms	611½ Cedar Street	Dolores Arnold, managed in part by Carla Loren	1968–86 or 1987

Brothel Name	Location	Madams or Owners & Proprietors	Timeframe
U&I Rooms	613½ Cedar Street	Fay Wilson	until 1960s
		Lee Martin	1960s–85 or so, possibly later
		Tanya Adams	1985–June 1991
"Red Door"	(Formerly Oasis or Luxette?)		(Named in *Idaho Statesman* article as one of only two houses remaining after 1987)
Sahara Rooms (This house is associated with four police records.)	Unknown (In *NYT* article, Sahara is named instead of the Arment.)	Unknown	1973

There were five houses active from the 1940s through the late 1970s, which was when the Arment shut down, leaving four houses in operation until 1986 or 1987, when Dolores finally closed her two houses. The Oasis continued until 1988 and the U&I Rooms lasted until 1991. Dolores ran the Lux, while Loma managed the Jade, which later turned into the Luxette under Dolores's management. All of the houses were located on the second floors of their buildings. The Arment was above the Silver Corner at 601½ Cedar Street. Ginger managed the Oasis at 605½ Cedar, and the Western at 611½ Cedar turned into the Jade Rooms in 1953 and then the Luxette when Loma left town in 1967. Lee Martin ran the U&I Rooms at 613½ Cedar, and in later years, she began to leave more of the management responsibilities to Tanya, who arrived in Wallace around 1985.

The original Lux was the only house not located on the north side of Cedar Street between Sixth and Seventh. It was located at 212½ Sixth Street with the entrance in Kelly's Alley. Then in 1977, when the State of Idaho bought the building with the intent to demolish it to make room for the freeway, Dolores's flagship house moved to replace the Arment. The four Cedar Street brothels featured both front and back entrances—the front doors were used most often by out-of-towners while local patrons more often used the back doors. The back-door access stairs rose up from the area of the former restricted district once known as "Avenue A" but often called

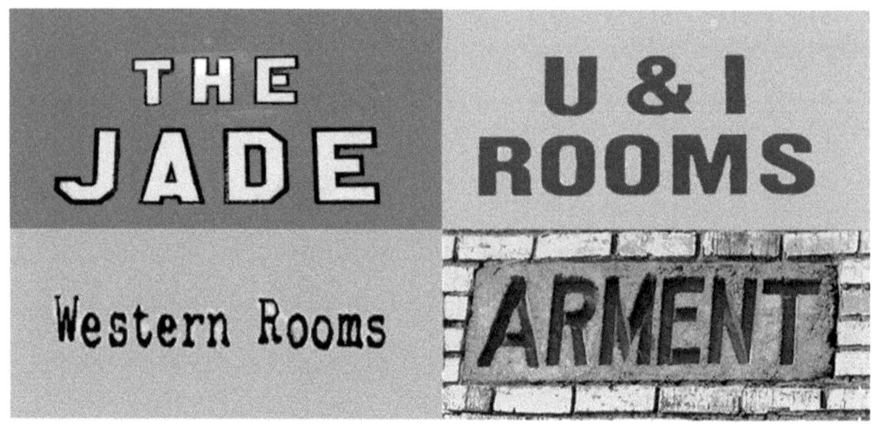

"It's A Pleasure To Be With You"

Wallace, Idaho

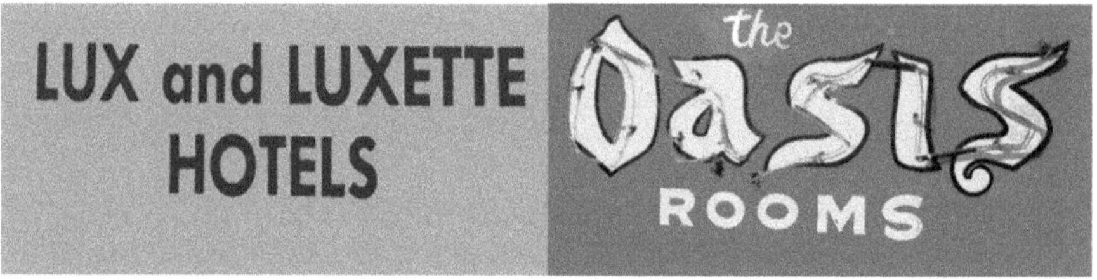

Post–World War II houses. *Pictures altered from actual signs or text from calendars, matchbooks and similar; photos and design by Heather Branstetter.*

"Chicken Shit Alley" during this time because it featured a more discreet entrance. Most of the houses had business signs until a temporary shutdown in 1973, when the signs were replaced with notices that said, "We're closed—beat it."[158] Signs with the houses' names never went back up after that. This chapter documents how the sex industry was balanced with the interests and identity of the community from the Second World War until the time when the houses closed. It also discusses the standardized practices of the houses and closes with a spotlight on Dolores's impact.

"You Don't Have to Obey the Laws, but You Do Have to Follow the Rules"

Almost every person I talked to during my oral history interviews repeated phrases like "The houses offered relief for single miners and kept local women from getting raped," "The women were checked out by the doctors and didn't solicit around town or on the streets" and, especially, "The houses gave so much back to the community." After Dolores expanded her operations with the Luxette, people used to say, "It's even become corporate."[159] Pithy puns and jokes consisting only of a single punch line, both innocent and suggestive, were repeated freely in Wallace. For example, many people related versions of a clever story about bar owners beneath the houses complaining, "Business is great, but there's too much fucking overhead."[160] Another man told me about running into the father of his girlfriend at the time as he was coming back down the stairs on his way out the door. His apprehension quickly dissolved when the father said to him, "Boy, am I glad to see you here."[161] Men who were grocery boys back in the days love to tell stories about their jobs delivering to the houses, which were known for handing out generous tips.

It's no accident that such phrases and stories are the chorus around town to this day. The madams appealed to the sense of humor and common sense values of the community, both in language and in deed, as they set the tone to subtly align the city's rhetoric about the houses. As former Day Mines and Sunshine Mines employee Rod Higgins explained, Wallace's embrace of the commercial sex industry was the result of the brothel managers' purposeful persuasive strategy: "Everyone viewed them [the brothels] as being an advantage, thanks to the madams' marketing efforts." Men and women alike repeatedly told me how "fun" Wallace was during this time, as they expressed gratitude for having the opportunity to grow up in such a great town.

Talking points about the benefits of the sex work in Wallace also offered direct rebuttal to threatening critiques of prostitution that arose periodically during the years. Specific practices, such as doctor's visits, solidified the madams' words into a "code of conduct" and built a foundation for the town's present-day understanding of its past. It was said that the brothels: 1) operated in accordance with a "live and let live" sense of order, providing services that helped keep the local streets safe at night; 2) were restricted to the northeast corner of town, where they were regulated and mostly free from sexually transmitted infections; and 3) contributed to the economy in both direct and indirect ways. Written records of history affirm variants of these arguments, which persisted through the years. The industry served local miners and regional loggers, contributed to the schools and attracted business from truckers, college students and Canadians, drawing men and their money into the community from distant places.

In Wallace, it was said that prostitution's "image was different—the image they presented and your image of them was different. The community had a high degree of acceptance of the girls and the business."[162] One newspaper article featured a sex worker saying she preferred Wallace to Nevada, where she encountered "a rougher clientele" and was not as "free to come and go as she please[d]," unlike in Wallace, where she could "come up [and work] when I feel like it, work till I'm tired of working, and then I go home."[163] By the mid-1950s, the town of three thousand people would elect only city leaders who allowed the prostitution industry to continue, driving away the few pastors or priests who advocated for reform. As late as the 1980s, former mayor Pellissier told me, a group of women he called

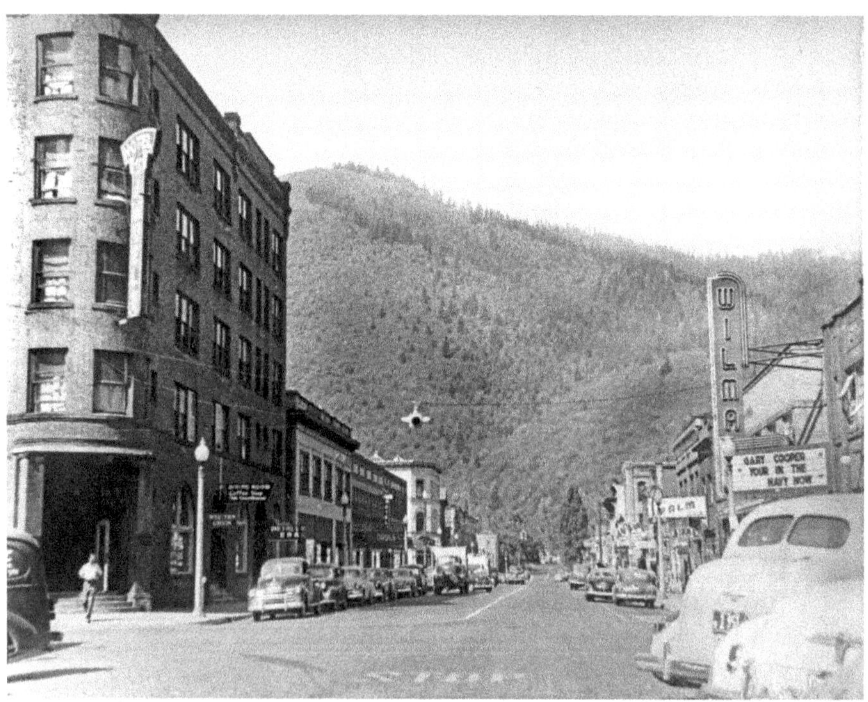

Looking west along Cedar Street from Seventh Street, 1951. Most of Wallace's houses are upstairs along the right side of this photo. The sign for the U&I Rooms is visible below the Palm Bar sign. *Historic Wallace Preservation Society.*

the "Golden Girls" said they would not support his bid for mayor unless he promised not to shut down the sex industry; they threatened to campaign against him if he closed the houses and they'd convinced him they wielded enough influence to derail his election.

Evidence for the residents' continuing acceptance of the brothels is not limited to quotes appearing in old newspaper articles and the oral histories I conducted. A study conducted by Robert Miles, who looked at prostitution in Wallace for his master's thesis in criminal justice at Washington State University, documents community perception during the late 1970s. Miles's research revealed that both men and women in Wallace accepted the houses as integral to the town's way of life. Throughout the study, a large majority of respondents agreed that prostitution was not morally wrong, did not lower respect for women and should be decriminalized.[164] For example, 69 percent of respondents disagreed with the statement that "decriminalizing prostitution would seriously weaken the social fabric of our community," and 75 percent disagreed with the idea that "decriminalizing prostitution decreases respect for the institution of marriage."[165] In 1984, historians Hart and Nelson wrote that Wallace's "unabashed and unrepentant acceptance of drinking, gambling and whoring, seen as commonplace…even acquired a certain civic respectability."[166] What's more, they added, people in the community believed that "prostitution kept together many respectable marriages, that Wallace madams gave generously to deserving charities, and that revenues from prostitution kept the city coffers filled and the streets paved."[167] The madams framed their business as central to the community and then followed up by donating in visible ways.

The houses had historically been a central part of the economic life of Wallace, but madams increased the publicity and scope of their monetary contributions to the town during the 1940s and 1950s. The women wove their work into the structure of the community by circulating small talk that appealed to values like civic service and philanthropy—appeals that were represented by monetary contributions that supported the town's families, churches and schools. During the 1940s, Magnuson told me, the Salvation Army used to collect every Friday night from the houses and the card tables, and they "did a lot of good with that money."[168] Many research participants told me the madams also contributed in less visible ways, citing as an example the way they would quietly purchase food and leave it at the grocery store available for the clerks to distribute to families in need according to their discretion.

It is difficult to find people who opposed the industry, but Holly Shewmaker, who went to high school in the valley during the early 1960s, spoke with me at length about some of the ways the presence of commercial sex influenced the lives of women who were not madams or whores:

> *Sex work affected my marriage and degraded my ex-husband, who taught me things based on what he'd been taught up there. "Being with you was like being with a courtesan," he once told me. I came to think sex was something you did in service of men, got pregnant at sixteen, and had a baby at seventeen.*[169]

It would be a mistake to glorify the madams in any way, Shewmaker cautioned me, because their profession was "based on lies. Prostitution is a lie and it erodes the soul. It destroys something meant to unite people." Shewmaker added that her dad had "tried to make me feel better because he was a city councilman. 'Whores built the viaduct,' he said."

Even though most women in town believed the sex industry was in their interest to promote, some women felt a tension under the surface because it "was like a secret club in this town between the men and women in the houses, but the other women in Wallace weren't allowed into the boys' club. Dolores had a relationship with men that other women were excluded from."[170] Visitors from out of town used to drive by and catcall young girls as they walked down the street. Some men from the region presumed most women in town were sex workers and were blatantly disrespectful when a Wallace girl revealed where she was from. Shewmaker related a story about high school cheerleaders participating in a Spokane parade:

> *Wallace girls marched in their black sweaters with the large "W"* [for Wallace] *across their chests. Coins were tossed at them and jeers of "W for whore" rang out.... At this point, I had come to believe I would rather be a madam or a whore than one of the "protected" women of Wallace.*[171]

She added that one of the girls went home and recounted the story to her mother, who told her never again to speak a bad word about those women because they protected young women from being raped and supported the community economically, including their own family's business.

These stories demonstrate how negative perceptions were countered through sayings that became folded into collective memory, layered within narratives repeated over time and embodied by the madams' respectability in deed as well as discourse. The women who worked upstairs knew that word would travel as long as they maintained a consistent image. And word did spread. The situation in the Silver Valley became widely known. One of my research participants told a story about working on a radio show in Los Angeles during the early 1970s; when the host, Sammy Jackson, asked her where she was from, she answered, "You would not know where I'm from, Sammy. I mean, it's a small town in northern Idaho." After she finally admitted she was from Wallace, Jackson answered, "Oh baby! I spent the best month of my life in Wallace, Idaho." Then she added to me, "I was just stunned that he would even know anything about northern Idaho."[172]

When reporters from around the region would come to town to do a story about the houses, the madams promoted their business practices openly and in accordance with the town's values. Emphasis on the women's care for single men and physical cleanliness countered the stereotype that sex work is immoral and spreads disease. One *Seattle Times* newspaper article, for example, quotes a madam saying that the "men need relief" and "are well taken care of here," featuring a photo of a neatly prepared bed and narration promising a "spotlessly clean room" because the madam "will not have anything dirty!"[173] The women created the perception that their profession was advantageous to the town because the industry operated in an orderly fashion according to community wishes. An article appearing in Boise's *Idaho Statesman* features one of the town's female residents professing, "A mining town needs brothels" and quotes the manager of the U&I Rooms promoting an understanding of justice congruent with the town's historic mining camp roots: "You don't have to obey the laws, but you do have to follow the rules."[174]

The women were said to bring money into the area and keep that money local. Most often noted, both in the newspapers and around town, was the way in which the sex industry supported the schools. In 1991, the *Seattle Post-Intelligencer* reported that "madams, for example, helped buy the scoreboard for the high school football team. They also pitched in to help with youth baseball uniforms."[175] Madams notoriously bought the school's band uniforms, and rumor has it that they funded the uniforms partly in exchange for an agreement that the band would no longer march around the streets to practice early in the morning.[176] The houses were said to provide good jobs for women in the community, including those who worked as maids in the houses and others who supported the sex workers' food, grooming, clothing and transportation needs.[177] One woman told

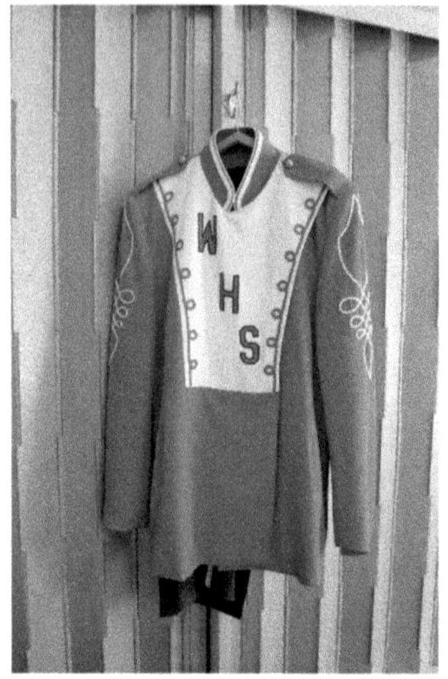

One of the famous school band uniforms paid for by prostitution in Wallace. *Oasis Bordello Museum display; photo by Heather Branstetter.*

me about how she used to give the women rides back and forth from Spokane to Wallace, where she worked at a bar called Sweets and ran food up to the girls during her shifts. She adds that she also "did make a lot of money selling Avon to the girls. They were great customers."[178] The madams' indirect economic contributions to the town and the residents' positive small talk about these contributions kept the sex industry integrated into the town's social and institutional fabric.

It is possible to estimate the numbers of women who came into town and worked in the houses from 1940 to 1960 or so because Nellie Stockbridge, whose photography studio was just across the street from the U&I Rooms, took pictures of all the sex workers during this time for licensing and record-keeping purposes. These photos are now housed in the Barnard-Stockbridge Collection at the University of Idaho Library Special Collections and Archives. Many are stiff and look like mug shots, but some of them are softer and feature the women in relaxed and smiling poses so they could buy the portraits and give them as gifts to relatives, friends and others.[179] The women were rumored to have been good customers of the Stockbridge business. The Barnard-Stockbridge Collection photos indicate that an average of 30 to 60 women came into town per year. The mid-'50s were particularly busy. During some of these years, 70 or 80 women moved into and out of Wallace's brothels. Old Shoshone County Sheriff's Office (SCSO) records document at least 531 women who worked in the houses between 1952 and 1973, although it's likely that some files were lost over the years.[180]

POLICIES, PROCEDURES AND PRACTICES

The madams operated according to an unwritten set of "rules" that promoted discretion and family stability, and the policies were well known around town. They were also enforced by small talk that became biting and judgmental if community residents began to feel threatened by boundary transgressions. Sex workers were discouraged from wandering around town aside from taking care of personal errands, and they were rather strictly prohibited from hanging out in the local bars. When research participants repeated variants of the rules to me, they were often related along with stories about notable exceptions. "You weren't supposed to date the working girls," but some people did, Penny Michael said, going on to tell a story about breaking into Quinn's Hot Springs with a woman who was dating her friend.

Sex workers also married local men and became homemakers. Although some of these marriages were socially acceptable, others were affected by stigma that haunted the women in gossip, and one family chose to move away rather than deal with the town's talk.[181] Local girls weren't supposed to work in the houses, and if they were discovered to be from the area, they were kicked out. This rule appears to have been enforced rather strictly—the Shoshone County Sheriff's Office files confirm that any time a local woman tried to get hired in the houses, they reported it to the madams and made a note in the file that she was not allowed to work there. One man believes a girl from nearby Mullan worked in one of the houses, but he's "not sure how she got away with it."[182] This woman may have been the same person described by Tammy Polla, who remembered a girl who came to Wallace to work in the houses and went to Mullan to try to get a high school diploma, which she'd never received. The girl was shamed out of school by the other kids, who made her life miserable after they found out.

Former maid Kristi Gnaedinger described her perception of "the rules" concerning the women's social life:

> *They were very discreet around town. They stuck to the rules, but not towards the very end. There was one girl who would come and party with us at my house when she was off. She came over and helped me move to Seattle. They occasionally had boyfriends in the community. They had favorite guys, but if they came up they had to pay. When you were there, you were working. The guys would sit in the rooms, the parlors up front where they could visit and socialize, and sometimes the guys would just come up and drink and drink and hardly ever go back into the rooms. So the girls could socialize, but if there were people who came in and wanted them to work, they would work. It was all money. It was very matter of fact. It was a business.*[183]

The sex workers were commonly referred to as "girls," even though they were officially required to be over the age of twenty-one. And the term "maid" in Wallace did not simply refer to someone who cleaned the houses. They were also called housekeepers, in a way that was very literal, insofar as they kept the house in order; they did sweep, mop and vacuum, but they also participated in much of the brothel management, answering the door, ensuring everyone stayed busy and knocking on doors to notify the couples that time was up after the timers went off. Sex workers set these timers as they dropped off their money into lockboxes after negotiating services and settling on an appropriate length of time for the encounter. The maids also shopped for food and cooked meals. Former maid Dee Greer said she liked to "spoil them a little bit" by taking them coffee when she woke the women up before their shifts.

The maids were primarily women who were from the area, but some local women were even limited from taking on this role as well. Gnaedinger

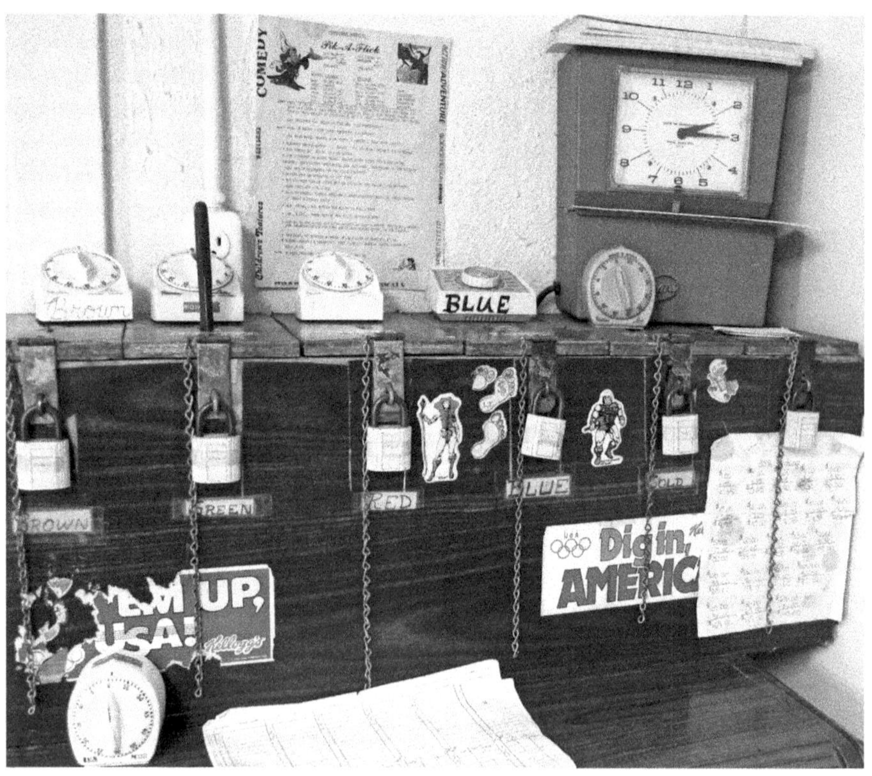

Lockboxes and timeclocks. *Oasis Bordello Museum display; photo by Heather Branstetter.*

thought her father "put some pressure on them [the city leaders and brothel manager]" to encourage her to quit because he was not happy with "the fact that his daughter was a maid up at the whorehouse." He would later become one of the doctors who conducted the sex workers' health checkups. Gnaedinger explained that she still maintained relationships with the women after she stopped working as a maid:

> *I still went up there to visit. I took my* [infant] *daughter up there to visit. At the time, Doc Peterson was still the doctor that took care of them and when he retired my dad took over. He really liked Tanya. He was very fond of her. She was a pretty special person. But my mother, probably more so than my dad, was worried about what people would say. "You can't do that. We have a reputation." Get a life, Mom. People were accepting of the houses, but you just didn't talk about it. My mother was worried about the family reputation. Lee told me that the city told her they had to get rid of me.*[184]

It wasn't just families worried about reputations who were concerned about the women who were employed as maids. The madams were also careful not to hire someone who could be perceived as personally connected to too many people in the town.

Sue Hansen related a story about applying for a housekeeping job at the Lux when Gennie Freeman was retiring.

> *So I went up to see Dolores, and Gennie put me in this room. I remember there was a jukebox in there. It was a nice room. And I waited for a few minutes and pretty soon, Dolores came in.* Beautiful, *beautiful, classy lady. And so she shook my hand and we started talking and she asked me if I'd ever done that kind of work before. And I said, well, yes. Because I used to clean for Millie Mara and a few other people. And she said, "Do you have any children?" And I said yeah, I have a little girl, about six months old. And she said, "Are you married?" And I said yes, well, and she said, "Does your husband mind, does he have a problem with it?" And I said, "Oh, no." So about that time Gennie knocks on the door, and she comes in and whispers something to Dolores, and Dolores goes, "Oh...I'm sorry honey, I was interviewing you for a different job."*[185]

The maids hustled the clients into and out of the rooms, calling out "man on the floor" when they walked someone from the parlor to the rooms or from the rooms to the door. This procedure prevented the men from running into someone they hadn't come up with. Housekeepers constantly kept tabs on the safety of the girls, and they monitored the patrons closely to prevent harassment or abuse. Greer explained:

> *At the Oasis they had peek holes in the doors. You tell people that* [and they say], *"Oh I'll bet you had fun." Well, it was if you heard something, a noise like somebody's trying to rough somebody up. Then you could go peek in the door and see if they were okay. Every place should have had it like that. And in the parlors…you know when you open the door downstairs a bell rings upstairs. And there's a window where you can see down, but they can't see you. And you always looked for somebody who had a sack, checked that out to make sure there wasn't any gun or whatever.*[186]

The maids needed to have tough personalities to deal with the customers, who could be disrespectful if they had been drinking too much. Greer told me she caught one young drunk guy pissing on the floor of the parlor room when the door was closed. She kept her cool and grabbed a wash bucket and soap, opened up the parlor door and handed the bucket to the kid, saying, "Now here, scrub that carpet." The guy pretended to be confused and then denied that he'd peed on the floor, to which Greer responded, "I stood here and watched you through the peek hole, dummy. Now—on your knees!"[187]

Both Greer and Gnaedinger had stories about men who tried to talk them into sleeping with them while they were maids. Gnaedinger said when she was pregnant she was uncommonly desirable to some of the clients, especially one who liked "really fat women" and another who wanted her to take him back to her place and tie him up. Greer admitted that the men were persistent sometimes, and she told a story about one guy who had come up with four of his friends:

> *This guy says, "And I'll have you."*
>
> *I said, "Oh, mercy, honey, if you'd seen my husband you wouldn't want me."*
>
> *And he says, "I don't care. I want you."*
>
> *I said, "Oh come on, you can shop* [meaning, find another girl you'd like to be with]*."*
>
> *So they all come in, and he says, "No, I don't want anybody. You can bring everybody in the whole town," he said. And pretty soon the other four took somebody and the madam comes out and we're playing music and I'm fixing him a drink. And he says, "I want you."*

> *I says, "You can't have me."*
> *And he got clear up to $500 for a quickie, and Billie's going, "Diane, Diane* [take the money and do it]*." Oh no, oh no, oh no. No. My husband is probably standing right around the corner. Nope, and I just went, oh my God. Nope. I knew better.*[188]

The policies were similar in each of the houses. The men would be ushered into the parlor to wait for the available girls to come in and engage them. This process was informal and often referred to as "window shopping." The houses kept liquor on hand for the men in the waiting rooms, and this was often as far as it went—many of the guys just went up to hang out around pretty women and continue drinking after the bars closed down.

If the men and women were mutually agreeable to having a sexual encounter, they would negotiate rates and services. A "straight lay" or "straight date" was conventional intercourse and usually did not last longer than ten minutes, although it was possible to pay more for a variety of positions or longer time on the clock. An old list of services at the Oasis Bordello Museum lists oral sex as "straight French." What was known as "half-and-half" was very popular. That was oral sex plus a straight lay, and it would commonly last about double the time. Gary Morrison, who grew up in Wallace during the 1950s and '60s, explained that he "was always stunned" about the amount of time typically set on the clocks: "I was like, whoa, what are you going to do in there? Did he pay like fifty cents for a kiss? The timeframes were so short!"[189] Some men proudly spent all of their money in the houses, staying there for a night or all weekend. One prominent man in town was known to rent the Lux for a week or two at a time, and Dolores would close down for him, sometimes taking the girls to a lake house for him.

The emphasis on cleanliness was solidified, even fetishized, in practice as the years went on. When any of the women acquired a sexually transmitted infection—and that doesn't appear to have happened very often—she was temporarily suspended from working and treated. The Shoshone County Sheriff's Office files verify this. Morrison described the cleanliness procedure much like everyone who spoke with me about the post–World War II economic boom era. After the parties negotiated rates, the guy paid his cash and was then asked to drop his pants and submit to "a pretty rigorous examination, trying to find any sign of rash, or, as they called it back then, a drip."[190] Gnaedinger, speaking about the 1970s and '80s, explained that the washing

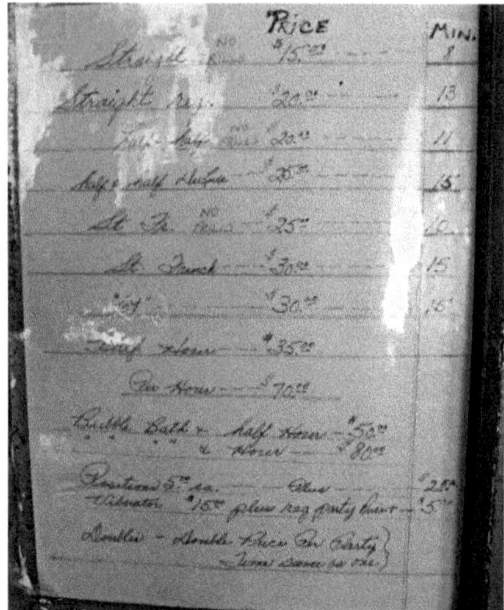

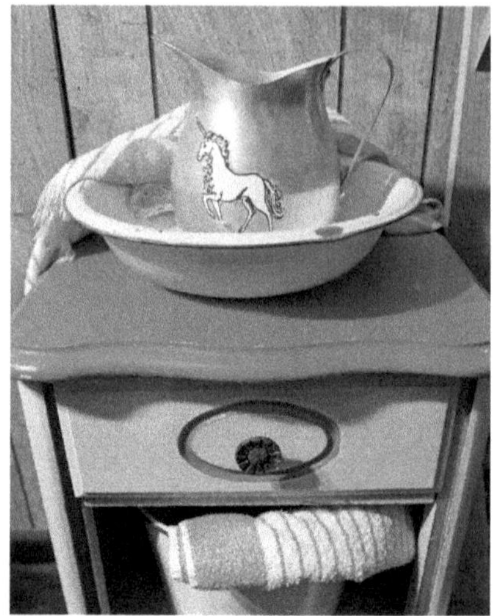

Left: Oasis price list, 1988. *Oasis Bordello Museum display; photo by Heather Branstetter.*

Right: "Peter Pan" washing basin used in many of the houses. *Oasis Bordello Museum display; photo by Heather Branstetter.*

helped maintain the image of cleanliness and also had a pragmatic purpose: "They cleaned the guys before they performed, and they'd clean them afterward. It was part of the ritual to get washed. And part of that washing was they were checking if they had any discharge, sores," she explained, adding that they didn't wear condoms until AIDS became a concern. The washing also made the experience more pleasant for both parties.[191]

Tim Johnson, who manages the hotel now located in the rooms that had been the Lux from 1977 to 1986, told me Dolores had a room dedicated to the washing process. She taught her employees they could speed things along there to avoid taking the man back into a room if they possibly could.[192] "Larry," who grew up in Coeur d'Alene, related the following story about a high school experience: "The whole defensive line of our football team came over and went up to the U&I once. One guy didn't know how it worked, paid thirty-five dollars to go up, and the gal put the warm washcloth on him and that was it."[193] The bubble bath was an incredibly popular service, even though it was also one of the most expensive.[194] Terry Douglas, who maintained the "coin-operated amusement devices" in the bars and jukeboxes in the houses, told me a story about his boss giving him money for a bubble bath experience, which he'd been hesitant to try out because of the cost. Douglas closed his story by saying with a smile, "And I've never forgot it. And we're thirty years later."[195]

"THERE OUGHT TO BE A STATUE OF THAT LADY IN THIS CITY"

The most famous and widely admired brothel manager was Dolores Arnold, who was largely responsible for the brothels' relatively strict operating procedures and shift toward civic contribution. Dolores's impact on Wallace, like her identity—an invented persona she assumed for forty years—is a mix of fact and fiction that became its own reality. She was born Mary Giacolone and died Maria Greer. But for most of her life, she was known as Dolores, a savvy businesswoman who quickly ascended from working girl to owner and manager of a successful brothel franchise. She led the madams' successful acquisition of increased economic independence, which eventually enabled the sex industry to exert greater influence on the social, political and economic life of the town. Dolores helped embed the industry within residents' sense of town identity to such an extent that one of my research participants characterized the brothels as "the United Way of Wallace because they gave back so much to the community," adding, "there ought to be a statue of that lady in this city."[196] Dolores moved quickly from an outsider position into a central role in the community; she knew small-town small talk could reveal, shape and solidify shared values.

Dolores promoted the idea that the brothels served the best interests of men and women alike. For example, "Dolores often said that she saved more marriages than any clergyman ever did."[197] She knew that stories repeated often enough could create a believable myth, and she harnessed this power to create a world where the sex industry could be relatively safe and supported by the vast majority of the community, despite its illegal nature. Those who knew her describe her as charming, funny, graceful and elegant. She made everyone feel special. She also had a reputation for professionalism in all of her business dealings, prompting a higher standard of excellence among subordinates, colleagues, clients and community members. Dolores had striking beauty, even well into old age. "People were in awe of her," Higgins told me. "She could have been a movie star earlier in her career." Another man said she looked just like the actress Hedy Lamarr.[198] People responded to her unguarded, empathic demeanor and confident way she carried herself, all of which she expressed through her eyes. Taller than the average woman, Dolores had long dark hair and a wide smile. She sensed the motivations of others and noticed details overlooked by most people.

Like many women drawn into the sex industry during the 1940s, Dolores suffered a traumatic childhood. Her parents were Italian immigrants who met in New Jersey before moving to Spanaway, Washington, where they bought a farm worth $2,600 in 1930.[199] Her mother died when Dolores was six, leaving her husband to raise Dolores and her three siblings, including her younger sister, Janet, and two younger brothers. Before Janet died, she met with local historian Dick Caron to talk about her childhood. During this conversation, Janet said they were left to raise themselves after their mother's premature death and dealt with "adverse conditions" as a result. They found out later that their mother had relatives they never met. Janet assumed they stayed away because they didn't want the relatives to feel obligated to take in the kids. "[We] were better off for being alone," Janet claimed; it "made us tough."[200] It did not, however, make them close. While Janet did not interfere with her sister's life, she refused to condone it.

Dolores did not finish high school and moved to Wallace in 1943 at the age of twenty-three after working for the navy in the shipyards at Bremerton, Washington, where she had been a "Rosie the Riveter."[201] Dolores had heard that Wallace was the place to go if she wanted to take advantage of an atmosphere that was friendly to illicit and lucrative sex work.[202] Morrison, who befriended Dolores in the 1960s when he delivered groceries to the Lux Rooms as a teen, said she was "like a family member" to him, and he characterized her move as "a business decision." According to Morrison, Dolores explained it in the following way:

> *I made up my mind that I could do that. Once I agreed that I could do that and just set that part of me aside, and say, "Okay this is business"… once I'd decided I could accept that, I got in the car and drove to Wallace. Somebody had told me about Wallace, having these—I had to hunt around and ask people—I didn't know where the houses were.*[203]

Timing contributed to Dolores's successful career in Wallace. She heard Wallace was a place with business opportunities for enterprising women, and she arrived at an opportune moment for the sex industry, after the introduction of penicillin, which cured most sexually transmitted infections, but before AIDS.[204] During this era, the brothels were open twenty-four hours a day, doing "booming business" serving military men.[205] The shore patrol from Farragut would walk the streets of Wallace, which was off-limits during the war.[206] The men came frequently nevertheless, traveling from the naval base near Coeur d'Alene, Idaho, and Fairchild near Spokane, Washington. They would get a bus pass for Missoula and then instead of going to Montana, they would get off in Wallace so they could visit the houses without leaving a paper trail. Then they would catch the bus as it came through again on its way back from Missoula.[207] Sailors were not allowed to wear anything but their issued uniforms, and the madams wouldn't let them upstairs unless they were in street clothes. But they found a way around this obstacle as well. A dry-cleaning business in the lot next door to the brothels would rent civilian clothes, so the military men could go in the back door with their uniforms on and out the front door in their rented clothes.[208] Even when shore patrol was present, sailors were invisible without their uniforms on, according to custom.[209] Most of the people in town knew exactly what was going on, but open secrets such as these permitted the sex industry to thrive while maintaining the appearance of propriety.

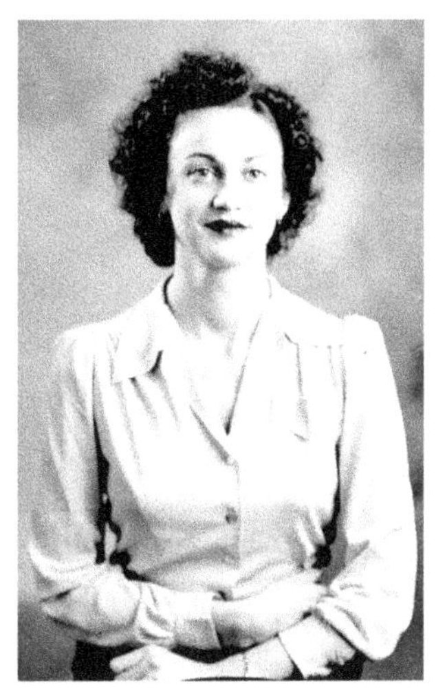

Dolores in 1943, when she first arrived in town from western Washington. *Barnard-Stockbridge Collection, University of Idaho Library Special Collections and Archives.*

Such word-of-mouth business practices offered Dolores insight into the importance of community perception in the small town of Wallace. As Higgins put it, "One thing Dolores was sticky on was regulations. Military men couldn't visit—she would not allow you up there in uniform." This pairing of a supposed rule with the answer to how you could bend it illustrates how small talk enabled insiders to distinguish strict rules from flexible ones while maintaining appearances in alliance with community values. During her early years in the town, Dolores easily identified the kind of information that circulated in local gossip: stories about people and their relationships, kids, family, sexual activities, work history, appearances, perceptions and social hierarchies all provided useful clues for fashioning herself into an eventual role as madam. The values and commentary accompanying the stories revealed the town's moral code. As an outsider, she needed to appeal to these norms in order to persuade people to sponsor her entry into the social and economic life of the town, which was historically self-protective and insular.

It's unclear how long Dolores worked before she was able to buy the Lux Rooms because there are conflicting stories about how she came into the means. These stories reveal what Wallace residents both admire and believe

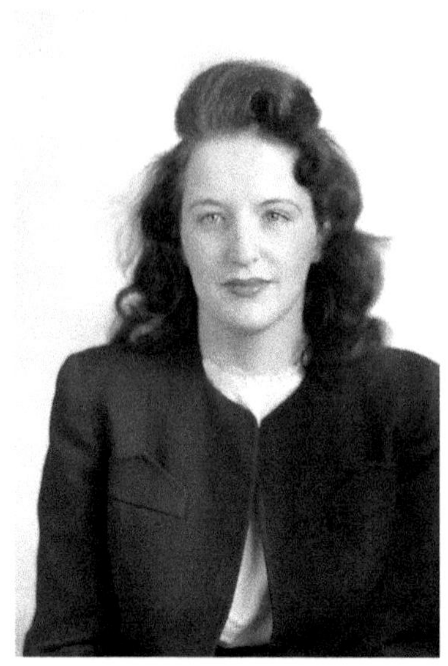

Dolores in 1947, as she transitioned into a management position at the Lux. *Barnard-Stockbridge Collection, University of Idaho Library Special Collections and Archives.*

to be true as they locate local values in the figure of Dolores: she was pragmatic and hard working. There are rumors asserting that she received the money from Hank Day, the affluent mining executive with whom she was connected. According to local gossip, "Everybody used to talk about Hank Day visiting Dolores at the whorehouses. And the story was that his wife drove him."[210] But many people around town believed that Day was apparently in love with Dolores, who was herself married to Lonnie Greer, the mayor of Mullan. One woman told me she thought Day and the madam had "a very special relationship."[211] Dolores likely invited the image of connection with Day, recognizing that the patronage of a well-known mine owner would be seen as endorsement. Two research participants told me Dolores saved her money and then rented the Lux Rooms until she could eventually afford to buy it.[212] Another man who worked at a bank told me she tried to get a loan but was turned down.[213] Others guessed she invested in mine stocks.[214] The written record shows that she and Lonnie Greer bought the building from Mary Albertini in 1953 for $7,000.[215]

Dolores quickly became well respected around town as she worked hard to build her business into an operation often referred to as "classy." She expanded into the Jade Rooms and turned it into the Luxette after her friend Loma retired and moved away. The walls of her personal room at the Lux, where she entertained especially privileged guests, were adorned with eighteen-karat gold-fleck paint imported from Italy for the price of $200 per gallon, and her closet was full of fur coats.[216] Dolores began advertising by giving away Playboy-style pin up calendars personalized with her business name, and other houses followed her lead by passing out similarly styled matchbooks. She was said to drive a 1958 baby blue Coupe Deville with a standard poodle named Mike riding in the passenger seat wearing a diamond collar.[217] Dolores cultivated an image as community caretaker and promoted prostitution as a profession as legitimate as anyone else's.[218] "In today's era,"

Higgins explains, "she would easily be a top executive in a large corporation. She was that good. She was instrumental in forming a consortium with the other madams" to support the community, developing a reputation for her business savvy and generosity.

The madams and women who worked in the houses emphasized—verbally, physically and spatially—the positive. Although there's no doubt that Dolores was generous, she was also very aware of public relations, and she purposefully tried to appeal to the classic "whore with the heart of gold" image.[219] Men and women alike continue to echo the ways that the houses were "symbiotic" with the town. Most of the people I've interviewed make sure to mention how the madams tipped large amounts for deliveries, bought most of the raffle tickets for various fundraisers and donated money to the local government and schools. Dolores was the biggest contributor, renowned for winning all the raffles and then turning the prizes into donations, passing along her Demolay turkeys to families in need.[220] A 1973 *New York Times* article discussing a temporary closure of the houses makes note of how Dolores donated baskets of food to the families of the ninety-one miners who died in the tragic fire at the Sunshine Mine.[221] Dolores knew she wouldn't be able to control what people said about her, but she wielded what power she did have, romancing the city leaders and civic clubs in the community with her visible good deeds, well-placed words and a consistent image.

"Dolores Arnold and her contributions to the town of Wallace are legend, and most of the legend is true," one newspaper reporter claimed, adding that a "rumor—that she has solid-gold bathroom fixtures in her apartment at the Lux and Luxette Hotel—needed clarification. Gold plate, Dolores explained, not solid gold."[222] This article, written during the 1980s, also corrects a popular legend about her Cadillac that nevertheless continues to be repeated: "The house madam seemed amused by another story that she orders a new Cadillac in Spokane every year and pays for it in cash. 'That's a lie.... My Cadillac is 14 years old.'"[223] Dolores's willingness to offer accurate information enhances her credibility even as it somewhat detracts from the image of luxury she sought to promote. The article reveals Dolores's ability to connect with

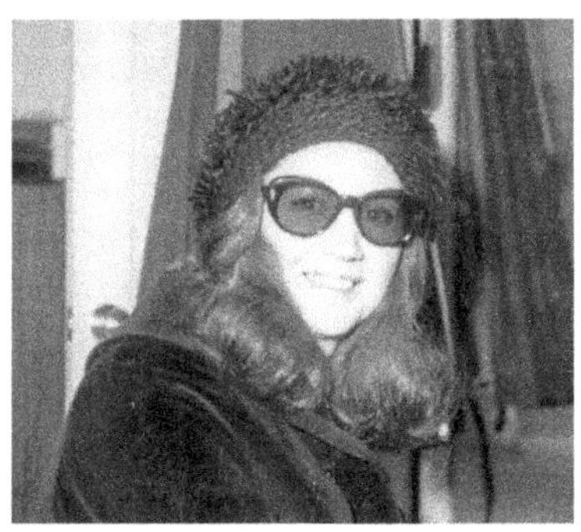

Dolores in 1965. *Richard Caron Collection.*

mining-town values; in spite of her gold-plated bathroom fixtures and showy car, she comes across as self-deprecating and down-to-earth. "People always think the worst of these places. But we do it right," Dolores added.[224] "Doing it right" probably contained some sexual innuendo, but she was explicitly referring to background checks and doctor's visits. When the women first arrived to work at the houses, police officers would run background checks and call the brothel managers with the information to ensure they weren't employing underage girls or anyone who appeared to have connections with organized crime.[225] "Doing it right" meant discretion as well. The working girls would never come up to a guy around town and let on that she knew him, several people told me. In short, "they kept their personal life personal and their business life professional."[226]

Dolores's discretion and strict management ensured she remained in the community's good graces. Many of my research participants made note of the fact that she hosted private parties for local civic or social organizations like the Gyro Club. There was no sex at these parties, which operated in accordance with the "underlying and rarely spoken agreement" that they "wouldn't fall into some kind of a debauchery, you know, a big orgy that then would be talked about in the community for the next century," as Morrison put it. He told a story about how upset his father was when someone had transgressed the code of conduct at one of the social club parties Dolores hosted. His dad said he'd seen a "community leader" at the party

> *slip off to one of the bedrooms with one of the girls, and he didn't come back out for about twenty minutes. And I'm pretty sure that they weren't in there having another drink. And he says, "That was just, just so* improper.*" I mean, he could care less if that guy went up there on his own, every night of the week, if that guy chose to do that, but to do it and to violate the unwritten rules of decorum, you know, for the club to be together up there, was really reprehensible to him.*[227]

Several other people I talked with noted this incident, which appears to have been exceptional and well known because it was not in accordance with the kind of social propriety required in a town the size of Wallace.

Dolores was not afraid to fire sex workers or housekeepers for overstepping boundaries. One story often repeated locally involves a robbery at one of the houses, resulting in a court case. One of Dolores's employees was called to testify as a witness and accidentally let on that the attorney cross-examining her had patronized the Lux often enough to be familiar to her. The way

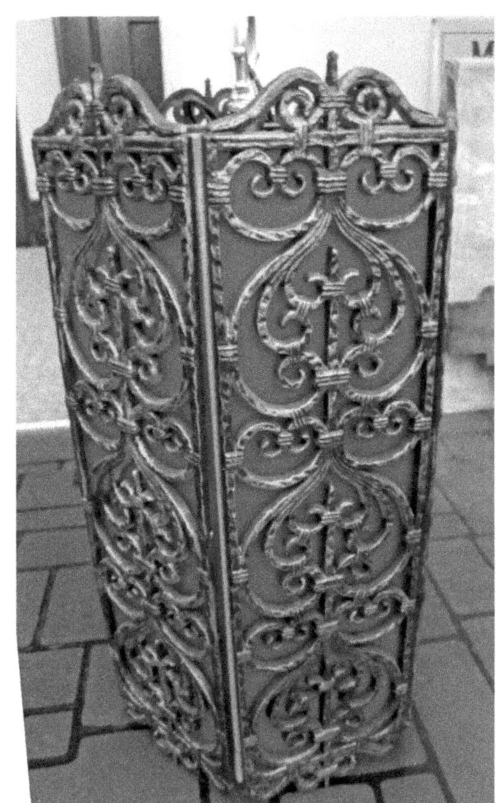

Right: Light from the Lux Rooms entryway. *Richard Caron Collection; photo by Heather Branstetter.*

Below: Dolores and her poodle, Mikey, in 1978. *Richard Caron Collection.*

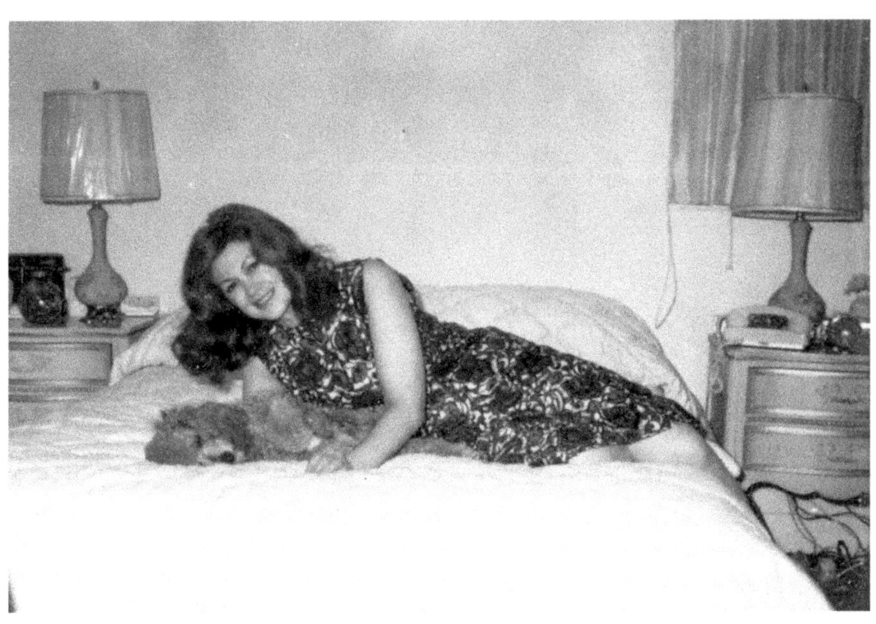

this tale is repeated often ends with the woman telling defense attorney Jim Keane, "You know damn well which way that door opens," as the court erupts with laughter. The actual court transcript (featured in the next chapter) reveals that her language is slightly subtler than this. In fact, she appears to have slipped up by accident only after Keane's questions disoriented her, but Dolores fired her for this lack of discretion anyway.[228] According to rumor, Keane tried to call his wife immediately afterward, but someone had already told her. He was embarrassed by the event until his friend gave him a copy of the court transcript for Christmas. The transcript contained a dedication in the front instructing the reader to make note of Keane's award-winning performance. "After that he was proud of it" and began laughing along with everyone else.[229] The anecdote spread, and Keane became infamous as a result; one day, he was sitting on a plane next to a man who'd heard a funny story about a lawyer from Wallace, and before he knew it, Keane was listening to a stranger tell him this tale about himself.[230]

5

Firsthand Written Accounts and Regulation

This chapter features written primary sources post–World War II. They add depth and complexity to our understanding of the houses and women who worked in them. I present them as lightly edited, accessible versions of the original documents. The first section is an account of an attempted robbery at the Lux, followed by an autobiographical narrative written by a former Wallace police officer. The third section offers a look into some of the handwritten ephemera left in the Oasis Rooms when the women left. Finally, the chapter closes with a sampling of files from the time when the Shoshone County Sheriff's Office regulated the houses and women.

"Not in This Whore House": Attempted Robbery at the Lux Rooms, 1957

On July 4, 1957, a man named Russell with an "odd hairline, deep set widow's peak, eyes close together with large eye brows, thin nose at the top, wide at the bottom" and a "very thin mouth" walked up the long steep staircase leading from Kelly's Alley into the Lux Rooms and attempted to rob it. This account of the event is re-created from a copy of the preliminary hearing transcript. Quotation marks indicate wording pulled directly from the original document.[231]

Self-described "professional prostitute" Edna was working that night. It was about 3:00 or 3:30 a.m., she said, and she was the only one available to meet with clients. When she encountered Russell alone in the back parlor, which seated between ten and twelve people, she was wearing a typical outfit for the time: white flat ballerina shoes and a one-piece that transitioned from white linen shorts with a green ruffle around the bottom into a sequined peacock leotard that zipped up the back.

"Hello and how are you, fine?" Edna asked Russell. They sat and chatted for two or three minutes. Dolores Arnold, who ran the house, poked her head into the parlor to check on her comfort and try to speed things along, asking Edna if she was going to be busy. Then she closed the door and walked away.

Taking the cue from her boss, Edna asked if Russell wanted to go to a room with her. They both stood up, and she held out her hand. Instead of answering her with his hand or a verbal response, Russell pulled out a switchblade, which he held to her stomach.

"Oh," Edna startled, looking down at the blade.

"I didn't come to give, I came to take," Russell said.

"Not in this whore house you won't," Edna put on a brave face.

"You don't seem afraid of me."

"I'm not," Edna lied, fearing for her life. She had made it a practice to "never show fear" and wouldn't begin doing so now. To show fear would be to reveal weakness to this man she believed wanted to steal money from the house.

Russell repeated, "I have not come to give, I have come to take, as I am tired of working my ass off."

"Don't feel bad, so am I." Edna looked into his eyes and smiled, trying to be calm and understanding as she explained to him that he had "made a mistake." She told him "he couldn't get out of it, because the joint was wired to the police station." Another lie, although she knew that in truth the officers were only a phone call away.

"If not tonight, tomorrow," Russell threatened.

Edna "told him he would never make it out of there, the boys would be up the stairs before he could get down the hall."

"If not tonight, tomorrow," he repeated.

"Take a word of advice, if this is the business you are going into, don't talk so much, learn to keep your mouth shut," Edna said, sensing he was not an experienced thief.

"What are you trying to be, a mother?" Russell asked.

"No, if I wanted to be a mother, I wouldn't be in this business."

Russell shook his head and put the knife back into his pocket as Edna threw the door open and called Dolores, who answered immediately. Edna told Dolores to "take a good look at the man...never let him back in again, as he had come to hold her up."

Edna then turned to Russell and said, "Come on, I will let you out," walking him down the hall.

"If not tonight, tomorrow," Russell said for the third time as they approached the door.

"There [will] be no tomorrow," Edna finally told him. And if he was wise, she advised, he would get out of town, since Dolores had begun dialing the police the moment they started walking to the door.

The man made it out the door, but police soon picked him up and brought him back in what was described as a "paddy wagon." Dolores and Edna were offered the opportunity to identify him.

In reality, Edna explained when she testified a week later, it would have been difficult for Russell to take any large amount of money from her that evening. "You have to go to the parlor and get your man, take him to the bedroom, talk with the gentleman" to negotiate services, "receive the money from the gentleman in the bedroom and then dispose of it" in a locked cash drawer containing individual boxes labeled with each woman's name. Dolores and the maids kept the key to the lockboxes except when they knew they would be busy. During the busiest times, they simply left the key in the kitchen.

There was an awkward moment in the courtroom when Edna was asked to describe her outfit and the attorney didn't understand how it worked. "I assume that you were clothed some way in the upper—" he asked, fading away, as she clarified for him. The purpose of the exchange about how she was dressed was supposedly to establish whether she had anywhere she could keep money. The lawyers asked her about the money situation at length. The only money freely accessible without a key might be "change for our convenience and juke box change and grocery boy and laundry boy and so forth," but Edna noted that "as the evening progresses and on into the morning, there is liable to be a great amount of money on the premises, yes," in the locked boxes.

Edna's testimony during Russell's preliminary hearing reveals that she is flirtatious and funny; she flustered the defense attorney, Jim Keane, on more than one occasion. He eventually asked her if it was true that the *only* way a person could access these "large sums of money" was by obtaining the key from Dolores.

"That all depends on what their talents are, Mr. Keane," Edna responded. Keane tried to keep his cool and began to grill her on exactly where the cash drawer was in relation to the door.

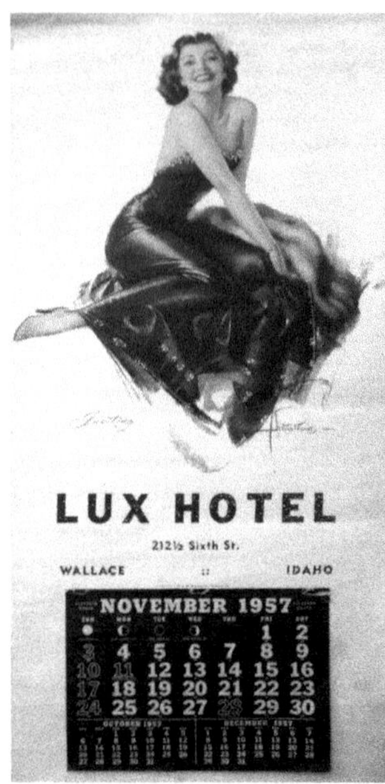

Lux calendar, 1957. *Oasis Bordello Museum display; photo by Heather Branstetter.*

Exhausted with his questions, Edna finally became flustered herself, and the result was a rare lapse in the sex industry's provider-client code of confidentiality. "You just open the door," she said, "*you know how the door goes* back this way against the wall."

It appears to have been unintentional, but Edna had let slip that in reality Keane knew exactly how the door opened because he patronized the Lux. According to Richard Magnuson, the deputy prosecuting attorney, everyone started laughing. Not only had she let on that he had come to visit before, but her tone also indicated she thought he was asking dumb questions.[232]

After the laughter died down, Keane responded, "I would hate to admit I did. I have been accused of a lot worse than that," which of course led to even more laughter. Magnuson told me they eventually "had to take a recess because there was such a commotion," and during the recess, Edna went up to Keane "and apologized profusely."[233]

In the meantime, Edna tried unsuccessfully to cover her tracks: "Mr. Keane, I did not mean it that way. When you open the door, the door usually goes back against a wall, well it went back, the cash drawer is right behind the kitchen drawer."

Keane likewise tried unsuccessfully to continue his line of questioning. He said, "And again I will ask you, oh strike it. That is all..." Finally he gave up, the laughter making it impossible to proceed with the interview.

Memoirs of a Cop

What follows is a slightly cut reprint of a narrative written by Reverend Dr. Jim Ranyon, sent to local historian Dick Caron in May 2008. A copy is available in the Wallace District Mining Museum. Ranyon grew up in the valley and was a police officer in Wallace during the 1960s.

I worked for the local grocery store and on occasion would be called upon to deliver groceries to the back door of each and every upstairs house. It wasn't easy, I'll tell you! First, you had to fight the other box boys for the job and then you had to carry those wooden boxes up those twenty back steps of the fire escape to the locked and windowed back doors. I'd ring the doorbell and press my eye to the window, trying to get a glimpse of whoever came to the door. Invariably, soon there would be an answer and some sweet voice calling, "Who is it?" "Grocery boy," I'd respond. The curtain would be pulled back to reveal a semi-naked lady.... She would say something like, "I'm gonna unlock the door and you can come in but don't you look because I'm not dressed! Now don't you look." Right! I'd follow her down the long narrow shotgun hallway to the kitchen while she disappeared to put on some "clothes." The clothes she donned always looked like something that might have been ordered from Victoria's Secret. And always there would be a large tip. Anywhere from one silver dollar to several silver dollars. Talk about the best job in the world. Naked women and money, too....

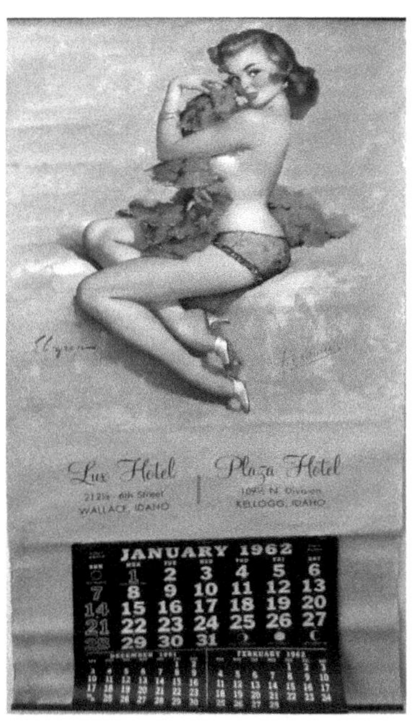

Lux and Plaza calendar, 1962. *Oasis Bordello Museum display; photo by Heather Branstetter.*

In 1962 I came home from U[niversity] of I[daho] and was looking for a job. Dick Mays was chief of police at that time and was in the process of transferring to the sheriff's department. We hit it off together, and I decided to stick around until a job came open. When it did, I was the first in line and Bill Lilly, the new chief, hired me right away. The job seemed kind of boring at first. There was very little crime on the surface of things. On weekends the population always increased exponentially. Normally there would be about twelve to fifteen hundred citizens roaming around.

It wasn't very long until I received a call of trouble at one of the houses. We raced down Cedar St., stopped at the Arment Rooms, double-parked the squad car, threw open the swinging door at the bottom of those 22 stairs and raced up. At the top of the stairway the door was opened and the madam directed us to room number 3. We walked up to the door, knocked briefly and before we received a response, opened the door to find a guy with his back to us and [a] girl backed up into a far corner of the room. In my best bad ass voice I said, "What's the trouble here?" Well, it was more than almost funny.

This guy had his trousers at half-mast, his shirt and jacket were off, and the girl was trying to get past him to the door. His face changed colors about four times then he stuttered, "Hey, this girl is a whore and that's illegal! Arrest her!"

I said something to the effect of, "Put your pants back on, zip up and you are under arrest!"

He sputtered some more until I said, "Shut up, *you're* the one who is being arrested!" We put the handcuffs on him and led him to the front door and the long stairway down.... Just as I passed through the doorway, I felt the madam kinda pat me on the ass and slip something into my back pocket. I never thought about it until we were back on the street hiking our "perp" back to jail.... Charge: Disturbing the Peace. Fine: 25 dollars and costs total $28.00.

We should probably state how the system worked: places of prostitution were allowed in Idaho and some neighboring states by city option. That is, it was left to the city to either allow or disallow the profession within city limits. Each house paid to the city a fine in the form of a misdemeanor of "running a disorderly house." A fine was paid to the city by the madam based on the number of ladies who worked in that particular house. Mostly there were five to nine girls working on a daily basis. You don't have to be a rocket scientist to figure that several thousand dollars went into the coffers each week. Yes, the fines were collected weekly. Again, these houses supported the city. The city paid [our] wages.

Therefore, when I discovered the twenty-dollar bill in my pocket after my first call to the Arment Rooms, I thought I should go back and arrest the madam for trying to bribe this conscientious cop. My partner said, "Like hell, one half of that twenty is mine." See, to them [the madams], it's a tip to ensure that whenever there is a call, we'll bust our butts to get there and solve whatever problem they have. It worked well, too. Being a low-paid cop, we needed some benefits. Christmastime always brought very nice bonuses for the individual cops....

The Lux Rooms: Madam—Dolores Arnold. One of the most attractive women to grace the streets of our town. Tall and willowy, with high cheekbones and raven black hair, she was a head turner from any direction. Dolores never went anywhere without her standard bred poodle, Mike, a beautiful three and one half foot tall [dog]. Mike always looked like he had just come from the groomers. I don't know how that is possible because the

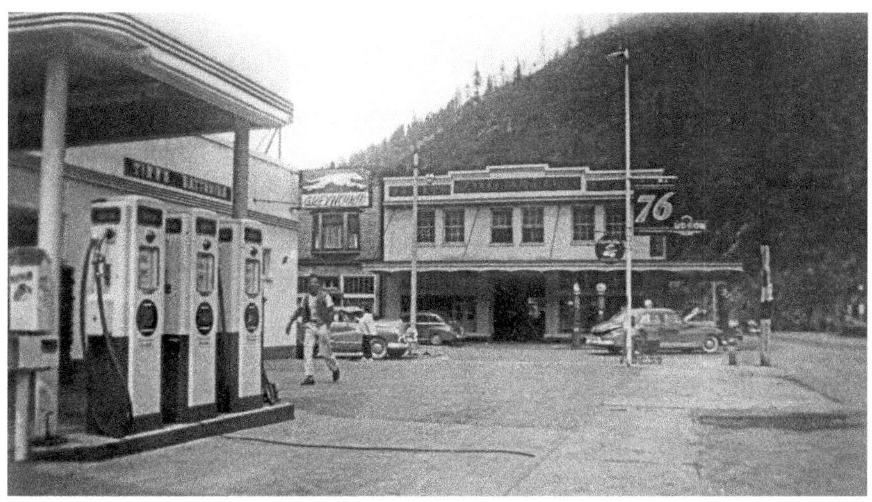

Union Oil, the Greyhound bus station at Fifth and Pine Streets that some of the women used to travel into and out of town. *Historic Wallace Preservation Society.*

last time I checked, there were no dog groomers within a fifty-mile radius. Dolores drove a baby blue 1959 Cadillac that was always parked in the garage that abutted the Greyhound Bus Depot....

I don't remember the madam's name [at the Arment Rooms], but I do remember many of the girls. I learned to appreciate and truly respect them as individuals. They were just like everyone else, trying to get by in a sometimes rough world. It became known to me and the other cops that many of these girls were supporting children the best way they knew how....

Ginger was a case and a half! Great personality, outgoing and funny, Ginger knew how to have fun—all the time....

The Jade Rooms: Madam—Loma Delmonte. A heavyset woman, Loma had a filthy mouth when she was upset, which was quite often. When her street door opened, she would pull the curtain away on the door at the top of the stairs to see who and what was going on. If you were a customer, fine. If you were merely moving off the street to avoid being seen whilst you took a whiz, the upper door was opened and you were treated to the most vile dressing down you ever heard. While she was cussing you and delving into your momma's history, we would be called. Many times we arrived while the wrong doer was standing in the doorway with his mouth open in amazement and his whizzer still in his hand. I still laugh when I think about that. Not only did he get a superior chewing out, he got arrested too—you guessed it—"Disturbing the Peace."...

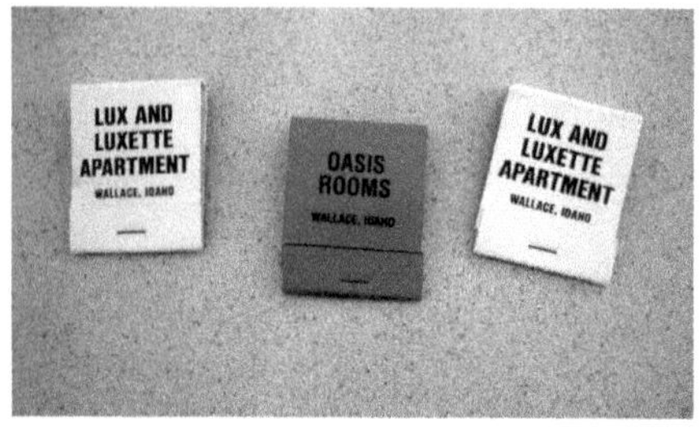

Above: Matchbooks advertising the houses. *John Hansen Collection; photo by Heather Branstetter.*

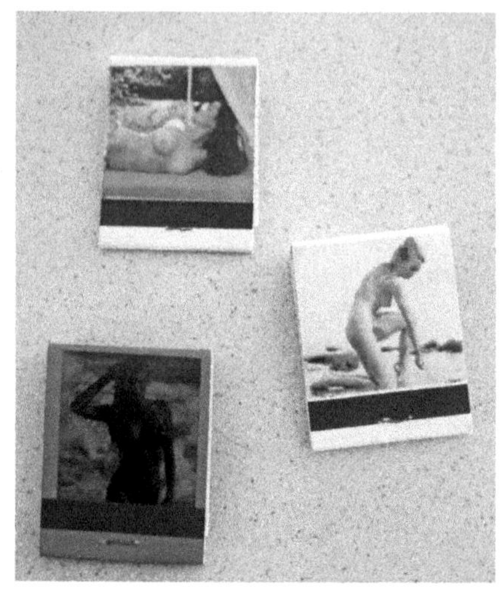

Right: The brothels' matchbooks also featured revealing photos. *John Hansen Collection; photo by Heather Branstetter.*

One of the most interesting stories about Loma was in 1958, she bought a Lincoln Continental Mark III. She went to Spokane, to Empire Lincoln Motors and placed the order for her new car. The new car had to be painted the exact color of a pink hairbrush she carried with her....

"The girls" were, for the most part, good neighbors. Some had college educations, some had very little formal schooling. One thing they had in common is that they filled a very special need in the community....

Other than creating conversation about the time "when," I think the need for "the girls" is just as strong now as it ever has been. I miss them. I miss knowing they were there taking care of business. They were a part of town. In some cases, the best part—that part that takes the cutting edge off humanity. Think about it!

"Look on the Sunny Side": The Oasis Bordello Museum Collection

The following notes and letters are from the files of the Oasis Bordello Museum. Darlene Murphy, who preferred to be called "Ginger," began running the Oasis Rooms in 1963. Documents confirm that she bought the Arment Rooms in 1966 for $19,080 and hired women to help her manage it while she spent the majority of her time at the Oasis Rooms.[234] The letters featured here are edited to protect privacy. I have tried to reproduce the language in a way that is as faithful as possible to the original documents, which were written by hand. They reveal a more personal and intimate look at life in the houses.

The following two letters were addressed to Ginger. The first was from a woman who used to work for her, and the second was from a woman who had just received a job offer from her. Both letters indicate a great deal of respect, admiration and love for the Oasis owner and manager.

November 9, 1982
Dear Ginger,
Just these few lines to let you know that you have been in our thoughts and prayers. I also hope that this letter finds you and yours all in great health and spirits.

I'm sorry it has taken me so long to write you but it just seems as though everything just happened so suddenly that I haven't had much time for myself lately. I hope you understand.

Thank you so very much for the beautiful flowers you sent. My mother just couldn't get over them and it really meant and still means a lot to her....

As for me I'm still working and keeping myself very busy with that and of course my animals take a lot of my time too, which I don't mind at all, they have all been a great comfort for me.

So how's life been treating my favorite and dear friend?

I hope that all is well with you, by the way how are your little ones doing? (your kids/dogs)

Could you please thank the girls for the nice card they sent for me. I'd do it but after I finish this letter to you I need to send out some cards for my mother and that's not going to be easy.

Ginger thank you also for being there when I really needed someone. I love you for that, but I love you more for the many, many things you taught me while I was up there. You'll always have a very special place in my heart forever.

Gotta run now but I'm hoping to hear from you soon cause I'd love to keep in touch with you.

Loving thoughts and warmth from my heart always,

[name redacted]

P.S. Thank you so very much for all that you have ever done for me. Love ya bunches!

[Postmarked July 10, 1984]
Dear Ginger
How are you doing? I hope this letter finds you in the very best of health.

I must admit that I was happy when I heard that you were trying to get in touch with me, because your job offer may be very important at this time in my life. I came back to San Francisco to bury my mother and having done so I am prepared to leave again and probably never return. In the last three years I have tried a number of things in a search for something permanent but I have discovered that there is nothing that suits me more than being around a house.

Another thing is that me and my man have been together 16 years and we both are ready to find a home not a place. We both knew that we are not getting any younger and it's time to settle down to do something with at least a promise of stability. I don't expect you to tell me that I have a permanent job without finding out how I am going to work out but if staying there is dependent on my willingness to learn, my ability to do my job and my sincerity, then I will have no problem in satisfying you. I am very interested in finding out what you have in mind.

At this I am working [as] *a maid in Nevada, there is no problem leaving. But I would like to have a idea of the position Ginger. Let me knew, and I will call you and let you knew my time and date that I'll be at the door.*

Love Always
[name redacted]

A woman who called herself "Casey" was one of the last girls working at the Oasis. She was well liked, according to a research participant who was one of her many admirers.[235] In the museum, her room was preserved and little bits of her life remain, including a pencil drawing of her face signed by someone named Mike. Her room also features a little wooden sign that says, "IN GOD WE TRUST—ALL OTHERS PAY CASH!" A trucker sent her the following two letters:

8-10-86—Sunday Morning—Rain—
Casey;
A short note to say how much I've enjoyed your company the last few months, we had some good some bad but they go together like us.

This morning will be extra hard for me because I'll have to let you go back, but it will all work out I'm sure, we will see more of one another in the very near future. So don't think that I'm not thinking about you all the

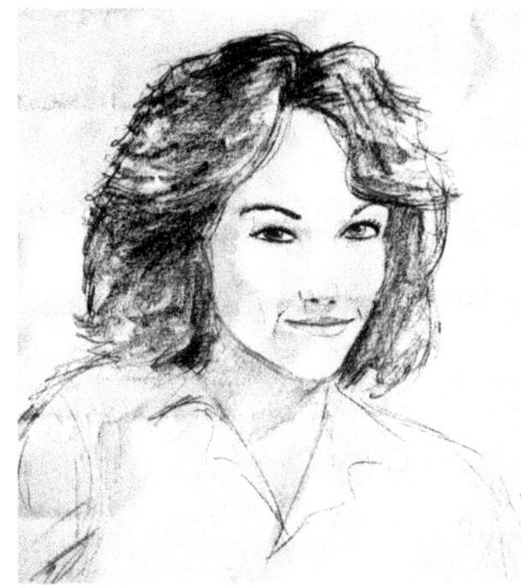

Left: Drawing of Casey by Mike. *Oasis Bordello Museum display; photo by Heather Branstetter.*

Below: Sign in Casey's room. *Oasis Bordello Museum display; photo by Heather Branstetter.*

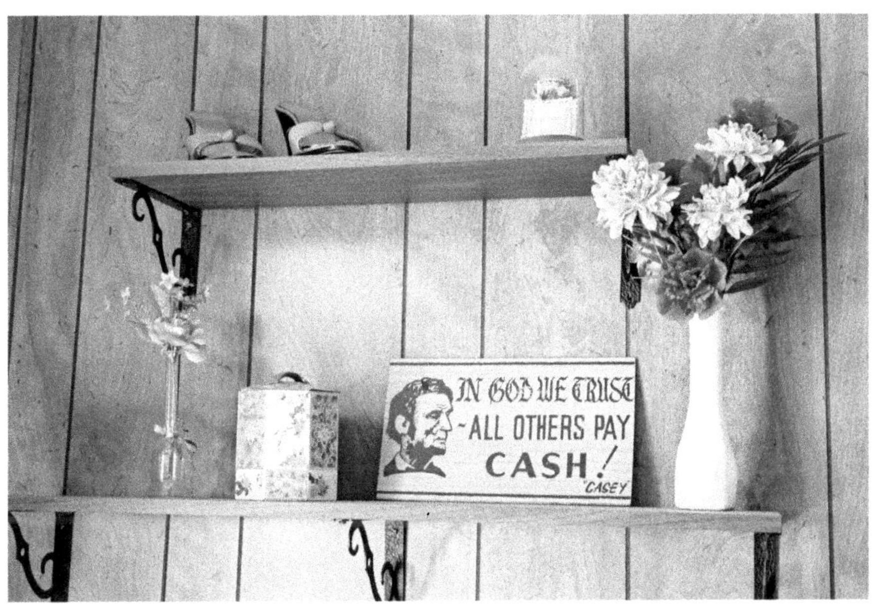

time, the ring is small and so are you, but the love you have inside is quite large and will hold for a long time. So do me and you a large favor. Stay the way you are and remember I also love you too. Take good care of yourself and don't let mom get under your skin.

I'll see you soon if possible.

Love [name redacted]

"Be Good" [quotation marks in original letter]

try [added as though it were an afterthought to the instruction to be good]

8-19-86
Tuesday Night
Casey,
Here I am again in Bed Bugger Heaven. Detroit, Mi. [Omitted: many details about shipments in a variety of cities throughout the East and Southeast. He urges her to remember Nashville, Tennessee—"good time!"]

I never sent any cards to the house in Salt Lake City, I'm not sure mom would like that, you know how long it's been since I've written to anyone. (Long time). Tonight just isn't right your not here watching T.V. in the truck, sure is real different with out you. I guess you were right about me being Spoiled! O' Shit I sat down to supper tonight and had Spaget—sure I almost order a Ruebon Sourdwetd. I talked to dispatch and I might be able to line up a load to Spokane or Seattle not for sure yet! but I'm working on it. I don't have a P.O. Box yet but I will soon. The truck seem to be running o.k. I hope the flight was ok. I'd have give anything to see the look on mom's face. You know it's almost my bed time 9:00 P.M. So for now, take good care of yourself. Ok. I miss you a lot. I'll write later,

[name redacted]

P.S. Say Hi to Ginger

This letter, featuring a Seattle postmark, was from a different man writing to three women who worked at the Oasis.

April 16, 1984
Dear [names redacted],
The time I spent with you last Thursday night and Friday morning was like heaven. If it wasen't for this physical nuisance I've contracted I'd swear I was dreaming. Thank you so much for the idealic [sic] *vacation. See you again this summer.*

Love,

[name redacted]

A woman who worked at the Oasis during the 1980s left a small notebook behind in a drawer in one of the rooms. It contains phone numbers, times, city names and a few scattered phrases, including the sentiment that "at least my kids will make me happy I knew that they really do love me. I love them to they don't expect anything from me they love me for just myself and that's a good feeling."

Ginger's room at the Oasis offers a partial window into her system of values. On the dresser sits an empty bottle of Black Velvet whiskey and a book about Nostradamus beneath a poster showing two birds flying under the sun. A poem on the poster instructs, "If you love something, set it free. If it comes back to you, it is yours. If it doesn't, it never was." There is also a framed comic that portrays a woman dressed in red, cleavage for miles, holding a cigarette as she tells a police officer, "Well, I would have reported it sooner sergeant…but I didn't know I'd been raped till the check bounced!" The documents reproduced below were written in Ginger's elegant handwriting. They appear to be personal reminders and/or instructions for the girls. Although Ginger was not known for being very religious, these documents indicate Christian beliefs.

By Reverend Dr. Gaines *Sun. April 20, 1980*

Look on the Sunny Side

There are always two sides
The Good and the bad.
The Dark and the Light
The Sad and the Glad

But in looking back over the good and the bad
We are aware of the number of good things we've had
And in counting our blessings
We find when we're through
We've no reason at all to complain or be blue
So thank God for good things
He's already done
And be grateful to Him for the battles you have won
And know that the same God who helped you before
Is ready and willing to help you once more.

Daily Prayer

Lord, when we are wrong,
Make us willing to change;
And when we are right,
Make us easy to live with.

Read written prayers—say Lord's Prayer

Read Scriptures:
1st John 2:13–17; 4:4–6
Matt. 6:24
James 1:13–15, 20–27
14th Chapter St. John
Joshua 2:1–22
Hebrews chapter 11
2nd Samuel 18:18
Proverbs 15:8, 11:29, 1:7, 3:35, 1:32
Psalms 121
Proverbs 3:5, 6
Matt. 6:9–13, 24:36–42
1 Corinthians 13:5, 6, & 7
Psalms 46:1, 28:8–9, 119:105
Matt. 5:15, 16

SHOSHONE COUNTY SHERIFF'S OFFICE FILES

Until 1973, the women who came into town to work in the brothels were fingerprinted and photographed by the Shoshone County Sheriff's Office (SCSO), which then ran a background check. Police worked together with the madams to look into the histories of the women and their connections. They kept physical records in filing folders containing rap sheets with photos, birthdates, aliases and ephemera such as newspaper articles inserted alongside the rap sheets. These files show that some of women who worked in Wallace's houses began selling sex after suffering incest, abuse, sexual assault or an unstable home life growing up. They also reveal evidence of the profession's mental health and substance abuse hazards. It is important to recognize that the women featured here are in some ways different from the majority of the women who worked in Wallace—the sex workers who led more "normal" lives are not as visible because their files are not as attention grabbing as the exceptional ones. Inevitably, the records offering the richest information focus on the negative aspects of sex work and its intersection with criminality.

The rest of this chapter provides a brief snapshot of only a few of the 531 women who appear in the SCSO records from 1952 to 1973. As I surveyed what turned out to be in excess of two thousand pages, I looked for patterns and made note of trends. The women worked on what was known as "the circuit," moving into and out of town in a transient way, traveling from one town to another like many of the miners did, and the files document other cities on the circuit. In part, the women moved frequently to ensure variety for the customers ("fresh inventory," as one of my research participants crudely explained). The files also reveal rates of turnover within the houses during this time. One remarkable case, which I discuss in some depth, includes an intake form and personal history sent from a mental hospital in Nevada, where the woman had been committed.

Police officers made notes in the files as they evaluated the women from the perspective of "what kind of trouble might she cause for us?" While these records offer only an incomplete and slanted picture of Wallace's sex workers' lives, they also fill important gaps that don't appear in the oral histories, which are featured in the last part of this book. The police were working with the madams in a collaborative way; they exchanged information to manage the industry together.

"Do not let back in town," "Not to return to Wallace," "Told to check out" or "Keep out" were the most common notations written in the files—these phrases indicated flagrant disobedience of the madams' or town's unwritten rules of discretion. One woman, for example, was "told to check out" after two weeks, following a night when she got drunk at Sweets, a local bar.[236] The madams were strict about preventing the women from patronizing the bars, mainly because they wanted to avoid the perception that the women solicited on the streets. Some women earned the label "pillhead" or were "chased out for good, supposed to be on drugs."[237] They were evicted and prevented from returning to work in Wallace if they engaged in behavior like stealing the madam's credit card or trying to "roll [rob] a guy."[238] Other common descriptions included "Trouble" or "watch out for this one."[239] One woman earned the label of "lesbian" after a police officer saw her kissing another woman at the Stein Bar, and she was noted to have "all the potential for a real trouble maker."[240] Her file reveals that eventually she married a man who was a miner from Kellogg.[241]

So many of the files contain patronizing language alongside matter-of-fact and sometimes brutal assessments of the women's appearance or character. In more than a few cases, there is a tinge of voyeurism in the commentary by the police officers in the notations. The files provoke visions of the women finishing their intake interviews with the madams before walking down the street to the sheriff's office for processing, where

FEDERAL BUREAU OF INVESTIGATION, UNITED STATES DEPARTMENT OF JUSTICE
WASHINGTON, D. C.

CURRENT ARREST OR RECEIPT

DATE ARRESTED OR RECEIVED	CHARGE OR OFFENSE	DISPOSITION OR SENTENCE
12/19/55	Inv.	FP&R

CRIMINAL HISTORY

CONTRIBUTOR OF FINGERPRINTS	NAME AND NUMBER	ARRESTED OR RECEIVED	CHARGE	DISPOSITION

INSTRUCTIONS
1. TYPE OR PRINT all information.
2. Include only FINAL dispositions.
3. INSTITUTIONS: Include date sentence expires.
4. Note amputations in proper finger squares.

SEND COPY TO:
Out – 3/4/56 – Oasis Rooms
In – 7/17/56 – Lux Rooms
Out – 9/10/56 – Lux Rooms
In 11/20/56 Oasis Rms.
Out 12/23/56 Oasis Rooms.

FD-249
(5-26-55)
U. S. GOVERNMENT PRINTING OFFICE : 1955 O - 348140

"Kim" in 1955. *Scan slightly altered to enlarge photo and hide full name; Shoshone County Sheriff's Office Files, Wallace District Mining Museum Archives.*

the officers relish their own personal preview of the incoming women as they take mug shots and fingerprints.

Wallace's pre-1973 regulation model would not be considered "decriminalization" by contemporary sex worker standards. Despite its entanglement with the criminal justice system, Wallace's pre-1973 system would more commonly be called "legalization" because it tracked the women by fingerprints and photographs. Not only are these kinds of regulatory practices invasive, but they also discourage compliance. The continuing stigma associated with prostitution makes such a system risky for sex workers. What if the laws change? What if a woman studying the history of prostitution in her hometown goes through the records fifty years later, when you are happily married to someone who never knew you were a whore, and now your past is coming back to haunt you? From a pragmatic perspective, it doesn't appear to have been necessary to involve the police in regulating prostitution. The system apparently evolved the way it did because of a combination of convenience and politics.

Police regulation ended in 1973 because Idaho's state law changed, effectively criminalizing Wallace's system, which before had not been illegal in the eyes of the state.[242] Sex workers continued to receive doctor's checkups, but around this time, police participation in the regulation appears to have ended. The legal changes relevant to Wallace's brothels concerned prostitution's criminality and punishment. The revised laws prohibited "interstate trafficking in prostitution," which forbade women from entering Idaho for the purpose of sex work; "accepting earnings of prostitution," which applied to the local government, schools, madams and police; and "harboring prostitutes," which outlawed brothels.[243] Laws specifically criminalizing prostitution and "patronizing a prostitute" appear to have been absent until a 1977 revision.[244]

In many parts of Nevada, where the culture of symbiosis connecting mining to sex work was much like Wallace's, prostitution was legal and

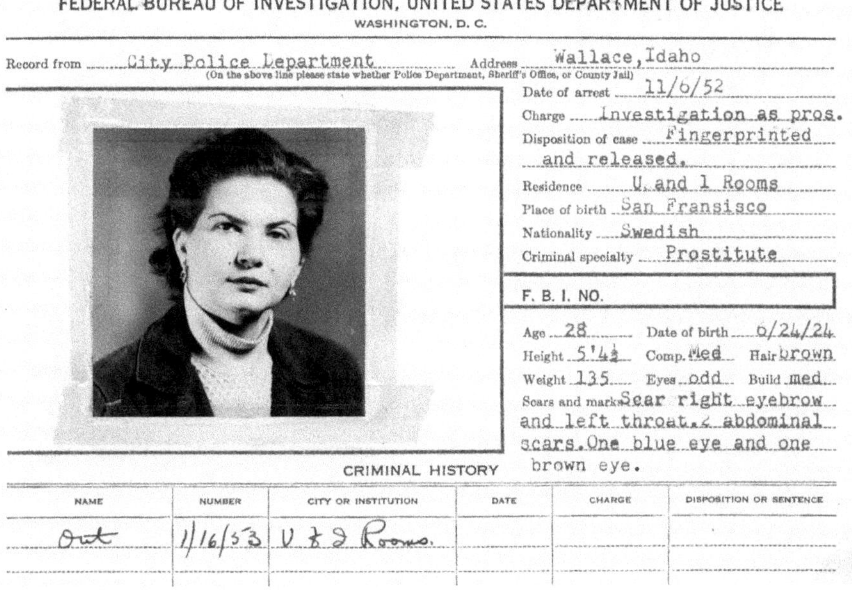

FEDERAL BUREAU OF INVESTIGATION, UNITED STATES DEPARTMENT OF JUSTICE
WASHINGTON, D. C.

Record from City Police Department Address Wallace, Idaho
(On the above line please state whether Police Department, Sheriff's Office, or County Jail)

Date of arrest 11/6/52
Charge Investigation as pros.
Disposition of case Fingerprinted and released.
Residence U. and I Rooms
Place of birth San Fransisco
Nationality Swedish
Criminal specialty Prostitute

F. B. I. NO.

Age 28 Date of birth 6/24/24
Height 5'4½ Comp. Med Hair brown
Weight 135 Eyes odd Build med
Scars and marks Scar right eyebrow and left throat. 2 abdominal scars. One blue eye and one brown eye.

CRIMINAL HISTORY

NAME	NUMBER	CITY OR INSTITUTION	DATE	CHARGE	DISPOSITION OR SENTENCE
Out	1/16/53	U & I Rooms			

"Bobbie" in 1952. *Shoshone County Sheriff's Office Files, Wallace District Mining Museum Archives.*

remains so. The SCSO records indicate that there were many other towns across the West on the circuit, and they reveal that about one-fifth of the women working in the houses during this time also rotated between houses while they were in Wallace. Some women came to Wallace from as far away as Florida, Texas and Illinois, while others were immigrants or characterized as "runaways." By looking at the notes on the rap sheets, it is possible to see which other towns also decriminalized prostitution: if the charge was "inv" or "venereal control" or sometimes "prost." and the disposition was "fingerprinted, mugged, and released" (often shortened to fmr), it meant that prostitution was regulated in those towns. Montana seems to have been particularly permissive: Butte was well known for its illicit yet tolerated prostitution until 1982, and the records indicate that Great Falls also regulated illegal sex work well into the latter half of the twentieth century.[245]

The sheriff's office files even reveal that the unlikely town of Burley, Idaho, nestled in the heart of Mormon country, permitted and regulated prostitution until at least 1970.[246] Many women came from towns in California, Washington and Oregon that were known for male-dominated labor industries like mining and logging. Prostitution appears under various guises in different towns, depending on the time frame. For example, it was common to see the charge of "immoral woman" and uncommon to see the charge of "taxi dancer," which appears to be specific to Oakland and San Francisco around the time of World War II. In Los Angeles during the 1950s and 1960s, prostitution was called sex perversion, lewd conduct or indecent exposure, and in Ephrata, Washington, it was referred to as "carnal knowledge."

When a woman arrived in town, she interviewed with the madam and then went to the police station to be fingerprinted and offer up her legal name for a background check. During the earlier years, the mug shots were actually portrait photos taken by local photographer Nellie Stockbridge. After her studio closed in 1962, the photos became more traditional mug shots taken at the police station, although even in these pictures, many of the women pose in friendly ways, smiling for the camera with hands on hips. The police would then begin keeping a file that noted aliases and information on spouses or male associates and the date she "checked in" to one of the brothels. When the women left town, the file makes note of that as well, mentioning it as a "check out" or usually just "out." Four out of five women who worked in Wallace chose one house exclusively during the duration of their stay. Most commonly, the women worked four to six months and returned after leaving for a while, but some women stayed for years.

Conditions for women in Wallace appear to have been more generally positive than in many other places, but most often they ended up in Wallace because they needed money. During this time, women did not have a variety of choices for work, and many of those who engaged in sex work did so because they didn't believe they had better options for comparable wages. The files contain plenty of evidence that the women needed money. A number of the women's rap sheets include crimes such as theft, larceny, forgery, fraud, writing bad checks or the more generic "obtaining money through false pretenses." Many women were raising children after turning to prostitution at a young age, having found themselves in a socially unacceptable circumstance, such as pregnancy out of wedlock. Several files offer evidence that some women had been coerced into the profession. They became easy targets for coercion after they were raped or turned out by relatives, ran away from abusive households or somehow found their way into the "correctional" system. Some women may not have characterized the guys who coerced them into the business as pimps but instead thought of them as boyfriends or father figures they supported financially in a reciprocal relationship that offered companionship or protection. Other women simply wanted financial independence and were willing to sell sex to achieve it.

There are several women who entered the sex industry after their stay in a California institution called the Ventura School for Girls, where each was labeled a "wayward girl." The Ventura reformatory, "whose picturesque location and academic name masked a repressive atmosphere, typically housed girls with long histories of delinquency, sexual promiscuity, and unsatisfactory stays at other reform institutions."[247] Historian Elizabeth Escobedo has documented incarceration at the institution as so threatening that young women went to "drastic measures" such as "swallowing safety pins the night before in order to get out of it."[248] It seems unusual that this particular institution, with its draconian punishments labeled a "disgrace to the state," shows up several times in the SCSO files.[249] It is possible the madams had some kind of personal connection with the "school" (which actually functioned more like a prison), or it may be the case that the women who were sent there were more likely to end up in the sex industry afterward.

The sheriff's office files confirm that women were turned away if they were discovered to have been "a hometown girl" or if their FBI background check revealed they were younger than twenty-one years old. Some women slipped through the cracks, obviously, but the effort appears to have exceeded due diligence. If the rap sheet indicated involvement with organized crime, they might also be turned away, although some women were associated with gangs that operated out of Texas and Great Falls. The records also make note of women who had been material witnesses for Mann Act cases in other cities, compelled to testify about an experience relating to someone facilitating their travel across state lines.

"Kitty," SCSO File 705

Many women had pimps in other towns. This was sometimes noted in their records explicitly, as was the case for a woman who called herself Kitty. She was born in Chewelah, Washington, in 1919 and worked in Wallace for four months during the summer of 1956. The rap sheet notes that Kitty was first picked up by the police in Spokane, Washington, in 1940 and fined twenty-five dollars for "city vag" (code for vagrancy, used by many cities both to indicate homelessness and prosecute street prostitution). Eight months later, she is again charged with vagrancy in Grand Coulee, Washington, when she was told to leave town. There was huge demand for sex work there during this time, when it was essentially a boomtown as men flocked there to work on the hydroelectric dam, according to a visitor's guide:

> *In the Grand Coulee, life changed dramatically and quickly once work on the dam began in 1933. Not only did the undertaking of this massive project change forever the shape of the river, but overnight it created towns where nothing but sagebrush, sand and rocks had previously existed. Thousands came to the Grand Coulee looking for work in the midst of the Depression. They worked around the clock to finish the dam by 1942.*[250]

During World War II, Kitty found gainful "legitimate" employment working in Puget Sound, Washington, as a mechanic for the navy. Like Dolores and many others, she was a "Rosie the Riveter." This element of Kitty's file is rather typical of the women who were sex workers in Wallace during this era. Our collective understanding of the "We Can Do It" history represented by Rosie the Riveter should include women who were in the sex industry both before and after the war. The rhetoric from this era celebrating patriotism and public service disguises the fact that many of these women joined the military workforce because they needed to work and

FEDERAL BUREAU OF INVESTIGATION, UNITED STATES DEPARTMENT OF JUSTICE
WASHINGTON, D. C.

CURRENT ARREST OR RECEIPT

DATE ARRESTED OR RECEIVED	CHARGE OR OFFENSE	DISPOSITION OR SENTENCE
5/19/56	Inv.	Fingerprinted Mug.& Released

CRIMINAL HISTORY

CONTRIBUTOR OF FINGERPRINTS	NAME AND NUMBER	ARRESTED OR RECEIVED	CHARGE	DISPOSITION
Admits;				
Troy Mont.P.D.	Kitty Black	1955	Prostitute	

INSTRUCTIONS

1. TYPE OR PRINT all information.
2. Include only FINAL dispositions.
3. INSTITUTIONS: Include date sentence expires.
4. Note amputations in proper finger squares.

SEND COPY TO: Out - 9/13/56 -

FD-249
(5-26-55)

U. S. GOVERNMENT PRINTING OFFICE : 1955 O - 348140

"Kitty Black" in 1956. *Scan slightly altered to improve photo quality; Shoshone County Sheriff's Office Files, Wallace District Mining Museum Archives.*

were unable to find other jobs that paid comparable wages. The Shoshone County Sheriff's Office records reveal a large number of women who were sex workers in Wallace preferred to work "square" jobs when the military was hiring widely but felt the need to return to prostitution after the war ended and these jobs dried up.

In 1945, Kitty was picked up in San Bernardino, California, for grand theft and drunk driving. She made her way to San Diego shortly thereafter, was charged with being drunk and served a fifteen-day term in the city jail. Two years later, she was back in Spokane, where she was arrested for "Inv," which means that she was investigated but not charged with anything. There is a noticeable gap between her 1947 Spokane arrest and her 1956 appearance in Wallace, where she arrived at the age of thirty-seven and began working in the Arment Rooms. Her record also notes that she was a prostitute in Troy, Montana, in 1955.

It's unclear whether Kitty's pimp coerced her into the business or whether he found her after she was already working in the industry. The file notes her pimp lived in Spokane, which is where she was first arrested, so both are possible. When women have pimps, it often indicates coercion—they are men skilled at targeting vulnerable women, sometimes by trolling the jails and paying for their release. Other men target young girls with an unstable family life, victims of financial insecurity and those who have been labeled promiscuous or run away from home. These men know how to find and exploit desperation or naïveté. Then they con their marks into thinking that they are loved or protected. For some women, their pimp may feel like a father figure. In other situations, the women have been manipulated or emotionally abused to feel like they can't do any better, or they were raised in circumstances where this kind of treatment was the norm. Some women—for a variety of reasons, including cultural influences like sexism and religion—simply feel obliged to please men. Physical abuse and intimidation are only the most obvious tactics. After grooming their victims by earning their trust, either through psychological manipulation or circumstance, these men use whatever means are at their disposal to further and continue their control, including threatening to hurt the women's children. Even though tattoos were uncommon for women during this time, many sex workers who came through Wallace's houses had men's names tattooed on their bodies, and these names may have been boyfriends or husbands, men they supported financially or men who coerced them into the business.

Many women who found themselves in the Wallace cathouses likely felt coerced by their financial situation and lack of better options. Crimes indicating an addiction that created the need for money often show up on their rap sheets. Narcotics, burglary, shoplifting, forgery, drunk and disorderly, "justifiable homicide," drunk in public, stolen credit cards and embezzling appear in the records. It was easy for just one disruptive life event to lead a well-functioning woman into a downward spiral of addiction or financial insecurity. Kitty had clearly become an alcoholic by the time the war ended, and she needed a means to support herself at least by the time she turned twenty-one.

"Jeannie," SCSO File 1058

One of the more recent SCSO files describes a woman called Jeannie who was born in North Dakota on June 28, 1947, and characterized as "running with Mike Shelley" while she was in Wallace from May to August of 1970. According to the *Missoulian* newspaper, she married a twenty-two-year-old army veteran within four months of leaving town and then shot him with a .22-caliber pistol in their trailer home in neighboring Mineral County, Montana, around one thirty in the morning less than ten months later.[251] The paper described her as a twenty-two-year-old housewife and reported that the coroner's jury believed she "'willfully and feloniously' shot her husband to death."[252] Her police file notes a gunshot wound on her arm from a hunting accident but confuses the two stories and says she shot her husband in a "hunting accident"; in fact, she was the one who had been shot, by her father, at the age of fourteen.

The details of this case remain unclear, in part because the court has sealed the records. We know she pleaded innocent to manslaughter in the district court, and we know the couple fought in the middle of the night.[253] But why did Jeannie shoot her husband? He had been to Vietnam and perhaps suffered from post-traumatic stress disorder after he returned. Did he drink to numb his pain and then take it out on her physically, beating her? We know that she told him she was from Missoula and married him four months after leaving Wallace. Did he know her while she was working in Wallace? Was that how they'd met? She was beautiful, with shoulder-length black hair flipped at the bottom.

Maybe one day, when Jeannie's husband was drunk and angry, he said something like, "You can just go back to what you were before." Or maybe he didn't even know she had been a whore. She lied about her age and name, so perhaps she lied about other things as well. Many of the sheriff's office files include mysterious partial stories like this one.

"Doris," SCSO File 475

The story of Doris's suicide attempt and later "belligerence" with the nuns at the hospital was told to me in a recent oral history.[254] Her SCSO file mentions the Owl Taxi and indicates she was sent to Spokane, "not to return." This woman is characterized as Irish and was born in 1926 in Tacoma, Washington. She worked in the Arment Rooms from August 1,

1952, to January 19, 1953, and then again from April 1, 1954, to April 4. The police report from the "Sisters" at the Providence Hospital on April 4, 1954, seems most concerned about her disrespectful attitude toward the nuns:

> *Who: Doris Johnson*
> *What: Belligerent Patient*
> *Called to the Providence Hospital, at 1:15 pm this date. Was asked to come pick up a women* [sic] *who was giving the Nurses and Sisters plenty of trouble. When Jerry and I went up there Jerry thought it was the big house keeper that had been working at the Arment. We were both surprised to see this little red head. I don't think she weighs a 100 lbs. The hospital had cleared through Dr. Petterson and had been advised to call the Police and have said women taken to County Hospital. The women was very belligerent and using foul language, at all the Sisters at the hospital. We took this Doris Johnson, to the County Hospital. She was wearing just her sleeping cloths* [sic] *and that is the way we took her to the Hospital. Her cloths are still at the Providence Hospital.*
> *Report Received by Jerry-Bert*

Handwritten on the back of the sheet is the follow-up:

> *Checked Arment, and Sandy, said that her and Vick of Owl Taxi took this woman to hospital at 7:17 am this date. The girl had taken a bunch of sleeping pills. Sandy had tried to get Dr. M* [illegible] *but couldn't, finally got Dr. Petterson on phone and he advised Sandy to take her to hospital. This woman doesn't have any cloths at Hospital, all Sandy could get on her was her bath robe. Sandy is getting all the girl's stuff together and I told her you would see her tomorrow.*
> *Put on bus 4/6/54 for Spokane—not to return.*

It's almost shocking to read that final line, which looks so callous and insensitive, considering she had felt so hopeless she tried to end her life.

"Bobbie," SCSO File 490

A Swedish woman named Bobbie, born in San Francisco in 1924, worked in Wallace from November 6, 1952, to January 16, 1953. Twenty-eight at the time, she is described as five feet, four and a half inches, with a scar on her right eyebrow and left throat, two abdominal scars, one blue eye and one brown eye. The rap sheet says that her 1943 San Francisco arrest classified her as "quarantined" for "vagrancy." There is a history of permitting sex workers to be quarantined for sexually transmitted infections, going back to the reform era extending from the early 1900s to the 1920s. In this case, however, the code probably just indicated prostitution regulation.

In February 1945, Bobbie is called a "Taxi Dancer" in Oakland, California. This label might have referred to the practice of charging a fee to dance with men at dance halls, or it could have been code for prostitution. By 1946, she is in New York City and receives a suspended sentence for what looks like a vagrancy law. Such laws were used to regulate everything from sexuality to radicalism because they were both broad and ambiguous and thus used to sidestep the Fourth Amendment's proscription against arrest without probable cause.[255] Bobbie worked at the Rose Rooms in San Francisco eight months before arriving in Wallace. By the time she landed in Wallace, she was associated with a pimp named Chuck Johnson, who was hanging out with Clyde McLean, who ran a game at Silver Strike.

By Christmas, Johnson was in jail in Yakima with a guy named "Corky." McLean was a pimp and gambler who stayed at the Samuels Hotel in December 1952 and had connections in Miles City near the oil patch in Williston, South Dakota. He was likely the pimp for Wallace sex worker Shari Shores, who is in the Wallace Police Department files, and Billy Banning, who was a sex worker at the Rex Rooms in Kellogg. Banning sent him money by wire. The men were probably connected with a gang out of the Great Falls/Billings area in Montana. The sheriff's office and police departments in the valley tried to run off girls who were associated with pimps involved in organized crime because the conflicting power dynamics led to instability. The file notes that Wallace police chief Hugh Marconi had been "playing Shores very strong—seen in various places in district also going in back way early in morning." Bobbie left the U&I in a taxi shortly before 6:00 p.m. on January 14, 1953, and Shari left at 6:00 p.m. the next day, also by taxi.

"Peggy," SCSO File 913

The sheriff's office files contain a particularly remarkable case file detailing part of one woman's life story. Peggy was admitted to the Nevada State

Hospital, a mental institution, in 1965. While there, she helped in the kitchen and was placed in a "square" job locally, but she only stayed "about two days and then left" for "Winnemucca, Nevada to resume her former occupation as prostitute." Within five months of her release, Peggy turned up in Wallace and began working for Loma Delmonte in the Jade Rooms, where she would remain for five months before getting chased off. Her SCSO record indicates she was "run out of town" after the police characterized her as a "Hope Head" (the intended word was "hophead," slang commonly used at the time to refer to an addict).

Peggy's Nevada State Hospital admission history and mental health examination, recorded by male psychiatrist Jules Magnette, was sent to the Wallace police chief on January 14, 1966. After 1996, a federal comprehensive health information privacy law would prevent this sort of information exchange without a patient's permission, but health information was not yet protected the way it is today.[256] Accompanying the file is a note from the hospital's administrative secretary explaining that Peggy spent about a month in the institution.

Dr. Magnette's account of Peggy's life often reveals a voyeuristic tone. He described her as a "young blond" who "tells you all about her checkered career of prostitution." Dr. Magnette went on to write, "This young woman has had quite a career," adding that it was possible to "talk to this patient for half a day and continue to gather various material," as if she had been simply a fascinating object to study. It is also disturbing that he described her childhood experience of incestuous rape in the following way: "Her father even carried on sex previously with her when she was a very young girl and has tried since she has grown up but she will not let him do that any more." The fact that the doctor calls it "sex," adding that "she will not let him do that any more," undermines his professionalism, credibility and judgment; his wording implies Peggy initially had a choice in the matter and fails to acknowledge she was unable to give consent as a little girl.

The doctor's account of Peggy's experiences as a sex worker goes into some detail, describing her entry into prostitution in 1959, when she was eighteen and still living in Montana, where she was born and raised. After Montana, she moved to Vegas briefly but primarily worked out of Winnemucca before arriving in Reno. She also spent time in Tonopah, Beatty and Ash Meadows, Nevada, where most of her customers came "from the men working in [the town of] Mercury" for the nuclear program there. Peggy told the doctor that the money she made from sex work was best in Winnemucca during the hunting season. There is some discrepancy in the

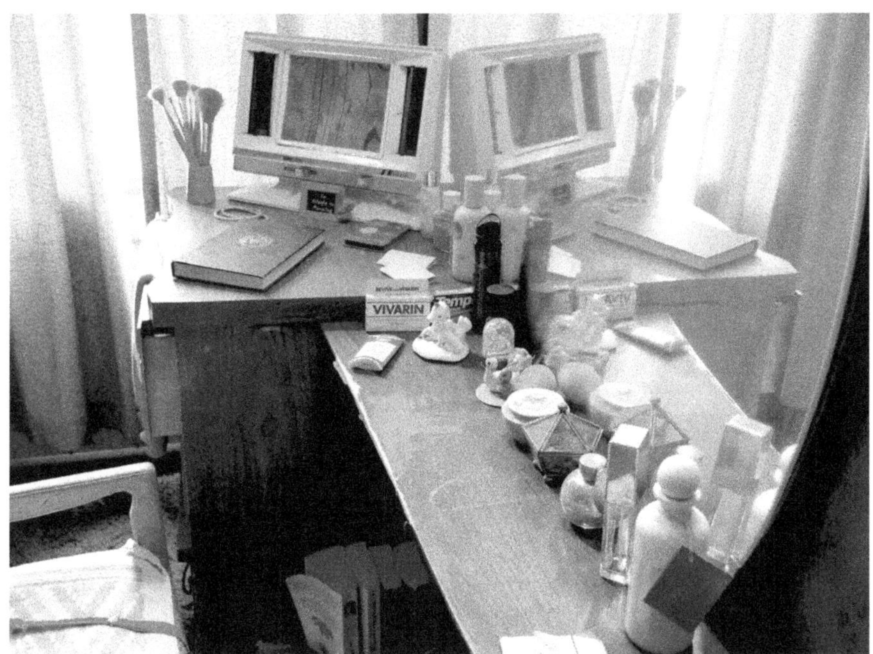

Narcotics Anonymous book on vanity. *Oasis Bordello Museum display; photo by Heather Branstetter.*

amount of money she made. She initially said she made as much as $500 to $600 in one day, "but when seen later she says the most she would make in a day for her own so-called 'take home money' would be about $150 or $165. The madam in the salons and houses takes 40% of the money." The amount of money the houses kept, according to this account, was also consistent with what people say about Wallace's practices.

At the conclusion of her admission history and mental examination, Peggy was assigned a "provisional diagnosis" of "personality trait disturbance" and "emotionally unstable personality, with alcoholism and drug addiction and prostitution." It seems strange that the doctor treated "prostitution" as a diagnosis. He described her thoughts about her means of income as follows:

> *This patient absolutely vows that she does want to change her life. She says she has never been satisfied with it. She doesn't feel its* [sic] *right to take the money from some of these poor men who have been her customers. She is ashamed of her life. She is ashamed, she says, when she faces other people. She said she would like to go to an LPN school. She likes to take care of the sick.*

Peggy's assertion that she would like to become a nurse aligns with Alexa Albert's findings from her time spent conducting research in a Nevada brothel; most of the women who worked at the Mustang Ranch while she was there in the 1990s expressed an interest in "helping professions," such as "social work, nursing, teaching, [and] daycare," as alternative "careers they would want to pursue" if those jobs paid better.[257] It's impossible to know if Peggy truly felt sorry for "these poor men who have been her customers," whether that was doctor-added interpretation or whether she was telling Dr. Magnette what she thought he wanted to hear. Prior to the publication of the *Diagnostic and Statistical Manual of Mental Disorders, Third Edition* (*DSM-III*) in 1980, psychiatrists relied on a narrative case history model of mental health pathology that reported a patient's words "as close to verbatim as possible by the physician."[258] These accounts, however, were not literal unless quotation marks were used; the clinician was most often "'recontextualizing' what the client said in the initial oral interaction."[259] Throughout Peggy's case history, her doctor did not use quotation marks. According to the psychiatric custom of the time, then, he did not record her words directly but instead filtered them through his own interpretation.

Dr. Magnette's notes imply that he believed Peggy was eager to please to the point of being insincere. In a patronizing tone, he explained:

> *This patient was told that we will observe her here a while and that the main thing that we go by here is what she does and how she acts and not how she talks. She has been told that her promises and her possible trying to impress the examiner mean nothing at all, that everything she does must be evidenced in her action—good ward behavior, willingness to work, some sort of a vow and sticking to it that she does really want to change her life and not just talk about it.*

Social and behavioral health workers are often justifiably skeptical of their patients' motivations, but Peggy's file offers evidence that she genuinely wanted to change her life, which makes Dr. Magnette's cynical assumptions seem unfair. For example, the doctor indicated she *voluntarily* "walked into Washoe Hospital about a week or so ago seeking aid" just prior to her commitment, which lasted from February 24 to March 22, 1965. But Dr. Magnette clearly believed Peggy was trying to manipulate him and exhibited drug-seeking behavior. Twice, he described her as a sociopath who tried to convince him to prescribe medicine for her.

According to Peggy's description, prostitution preceded her drug use. Her husband facilitated her addiction to painkillers before he was sent to prison, at which point she began to rely on her wages from sex work to pay for her addiction. The doctor used a doubtful tone of voice as he wrote, "She claims" her husband influenced her to begin using drugs like "Dilaudid, Morphine, Demerol, Cocaine, and Dolophine" obtained by robbing pharmacies until the time came when "she had to use her money from prostitution to go out and buy the drugs" herself. Dr. Magnette then diminished her to "nothing but an addict" while noting how other doctors knowingly enabled her addiction: "Most of her medication was obtained [legally] from doctors," and "there was a doctor or two in Las Vegas who even knew she was nothing but an addict," yet they "continued to give her the drugs at $12 a visit, or give her the drugs to take."

The doctor's report concludes:

> *In the search for real psychotic material, there is none. The patient has never had any hallucinations, delusions, paranoid material or ideas of influence or reference. She says she knows she has been listed as a sociopath. She has done a little reading like most of the sociopaths have and is able to discuss her case, at least in a superficial fashion in a fair way.... She herself has never been in jail. She denies homosexuality.*

It is unclear why the report ends with a statement about her sexual orientation. The doctor may have associated the willingness to sell sex with sexual deviance in general; at the time, homosexuality was still classified as a mental health disorder, and it is not uncommon for women sex workers to be bisexual. Peggy's file indicates that after leaving Wallace, she returned to Montana. In a letter from the Miles City police chief to the Wallace police chief, we find out that she was "run out of town" there, too. The Miles City officer went on to write, "I heard last week a couple of her girl-friends worked her over in Billings, Montana and put her in the hospital."

Part III

ORAL HISTORIES

6

1945–1973

Memory is notoriously unreliable, as I saw firsthand during the course of this research. But written records alone often lack important contextual details or remain buried in basements until those who don't recognize their value toss them out. Oral histories are an especially valuable way to learn about the kind of history that tends to be hidden from written records. They allow access to the everyday history and stories that would be lost to future generations after the deaths of the elders because they were never written down. The subject of prostitution is well suited to oral history; it is "tricky to document, because people go out of their way to keep from chronicling the information."[260] After interviewing ninety-nine people for this project, it became apparent how you can discover unexpected truths through patterns and trends that reveal themselves in the stories people tell. In this final part of the book, I share some of these discussions, which I have edited lightly for clarity and to protect the privacy of those who requested it. This chapter covers the time from World War II through a temporary closure in 1973.

Loma Delmonte

According to Magnuson, Loma arrived around the time of World War II, and she left Wallace during the 1960s. During that time, she ran the Jade Rooms at 611½ Cedar Street. Loma wasn't as "public" as Dolores was.

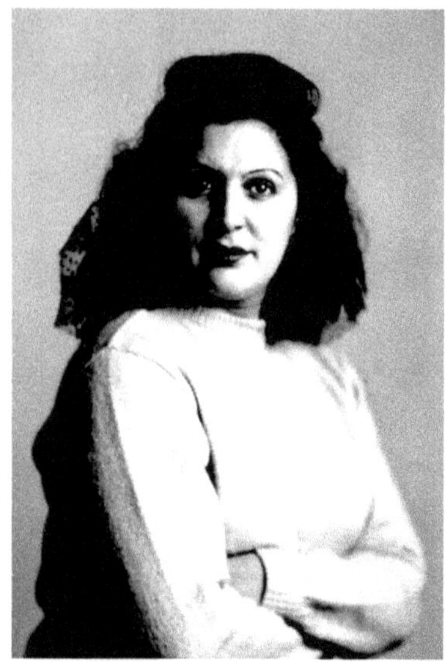

Loma Delmonte in 1945. *Barnard-Stockbridge Collection, University of Idaho Library Special Collections and Archives.*

They were in direct competition, but if you talked to either one of them, they referred to each other as good friends.[261] Another man compared Loma to Dolores in terms of their personalities and choice of cars:

Loma was more on the brash side. It was '58 when Dolores bought that baby-blue Coupe Deville. Loma had a '58 pink Lincoln with a purple Landau top and a really dark red interior. Now that was the difference. Dolores had the baby blue, Loma had the pink big four-door Lincoln Continental, she was more like what you'd think of as a madam being, raucous.[262]

Penny Garr, Former Maid at the Jade

Aunt Jane got me the [maid] job. Her apartment was close to the [Jade] rooms. My mother practically had a heart attack over it. I was naïve, twenty-one. Found a ten-dollar bill behind the radiator and gave it to Loma. If I would have known better I wouldn't have done that, because the girl had been "cheating" on her and got fired over it, for hiding some of the money she was making. I should have just given the money back to the girl.

Loma's room was a disaster, full of clutter. She was very religious, had crucifixes everywhere, gave a lot of money to the Catholic church.

She only had two girls working for her during the time I was there (1966 or so)—it was pretty small. The job paid really well, five dollars an hour. And Loma bought me a nice, monogramed passport wallet for my upcoming trip to Europe. It was a parting gift and was made of black leather, so it probably cost a decent amount, a nice gift.

I was just trying to get money but didn't tell a lot of people because they might get the wrong impression. I don't care who knows about it now, but back then I was shy about it and kept it pretty quiet.

Went in earlier around four or five. If someone rang, I would head to the back [instead of answering the door like maids did in some other houses].

Her room was so cluttery, full of religious stuff, it blew my mind. Guess she got married and moved to Seattle or Tacoma. She was heavy set, wore a lot of makeup.

I *know* she gave a lot of money to the church. Maybe it was guilt. Like she was compensating for something.

Didn't tell a lot of people in part because of how my mom reacted, didn't tell people for a long time.

But there were no rapes then. We stuck up for the houses as something that was necessary because of all the transient miners. So we never had any problems on the streets. You just got used to it.

And a lot of people went up there just to have drinks, not sex. Lots of things were different back then.

Loma was quite the pink. Lots of pink. Pink Cadillacs....

She did a lot for the high school, did the most for the kids. Those two [Loma and Dolores] were the most popular madams. Don't remember any of the others during that time.

Some of them had pimps. A lot of them were college gals.

I don't care who knows, now, I'm sixty-eight years old. My mom did care. I wasn't there that long. I was maybe a little uncomfortable, but I was mostly focused on my own life, and it was just a way to make money. Didn't know how people were going to take it if I told them. Little Catholic girl.

But that religious stuff, that surprised me the most. Just *overboard* with the Catholic stuff in her room. Crucifixes on the wall, pictures of Jesus. Like she was trying to make up for something.

But you'd see the girls during the day. They never went out at night.

And Doc Peterson made sure they didn't have any diseases—they did that religiously.

You always felt safe there [in Wallace]. Everybody always knew where Wallace, Idaho, was. I'd say I'm from Wallace, and everyone would know what that was famous for and laugh, even in New York. So you had to live with *that* your whole life.[263]

Anonymous 15, Graduated from Wallace High in 1963

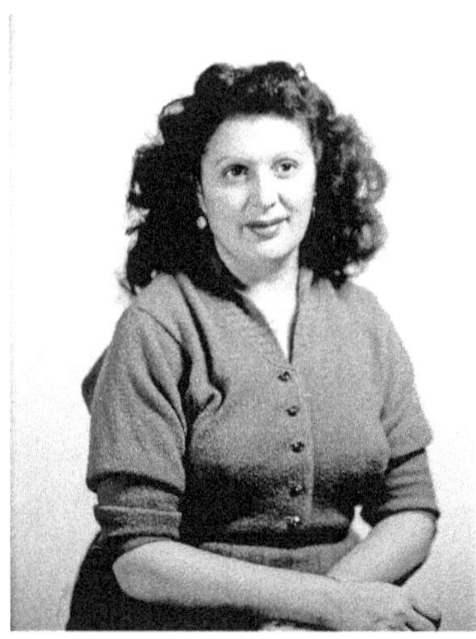

Loma Delmonte in 1955. *Barnard-Stockbridge Collection, University of Idaho Library Special Collections and Archives.*

A lot of guys had girlfriends up there [in the houses]. By 1963, I had a girl up there as a girlfriend. Most of the girls were nineteen to twenty-one years old; some were from Europe. I had an affair with a redhead girl named Anne Marie from France when I was nineteen or twenty but only saw her a couple of months....

Wallace was unique with the hook shops and open gambling. Made eighty-eight dollars working in the mine and then would just go lose that paycheck....

Loma was tough....Loma told me about a former mayor of Wallace who was "sick." [At first, he wouldn't tell me the details but then finally did.] This guy who had been mayor used to pay four girls to take enemas and then put it into a bucket. He was bottling it. Loma was upset about it when she found out and kicked him out because she didn't want that happening in her establishment.[264]

DOLORES ARNOLD

Dolores was perhaps the most beloved of the madams in Wallace. She ran the Lux Rooms at 212½ Sixth Street beginning in the 1940s. Then in 1967, Dolores bought the Jade from Loma and turned it into the Luxette. Ten years after that, she moved the Lux to 601½ Cedar, where it would remain for another decade, until Dolores became too ill to manage her houses.

Richard Magnuson, Former Prosecutor, Judge and Local Historian

There were small signs that just said "Rooms," for most of the houses. The houses were mostly called "cathouses," not brothels or bordellos. Never heard any called a bordello until the Oasis Museum opened up. They had "Reserved for Bordello Parking" signs that were stolen as quickly as they could put them up.

Most of the signs were very small, but there was an exception. Once during a city council meeting, Fred Levering—a real blue-nose, preceded your grandpa in the depot—was upset about a big sign with a flashing arrow that said "Lux" on it and pointed around the corner to the door in the alley. Most signs were not flamboyant, but this one was.

The thing that upset Fred the most, he said during this meeting: "And she's painted it titty-pink!"

One year, the madams got into an informal competition to provide bicycles for kids from town who caught fish during a fishing derby in the city pool, which had been drained and filled with water from Printer's Creek. The best prizes for the derby were the bikes from the madams. They didn't publicize it; the kids might not have known their prizes were from the madams.

Dolores and the other madams probably had influence around town because they spent so much money. My dad ran the meat market, and Dolores would only shop there when he was there, because she liked him. When he was on vacation, she wouldn't go there.

Dolores was a very warm person. Anybody needed help, any drive around here, even gave money to refurbish graves of men who had been killed during the labor troubles. She put on a real party every year. Started calling this one club [Gyro Club] the "ham and legs society." No women except her girls, in long dresses. No hanky-panky, no trick suits [slang for the outfits the girls wore while working]. Dolores hosted a lot of people.[265]

Anonymous 1 and Sonny Parsons, Grew Up in Wallace During the 1960s

Anonymous 1: Had to drive all the way down to Lewiston to play football, got back on the bus afterward, driver was drunk. The only thing that kept us alive was knowing that the cathouses would be open no matter what time we got home.

Parsons: I used to go with the madam of the cathouse right up here [at the Arment]. Her name was Tammy. I played in the drum and bugle corps, I didn't know how to blow the goddamn bugle, and the serpentine went to the Metals and then up into the Arment Rooms. The bugle corps left and I stayed.… I thought I had it made up there, I was young, single, used to help count the money up there in a goddamn Safeway sack, but I found out later, I wasn't the only boyfriend up there.

Anonymous 1: He wasn't the only one, honey. Cha Cha.

Parsons: Some of them had a kid back in Missoula.

Anonymous 1: Three weeks on, one week off.

Parsons: Their mom and dads had a normal life, didn't know anything. Nice girls.

Anonymous 1: There weren't a bunch of dogs up here.

Parsons: No. They were good-looking women.

Anonymous 1: And some of them were real professionals. And there was one who worked in the Lux Rooms during the '50s and '60s. Cha Cha. Unbelievable. She lived in Spokane, had a nice place in Spokane, and she'd come here to work. Stayed here for eight to nine years and retired.

Dolores and her sister Donna came over here during World War II and started working here in the Arment Rooms. Dolores was beautiful. She looked like Hedy Lamarr....

My grandmother would be there, and I'd go in my grandmother's when I was a little kid and she'd be sitting there chatting with Dolores and having a cup of coffee with her. Dolores Arnold looked and dressed like a movie star. She was gorgeous. And class. When the old madams like Loma and Dolores ran the cathouses, it was first class, no smoking, no drinking.… They were the old-time madams that understood what the deal was.

Parsons: They were prominent citizens.

Anonymous 1: Did you hear about when she [Dolores] bought the '57 Studebaker cop car? There was this big fat cop called Louisiana Jim, weighed about three hundred pounds. And Wallace had an old '54 Chevy van they called the paddy wagon. Why that paddy wagon couldn't catch nothing. Top speed on it was probably sixty-five miles per hour. That big Louisiana Jim goes up Nine Mile in the paddy wagon and he's drunk and he's got some broad in there with him and they're fooling around and he drives it right in the creek and he rolls it, so they don't have a cop car anymore. Dolores is good friends with the guy who owned the Studebaker dealership, so she tells him she wants to buy the police a new cop car. They put that new 289 supercharger engine in it. It would outrun anything in Idaho. So everyone was pissed at Dolores.

Dolores just worked and saved her money and as soon as she got enough, that was when she went down and rented that building. And she went and put her own place in it and she had the best. That place was the best in town. That was the class. Because of Dolores, because she had class. Did you know she used to be married to the mayor of Mullan? And he lived up in the Lux Rooms for a while. He was a great big tall guy.... She did [have a relationship with Hank Day], because he was in love with her. He'd pay money to shut the whole place down for a few weeks so he could have it to himself....

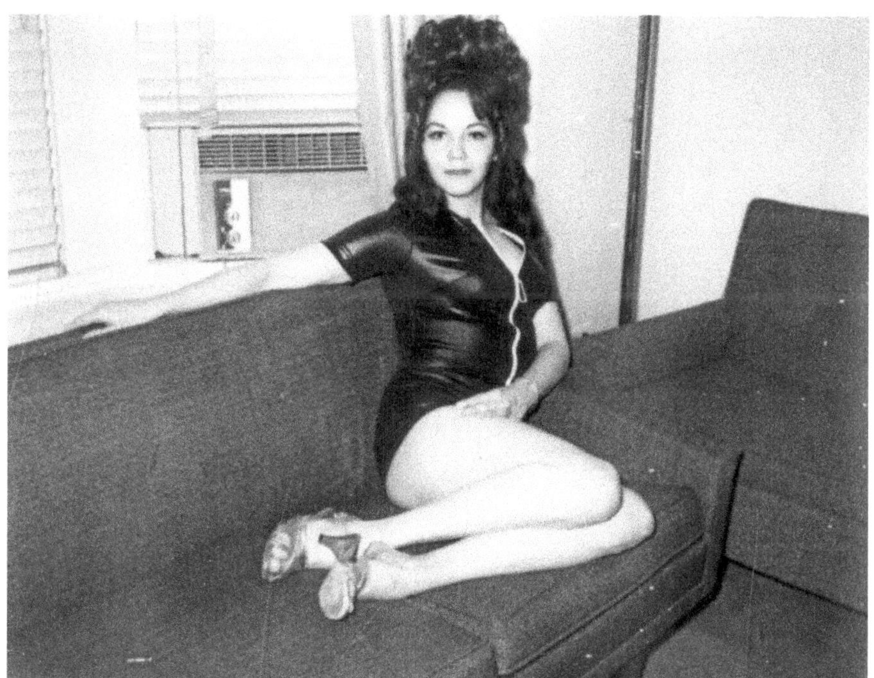

"Frenchie," 1970s. *Richard Caron Collection.*

There was a guy named Turpack who worked for the railroad and blew all $5,000 of his retirement savings in the Lux Rooms, said he'd like to be up there until the money ran out. Bubble bath, bubbles and booze everywhere.

This town here was the funnest place. I was born in 1945. This town, when I grew up in the '50s, this was the best place in the world to grow up in. This town was unbelievable.

You would have loved her. She was so gracious, and so classy.

Dolores had a big standard poodle named Mike, and Mike was white and he had a diamond choke chain collar. She'd take Mike out for a ride, and he'd sit in the passenger seat, the top fucking dog in the whole town. He was a dandy, that Mike. Beautiful dog.

The girls didn't drink or smoke—it was all business.... When Dolores ran those places, it was the cleanest place you were ever in in your life. The girls didn't drink. Dolores never drank, never smoked, never cursed. The lady, unbelievable. It was all business....

So with the cathouses they understood this, this was business. All of Dolores's girls loved her because there wasn't nothing she wouldn't do for them. She was pretty, she was just beautiful. Look at Hedy Lamarr, that's who she looked like.

Dolores she saved her money and then she went down and leased that place. You know what used to be underneath the Lux Rooms there? The Swan Bar. Joe Swan. Dolores rented the upstairs and put the Lux Rooms in up there. Then Dolores ended up buying the building, eventually.[266]

A Conversation with Sonny Parsons

Some of these guys, that's all they did was go up to the cathouses.... [Name redacted] said Tammy was *his* girlfriend. I said, bullshit, Tammy was *my* goddamn girlfriend. You're the one who *introduced* me.

He did introduce me. I was working down at the Osburn Club [in the town between Wallace and Kellogg]. She came in there. [Even though the girls didn't go out to the bars in Wallace, they often went to the Osburn Club when they wanted to go out on the town.]

He came up to me when I was working at the bar down there, and he says, "You see that girl down the bar there?" You couldn't miss her, she was like five-seven and blond. She was gorgeous.

[He] says, "You see that girl down the bar there? She wants a Manhattan, and she wants to give you fifty thousand dollars." I said, "Right on." Fix her a Manhattan. He's kinda giggling down there at the end of the bar. He comes back and says, "Fix her another one, and now she wants to give you a corvette."

I said, "Let's fix another damn Manhattan." Her and [him] are down there, kinda giggling and stuff. And when she left, she looked me right in the eye. I'm just a young man. And she looked right in my eye and said, "I'll see you later." And that's how it started. I went up there. I went up there after I closed the bar.

[He] later says to me, "You weren't her only boyfriend."

She treated me like I was her boyfriend and that's what counts....

It was a business. The girls were over here doing what they were doing. Tammy had her own apartment up there. We used to go to Coeur d'Alene, rent the finest places, do this and that. My opinion, the business she was running didn't bother me at all, because she was a nice, nice person. A very nice person. And I was kinda trapped between a moral issue, you know. I talked to a lot of the girls. One of the girls was from Montana, and she was a single mother, had two kids, mom and dad lived in Missoula. They didn't know what she was doing, but she had no other choice and she was over here making money, and would go back to Missoula as a normal person....

Put a little humor into it, my mother worked at the First National Bank on the corner [of Sixth and Cedar across from where Tammy worked], and I had a brand-new Thunderbird, and in the mornings it would be parked out right over here in front of the corner, Arment Rooms, and my mother was a great woman.

She called up, and she said, "Son, I've never gotten involved in your business, but I want you to park that Thunderbird around back from now on." Because she'd come to work and her son's Thunderbird would be in front of the Arment Rooms. Well, in my view, it was just like she had an apartment and she was my girlfriend.

Maybe a couple years, and then the padlock was on the door [in 1973], and I'd never see her again. Never seen her again. They shut it down for, I want to say, two or three months, opened up again, I didn't know anybody. Tammy was gone. It broke my heart when there was a lock on the door and I never seen her again since. Actually, I really thought she was cool. She had a lot of charisma. I'd go up there after work.... She'd cook a steak. A lot of kissing and hugging. Sex wasn't a big deal. It was just neat. That whole time in my life, I don't regret a bit of it. I thought it was just awesome....

Not many people knew about it except my mom because she saw my car. I didn't brag about it or anything.

Met them all. All of them were very nice girls, they all had their own story to tell. One of the things I never could understand, was all these drunk tramp miners would come in and all these girls were very nice, I just can't imagine them laying down some of these drunk miners. Picture that in your mind.

[Another guy interrupted our conversation to say that, in fact, his best friend met his wife in a Wallace whorehouse. He and his friends all bet money that it would never last. It did, but the couple is not alive anymore.]

The thing is, the sex is the sex. I don't know how much you want to elaborate on that. But as far as the women go, there were some neat women. I gotta defend them, you know what I mean.... It was mostly just girls sitting on your lap, mostly camaraderie. Sex wasn't really huge. If you wanted sex, you could have sex. You paid for it....

[The relationship with Tammy] was like a real education for me. Made me kind of a half a man instead of a little boy.... I wasn't up there screwing all the girls and all that shit when I was with Tammy. I was up there because her and I had a little deal going on. That's all....

But I defend brothels.... You know this, they were prominent women. They ran the town. And Dolores Arnold, really, underneath, ran this town. She gave more damn money to charities, to baseball uniforms. Dolores was a prominent woman. And she was a nice gal, too. I liked Dolores. Very nice. She was first class....

I was sad to see it go. We had a lot of people playing politics with us, a little self-righteous. And that's for the man upstairs, that's not for other people. That's the oldest profession. I don't think you're ever going to stop it....

Some people would say those women were disgusting for working in a brothel. I'd say, "You ever been to a brothel?" No. It's like prejudice. Prejudice is lack of knowledge. They're sitting there bad mouthing a brothel. You ever been to a brothel? Well, no, but it's this, it's that. Aren't you speaking with prejudice? You really got to try to understand what it's all about....[267]

Anonymous 22, on Relationships with the Girls and "Stag Night" at the Elks

Dolores would invite us up to have dinner in her suite or penthouse. She had a beautiful apartment in the top of the Lux Rooms. So we'd go up and have dinner while my mother did her hair. Dolores would talk about

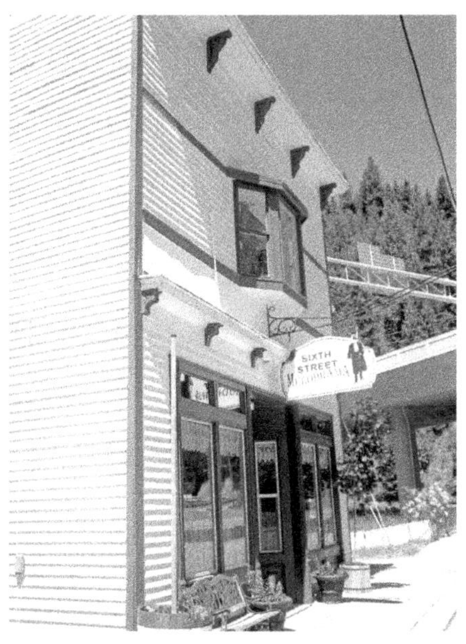

Kelly Building in 2010. The former brothel has become costume storage for the Sixth Street Melodrama Theater. *Photo by Heather Branstetter.*

anything. Very intelligent. Classy, very classy woman. Nothing but the best. She did more for people in this town than people really know about. Thanksgiving or Christmas would come along and there was a Combination Foodliner across the street here, down where the Depot is sitting now. And she'd buy $5,000 of groceries every year and nobody knew where they came from except people at the store....

I dated one of the girls at the Arment for three years. When I was younger. That was a great experience. I wouldn't trade that for nothing.... We would go to the Davenport Hotel on weekends. She had some businessman down there who would pay her a lot of money for a couple hours. And she would hand me a hundred-dollar bill and say, "Go shopping." He paid her a lot of money, a couple of thousand dollars. When we'd go to Spokane she always got in touch with this guy. She was a classy, classy gal, too. She had like eight years of college education. Her name was Barb. She could talk to you about anything. Very intelligent. Sports or economics or politics or religion. Whatever you wanted to talk about.

How come you didn't marry her?

Well, that's a long story. I was twenty-one. I had a girlfriend I was also going with at the time. She was a very strict Catholic. And that should tell you something, being a very strict Catholic and two young people. I was going elsewhere to entertain myself. And then I met Barb. I played golf at the time. I played well and was thinking about getting on the pro tour. At that time all you had to do was have $10,000 to get on. And she said, "I'll sponsor you, put you on the tour, but we have to get married."

And all I said was, "Let me think about that." And that was the end of that....

Was it because it came with a payment?
I guess. I wasn't in love with her. I didn't want to marry her. I was twenty-one years old, having fun.

What did Barb go to school for?
Don't know.

Did you ask her why she started working up there?
Money. Money was great.

Did she mind the job, have any qualms about it related to ethics or morality?
She enjoyed a boyfriend, but when she was with a customer it was strictly business. My mom did a lot of the girls' hair. Barb used to take my mom and my sister and me to the Davenport Hotel for the weekend. She had called up and said, "Going to go to Spokane for the weekend."

My mom couldn't go and she said, "[Anonymous 22] will take you," so I went and picked her up at the Safeway in Kellogg. Drove my '47 Buick down there, parked it in the parking lot.

She gave me keys to her Cadillac and said, "You're driving." That was cool....

After an Elks Stag Night, we'd go window-shopping, and go up and have drinks after hours.

Stag Night?
At the Elks, they'd have strippers come in, and it'd be wide-open for gambling. They'd have craps tables going and blackjack tables going. Girls would come up, strippers, put on a show for the guys. No touching. Stag Night at the Elks, once a month we used to have that.... Some prominent citizens of Wallace would take some of these strippers into the women's lounge and have their way with them. For money, I'm sure.

That's a big lounge in there.
Yes. The girls would pick up a few extra bucks. Most of them had a chaperone. Like a bodyguard type of guy with them. And they would strip. They would strip all the way. But they were protected. Nobody forced themselves upon anybody. It was all consensual....

[These were not girls from the Wallace houses;] these were girls from Spokane. They'd book them from strip clubs in Spokane. Yeah, you could find something to do every weekend in this town....

The town accepted the girls. Very few people didn't like the girls being here. They just accepted them. They weren't bothering anybody....

When you went on dates with the girl you were seeing, did you always go out of town?
Davenport Hotel in Spokane. Every time. I remember that first date I had with her, we went down and had dinner and she pays for everything. I guess that makes me a gigolo, but I offered to pay.

"No, no, no, no, no. I'm paying," [she said].

I said, "Do you want to go dancing, do you want to go to a movie or something?"

She said, "No, I'd just as soon go back up to the room."

And that was fine with me. Twenty-one-year-old kid, hell yeah. She taught me a lot. I have to say that. I thought I knew everything, but I didn't know nothing.[268]

Dee Greer, Maid at Several Houses

You want me to tell names about who visited the butt huts?

Whatever you feel like sharing.
Well that was one thing we never could talk about. You'd get your ass fired.

So you were really discreet.
Oh yeah. You'd be so surprised, I'd open that door and I'd say, "Good evening." Their mouth was just hanging down and their eyeballs were poking out. It's like, "Mum's the word."

Maybe we could start by talking about you and how you got started working at the houses.
I was working at Sweets Café as a waitress, and I was just getting fed up. And we had a cab driver; his name was Jerry. He said they need a maid up at the—and I said, "Oh, are you out of your mind?" I said, "I have kids."

"So? The other maids have kids, too."

Well for heaven's sakes.

I went home and I kinda—he [Greer's husband] said, "Well that would be okay." And oh dear, I didn't want nothing to do with that, it was just kinda—but I went up there. I was a gutsy old broad. And the first one was the Arment Rooms and you know that was above the Silver Corner and the madam, Vicki was her name. And the Oasis, I worked there. Billie was her name, she was the madam there.

One gal she wanted a car that was in the Steve McQueen movie *Bullet*. My husband found it for her. But it was too much car for her, and my husband kinda knew better. Billie was a really super nice lady. Call me up on Sundays, "Come on get the kids, let's go have dinner in Montana or some place." Vicki was a good gal, too, but she was just crazy. This would have been around 1973. When I first started at the Arment. And I was up there quite a while.

Then I had the pleasure of meeting one of the nicest ladies, Dolores. What a lady she was. She was a beautiful Italian lady. She was just awesome to work for. One time I'd left. We'd went down to Kansas where his folks were from. And I got all mad. He was out on the road looking for a job, so he said anyways. I just couldn't handle it, had no money, just out on the farm. I said, "I'm going." I loaded up a few boxes and sent them up here to Wallace. Loaded up my Thunderbird with a set of silverware, stereo—got to have your music—three kids, a cat and that's it.

We came to Wallace. And I sold everything in the house for a thousand dollars. Everything I bought was brand new. And I come home with that thousand dollars. And I went up to Dolores and she said, "You need a job, don't you?"

And I said, "Yes."

And she said, "Well I just happen to be needing a maid."

What year was that when you came back?

Mid-1970s.

We had this guy who used to come up and walk Dolores's dog, Mikey. And the guy's name was Federico. Did you know Federico? Italian. He was an Italian guy. Sweetheart. Anyways, he got up and left one night, and I was at the table and she looks over at the chair. "Oh, no, Federico left his coat."

And I go, "No."

And she goes, "Well whose is it, then?"

I said, "Well, it's my daddy's, but I have to wear it because I don't have one." And he was a big man and I only weighed like 120 pounds or something.

And she said, "Oh goodness sakes." She goes, walks down to her apartment, and she's gone for a little while, and then she comes back, she had this fur coat. "Here, try this on."

I said, "OK," so I tried it on. It was one of those rolled collars, with the A-frame. And I know when she bought it and what she paid for it. And I was being silly, going up and down the hallway, in the parlors, [showing it off for] all the guys and everybody.

Then I went back into the kitchen and took it off and handed it and she goes, "No, that's for you," and she handed me money to have it cleaned.

I said, "Oh, I couldn't take that, I know what you paid for it."

She said, "I just bought it to walk Mikey."

I said, "Oh, Dolores."

She said, "You take that." And I had that coat until just a few years ago. It was just falling apart, you know. But what a lady. And come to find out that she was married. She married the mayor of Mullan. Did you know that?

He had your last name, I believe. I was wondering if there was any relation.
Oh no. My husband was from Kansas. He had no relation up here. Yeah, that was really weird. I said, well, for heaven's sakes, we have the same name. And she was a working lady only two years herself, to get that place, the first place.

Did she tell you that?
Mmm hmm.

Did she ever tell you about the story? About how she came to be in Wallace?
You know, she might have. But I forget so much. I was kind of an alcoholic back then. And I quit twelve or thirteen years ago, but I can still go and have a couple drinks and be silly. And I just love to go bullshit, you know. And I worked at her other place, the Luxette. And Julie was the madam then.

But you were primarily at the Lux.
It depended. I spent a lot of time at the Oasis, too.... Julie had known Dolores for a lot of years. She was heavyset. But just a beautiful face. I can imagine what she looked like when she was a working girl. No she never told me the story that I remember about how she got here.... I met nicer ladies up there than I did down here. And most of them were married, you know, they had families. I go, "But you know, how do you do it? Your husband's OK with it?"

"Yeah, he knows that I love him. And this is my job."

And they said, "We just put dollar signs in our eyeballs and go wham bam thank you ma'am when I stand in the boogie van."

And I go, "Oh, I see." They were always trying to turn me out, you know. And I go, "You've seen my husband. [Clears throat] I don't think so."

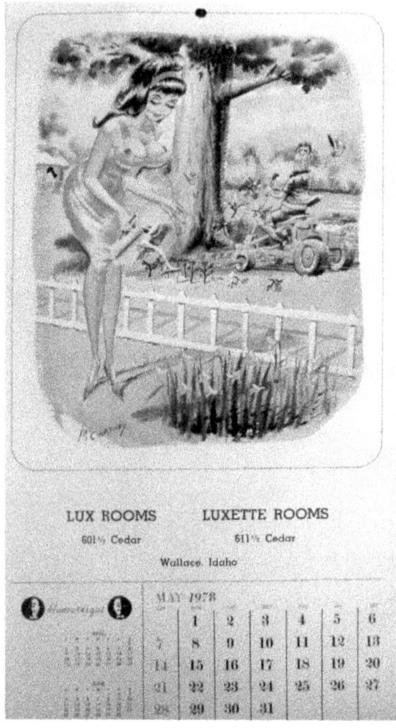

Lux and Luxette calendar in 1978, after Dolores moved the Lux from 212½ Sixth Street to the Arment Building on the corner of Sixth and Cedar. *Heather Branstetter collection.*

But I enjoyed working there. Boy the things you don't learn. Weird people—not weird, you know it's their choice, everybody likes something different, you know. Yeah. Yeah.

What kinda things?
Oh, dear. Well we used to have one gentleman that come up every Monday, and he only wanted this one gal, Tammy was her name at the time. Nobody ever knew their real names. And we all called him "Ringa Hands," and he'd be sitting in the parlor because there's always one girl on call all night, you know, she has to be in makeup and all that. He'd sit there in that parlor and go like this: [rubs hands together nervously]. So we called him Ringa Hands. And he liked to be dressed in a diaper and powdered and [fed] a bottle. You know. Yeah.

Wow. Every Monday, huh? Now was he local?
I think so. I can't remember where he lived or anything, you know.

Did you know how many men were local versus how many came in from out of town?
I knew the locals. Back then I used to know a lot of people because I tended bar for thirty-four years. I worked at the gas station also. I had three jobs. I worked for Gene Ussellman that had the old Metals for seventeen years.

One day, this guy come up. Well, he was there when I got to work. One of the gals on the left-hand side of the hallway, she was with somebody. And this other guy was [just waiting] in this other room, and I thought, well, that's strange.

And I'd been to the grocery store, so I went to the kitchen and was putting shit away, and the madam goes, "Would you take this gentleman some iced tea?"

I said, "Well, sure."

She says, "That's our load man." OK. And I come back to the kitchen. I sat down, and she goes, "You don't know what a load man is, do you?"

"Oh, yeah, sure I do."

"No you don't."

I go, "OK, so I don't. So tell me."

Oh, I don't think you want to hear what it is, but—

Yes, I do.

Oh, no, you'll puke. Well, this gal that's with the guy, as soon as he comes in her, then she runs right across over there [to where the other guy was waiting] and that guy over there eats all of that out.

Really? And they call him a load man.

A load man. First load man I'd ever seen. Like I said, different strokes for different folks.

And they could just pay for that.

Oh yeah, they paid for everything. You don't even get to look at a tit or nothing for nothing.

Could they pay for anything, or were there some things that were off limits?

No hurting, harming, you know, no anything like that. We used to have this big tall miner, he used to love it—this was at the Arment Rooms—when I'd come to work, because he'd buy the girls off the floor for the whole weekend. And he'd wait for me to come in, and he'd be hiding in one of those fucking rooms, just jump right out at me. He bought food from Albi's—that's when it was a good place—and always steaks and everything and always the bubble bath and all of that. Everything cost.

And Albi's delivered up there.

Yep, and we would tip very well. In fact, I got all of the furniture I wanted out of the Arment Rooms when I came back from Kansas that time. I needed that. Kids got the sheets. Oh they didn't screw in the sheets, though. Didn't fornicate, excuse me.

Did they screw on a blanket on top?

They had a towel. A big, you know, beach towel, whatever. And then if they were bought off the floor for the night, then they could crawl in the sheets, but it cost extra.

How much was it to buy someone off the floor?
Depends on what you wanted, but most generally a hundred bucks. That was back then, you know.

In the mid-1970s.
To buy them off the floor was probably more than that, $150, maybe. I know a bubble bath was expensive.

What was so great about the bubble bath?
Well it was what you'd do in it, whatever you wanted, I guess.

They [the girls] could go into the restaurants, but not the bars, you know. And they had to be off the street by five. And like I said, I tended bar also and people would get to talking about the girls and I'd put a stop to it: "You don't know anything about those girls up there," you know. "In fact, yeah, your husbands were probably just up there a while ago." I never let anybody bash them. They did their job, and they did the best at what they knew how. Just like you do your best at your job. Everybody's raised different, and thinks different, and nobody thinks the same.

Did some people badmouth? What kind of things did they say?
Oh just whores, sluts, pigs, whatever, you know. If my old man was going to cheat on me, I'd just as soon he'd a went upstairs, you know. At least they're clean. They don't got no disease or bugs.

And was that the case, you never saw anyone with an STI or anything like that?
If a guy had crabs or something, you'd just grab a bottle of Campho-Phenique and they'd just drown and you'd kill them right away, you know. But we'd sit and play pinochle on a slow night and when I'd day shift, I'd take the girls coffee in bed. They had to tip you every day and back then to take them to the airport in Spokane was fifty dollars and that was a lot of money back then....

How often did they go to the airport? Just for vacation?
There was always the period time. They would go home a week off. They would work three on and one off, usually. And if the girls were working for a car, or whatever, then they would just stay and work. And they could, couple of them would just take birth control pills, stops your period. And sometimes they would just use a sponge, cosmetic sponge and the guys didn't know it, that they were on their period.

How many men did they sleep with in a night?
Oh goodness sakes, it's hard to tell. Some of them might sleep with just one. And some of them, it's hard to say. I never really stopped to count it. But, if it's the quickie, ten minutes or twenty, you could do quite a bit if the guy would pick you. And we had one little gal when she came back on work after her week off, she set herself at a goal for what she was going to make that week. And if she didn't make it, holy shit, yeah she was not a happy camper and she was not a very nice person, you know. I'd say, "Well goddamnit, Jodie."

Do you remember what her goal was?
One week it was like $1,400 or $1,500. Yeah.

And do you remember if she met that goal?
She did. She was the cutest, the most petite, beautiful little gal I ever seen. I said, "You ain't no bigger than a pint of piss."

Do you remember much more about her?
That she was married. That she had a little boy at the time.

Do you know anything about her background?
No. They didn't talk a whole lot about their background and that stuff. We even had, well everybody knew that, one guy in town, I won't mention any names, he married one of the girls and they lived here.

Is she still around?
No. And you could not work in one of the houses if you were from Shoshone County.

Do you think they stayed longer than six months? If you were going to do an average, would it be like six months to a year here, or did some work longer than that?
Yeah, six months to a year. Some stayed longer. But you kinda want them to change because it would get a little old. But that was back when it was booming here. You know, it was romping, stomping. God, we had the loggers, we had the railroad men, we had the CF [Consolidated Freight truck] drivers because Osburn was their turnaround. We had the mine inspectors yowsa yowsa. And boy, oh, boy. It was nothing to do $500 or $600 on a day shift. And tending bar, you know. Back in the '70s. And, oh, it will never be that way again. I always thought it would go one more time, you

know. I always thought it would just boom, and now I'm too old to work it. Pretty interesting back then. I worked in a lot of places.

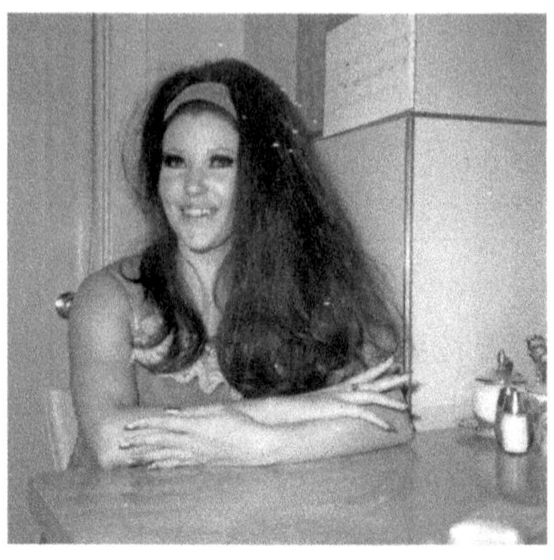
"Gypsy" in 1971. *Richard Caron Collection.*

How much did the houses take in each night?
Dolores worked sixty-forty and some of the others worked seventy-thirty. Trying to think which way it went, can't remember who kept what. Some of the houses had the little sinks in their rooms. The Oasis didn't; they just had a tin dish pan and a pitcher with water in it to wash the guys down before they went to bed with them. And then they poured in that pan and when that pail got full they'd set it outside their door and I'd go dump it.

I cooked one meal a day when I was working day shift, and the rest of the time they had to fend for themselves. You heard about that gal, there was a tour going through the Oasis, and this one gal asked the tour guide if she could go into this room. And she walked in and picked up this lamp and unscrewed the bottom of it, and this money come out....

How much money was made in total?
Oh, God, that's something they would never—because each girl had their own little box with a lock on it and a slot in the top of it, where you'd put the money down and the timer on top of it. When the timer went off, you went and knocked on her door, but you didn't know for sure. You could make an estimate amount. Like Jodie, probably in one night, probably $500 or more. She could make the money; lots of the girls could make good money. And it all depends on how you come across with the guys and stuff. You know that.

Did most of them work seven days a week when they were on?
Yes. For three weeks.

That's a lot of work.
Yeah, I'm going, "Oh!"

Did they ever complain about being sore?
I had one complain. This one guy would come in the morning, and he always wanted a blowjob. And she says, "Them filthy sons a bitches they take a shit and they never wash their goddamn ass and blah blah blah."

Somebody had said something about it being too big, she goes, "Yeah, I'm going to go to the doctor and see if he'll sew this fucking pussy right up."

Yeah there's a couple of them that would get, you know, all depends on what they did and what they used.

Did you feel like they enjoyed sex or was it mostly just a job?
It was a job. They had to pretend, of course. Otherwise some guys would really get pissed you know. Like when you'd give them a blowjob. If they don't think you're swallowing that, they're pissed. And they'd try to keep a napkin right by the pillowcase and they'd roll over, spit and drop it.

Did you get the feeling like any of them weren't there because they wanted to be? Were there times you felt like the girls had been coerced into doing the job?
No. Not really. That was their job and most of them, I'm not going to say enjoyed it, but that was their way of making money. I don't know that any of them had been coerced into it. Not that I noticed.... Couple of times, we'd sneak up there—[my daughter's] dad and I had matching motorcycles—and we'd sneak them on a little ride. They were very interesting. They were very nice. And like I said, I met nicer women up there than I ever did in the bars.

What about drug use? Everyone seems to want to know about that.
You know there was some of them. I didn't know anything about cocaine or meth or anything like that. Pot. There might have been a couple that smoked pot. They couldn't do it in the house.

You didn't get the feeling like addiction was a real problem?
I didn't...but just mostly pot was all I was around.

How long did you work in the houses?
About seven years.

How many women worked in the houses at one time?
Usually, you'd have five, four on and one off. Some houses had just four and there would be three on, one off. Dolores did so much for the town. More than you even knew....

Do you remember other things about them, like where they came from, what kind of stuff they liked to do when they were off work?
Jodie liked to go hiking with her boy and her husband. And Tammy wasn't married, didn't have any kids...just wanted that car like Steve McQueen's in *The Bullet.* And I really liked Billie, the madam.

And what was she like?
Straight up, tell it like it is. Explained things to you very well.

She walked with a cane and was small, petite?
Yep. She was probably five [feet], four [inches], at the most. Maybe 115 or 110 [pounds]. Most often wore a turtleneck with long sleeves and pants to match.

Do you remember violence? Did anyone ever experience violence?
One time, a guy was going to hit a gal. And we got it stopped. She whammed him one and I got the cops up there. That's all I remember.

And the relationship with the cops was good?
Oh yeah, they were always there to help if anything would go wrong. They would come up and have a cup of coffee, just bullshit, tell us how the night was going out on the streets.

Did they ever expect services for free?
Oh, no. Not that I know of. I couldn't say that anyway. I just don't think so. But maybe. Maybe. I never worked for the U&I. She wanted me to. She sent a guy down to the Oasis, and I said, "Now come on, tell me why you're here. You don't want a girl, you just want to sit here and bullshit with me or whatever."

So finally he goes, "Lee would like to talk to you."

So I said, "OK." I go over there to talk to her, if I'm going to make more money, that's where I'm going to go. And we talked for a little bit, Lee and I, and I said, "And what is the pay?"

She goes, "Well, I'll start you out at—" and I think she said $1.75 or something like that. And I said, "I don't think so. You know what I can do, and you know I'm good at it. Don't give me that. You know I'm well worth the two-something." And I never went to her house.[269]

TEMPORARY CLOSURE

Newspaper accounts confirm the houses closed for a brief time in 1973. The *New York Times* even covered the story:

> *Students at the University of Idaho referred to the U&I Rooms as the U of I, northern branch, and when the houses temporarily shut down in 1973, students at a football game let fly a banner that read: "Governor Andrus—Give Wallace Back its Houses."*[270]

In 2010, Mayor Vester told me he'd heard that the state had closed the houses down: "Harry Magnuson and Hank Day were the two most influential people around here and on Saturday morning, they called down to Governor Andrus and said, 'You run your end of the state, and we'll run ours.' The houses were back open on Monday. That's the way the story goes, as I've heard it."

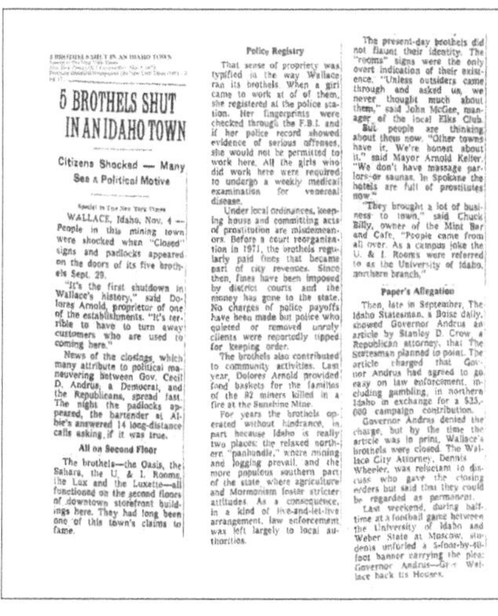

5 BROTHELS SHUT IN AN IDAHO TOWN

Citizens Shocked — Many See a Political Motive

Special to The New York Times

WALLACE, Idaho, Nov. 4 — People in this mining town were shocked when "Closed" signs and padlocks appeared on the doors of its five brothels Sept. 29.

"It's the first shutdown in Wallace's history," said Dolores Arnold, proprietor of one of the establishments. "It's terrible to have to turn away customers who are used to coming here."

News of the closings, which many attribute to political maneuvering between Gov. Cecil D. Andrus, a Democrat, and the Republicans, spread fast. The night the padlocks appeared, the bartender at Albie's answered 14 long-distance calls asking if it was true.

All on Second Floor

The brothels—the Oasis, the Sahara, the U. & I. Rooms, the Lux and the Luxette—all functioned on the second floors of downtown storefront buildings here. They had long been one of this town's claims to fame.

Police Registry

That sense of propriety was typified in the way Wallace ran its brothels. When a girl came to work at of of them, she registered at the police station. Her fingerprints were checked through the F.B.I. and if her police record showed evidence of serious offenses, she would not be permitted to work here. All the girls who did work here were required to undergo a weekly medical examination for venereal disease.

Under local ordinances, keeping house and committing acts of prostitution are misdemeanors. Before a court reorganization in 1971, the brothels regularly paid fines that became part of city revenues. Since then, fines have been imposed by district courts and the money has gone to the state. No charges of police payoffs have been made but police who quieted or removed unruly clients were reportedly tipped for keeping order.

The brothels also contributed to community activities. Last year, Dolores Arnold provided food baskets for the families of the 92 miners killed in a fire at the Sunshine Mine.

For years the brothels operated without hindrance, in part because Idaho is really two places: the relaxed northern "panhandle," where mining and logging prevail, and the more populous southern part of the state where agriculture and Mormonism foster stricter attitudes. As a consequence, in a kind of live-and-let-live arrangement, law enforcement was left largely to local authorities.

The present-day brothels did not flaunt their identity. The "rooms" signs were the only overt indication of their existence. "Unless outsiders came through and asked us, we never thought much about them," said John McGee, manager of the local Elks Club.

But people are thinking about them now. "Other towns have it. We're honest about it," said Mayor Arnold Keller. "We don't have massage parlors or saunas. In Spokane the hotels are full of prostitutes now."

"They brought a lot of business to town," said Chuck Billy, owner of the Mint Bar and Cafe. "People came from all over. As a campus joke the U. & I. Rooms were referred to as the University of Idaho, northern branch."

Paper's Allegation

Then, late in September, The Idaho Statesman, a Boise daily, showed Governor Andrus an article by Stanley D. Crow, a Republican attorney, that The Statesman planned to print. The article charged that Governor Andrus had agreed to go easy on law enforcement, including gambling, in northern Idaho in exchange for a $25,000 campaign contribution.

Governor Andrus denied the charge, but by the time the article was in print, Wallace's brothels were closed. The Wallace City Attorney, Dennis Wheeler, was reluctant to discuss who gave the closing orders but said that they could be regarded as permanent.

Last weekend, during halftime at a football game between the University of Idaho and Weber State at Moscow, students unfurled a 5-foot-by-40-foot banner carrying the plea: Governor Andrus—Give Wallace back its Houses.

Newspaper article documenting the houses' temporary closure in 1973. *From the* New York Times, *November 5, 1973.*

Former judge Magnuson offered his insight on the legal status of prostitution in Wallace before and after this temporary closure, which was a result of a change in Idaho's laws. Magnuson explained that this time signified a major shift in the madams' approach to advertising and the town's approach to regulating sex work.

RICHARD MAGNUSON, ON THE LEGALITY OF PROSTITUTION IN WALLACE

The following account is mainly excerpted from an interview that took place in 2010, but I fold in some information from a 2014 discussion as well.

The laws are always in flux, because they change every two years with each new legislature. For years, Idaho laws had designated three kinds of towns:

cities of the first class, cities of the second class, and villages. There might have been another class that was called "charter cities," which Boise and Lewiston might have been. Cities are the creation of the legislature, and they only have those powers that are granted to them by the legislature. State laws are called statutes, and city laws are called ordinances. But since Idaho statehood, the law had been the same, more or less; it worked under basically the same system. It was tied in with the city police and city court. So there were fees and regulation—the madams filed twice a month and paid $150 a month to operate, which totaled $9,000 a year.

After 1972 or 1973, the laws changed, so there was no longer a city court system in Idaho. They amended the statutes and redesignated cities. Up until this time, the law had provided cities of the second class (what Wallace was) the power to control prostitution—it was neither illegal nor legal in the eyes of the state, so whatever happened was determined by city ordinance. But everyone thinks they can improve on something, I guess, and shortly after 1972, the state legislature reached idiotic heights. They passed what was called "Model Penal Reform." That was the statute catchphrase for it, at least, and it referred to criminal law. That phrase used those words for the rhetorical purpose of making it sound good.

In 1972, the state legislature held committee meetings throughout the state. I was the only person to show up in Moscow to protest the reforms. But the state ended up passing this entirely new set of laws reclassifying everything, and for the first time, they made prostitution illegal, while legalizing adultery and lewd cohabitation, which before that had been crimes. As far as I could tell, the logic on this indicated that they didn't feel that the act [of sex] itself should be illegal, just the exchange of money.

But after six weeks there was a public outcry so much that the state legislature reconvened and passed all the old laws over again. According to some old provision, though, all of the laws had to be Xeroxed, and this guy thought he'd "pull a cutesy." Through Xerox editing, he omitted the line about prostitution being lawful again. But then someone else took out the penalty. So for a while prostitution was unlawful but didn't have a penalty, so there was no enforcement. They put the penalty provision back in around 1973 or so.

I think that the reason why they re-instituted the old laws involved lewd cohabitation with a minor, and there was a loophole in the new laws that led to a defendant in the Pocatello area going free—that was the catalyst for making the legislature re-overhaul the penal code back to the way it was. The vast majority of people wanted things the way they had been. But it meant that prostitution ended up becoming illegal, according to state law.

Periodically, the preachers during the '50s and '60s would come into town, expressing shock and awe about prostitution, but all of the old church women—didn't matter how conservative they were—would tell the preachers to back off.

In 1973, these moral crusaders, maybe Stanley Crowe was a ringleader, they started in Pocatello, moved through Boise, then up through Moscow, Coeur d'Alene and finally over to Wallace, looking for and finding sin under every rock. No trouble finding sin if you're looking for it. Cecil Andrus was governor then. I got a call from him asking about the houses by the time Crowe and the other guy made it to Moscow. Andrus was concerned about what they would find in Wallace.

I went down and checked the doors and saw padlocks on them and confirmed to Governor Andrus they were shut down. It was much ado about nothing because they were calling about what had already been closed. In the weeks when the houses were closed then, might have been up to three months, there was probably local access through the back doors. During that time right after they were supposedly closed there were sex crimes, a kidnapping, a child case. There was a direct cause and effect between sex crimes and the presence of the houses. But prostitution had existed for years. In mining towns—Wallace had 3,800 people and lots were single or had families far away or they worked mines in the winter—there often wasn't the typical family unit.

After 1973, when the Idaho laws changed, the [local] government had nothing to do with regulating prostitution anymore. The madams continued the system on a voluntary basis, paying money into an account at the bank. When the FBI raid happened, they tried to find it but they couldn't come up with anything concrete. As for the medical visits, they also continued that on a voluntary basis, because they were as interested as anyone in continuing to make sure the girls were taken care of in that way.

7

1973–1991

After the closure of 1973, things shifted a bit in the upstairs rooms. Since there was no longer written regulation or records, the "facts" become more difficult to track. Oral history stories feature colorful language and off-color humor. This section is incongruous in some ways, with darker details alongside light-hearted stories, but a history of selling sex in the Silver Valley needs to include both realities.

Ginger and the Oasis Rooms

From the 1960s through the 1980s, Darlene Murphy, known to everyone as "Ginger," ran the Oasis and Arment. Ginger was beautiful, even in old age. The girls called her "Mom" and thought of her as a mother figure. As she grew older, she was rarely seen in public.

A Conversation with Norval and Edith Pennington

I had the pleasure of talking with Ginger's son and daughter-in-law, Norval and Edith Pennington. We spoke over the phone because they live in Alabama. They were happy to share their stories; they believe that Ginger "deserves some documentation and credit in history." Our interview took place on July 20, 2016. The first half of the interview features Norval, and Edith closes the conversation.

I grew up in Colorado, was born and raised by my grandparents, Ginger's mom and dad. Because of her trade and business, I wasn't too involved in that. In 1950, I went to Vallejo, California. She had some houses there in Vallejo, and she was still very active; she was a young lady back then. Of course, she had two houses there. Reason she went there, was the naval base was there. When they brought the ships in to have them worked on, all these sailors had backpay coming. Well, that worked out pretty good.

One time, she had some fellow come in and he opened up a house not too far from her, a single house there in Vallejo, and she couldn't figure out why she wasn't getting any action over at her house where she had working girls. Well she caught one of the cabs, and he said, "He's paying ten dollars a head for everyone we bring out, and you're not paying anything." Well the next day, what do you think she did? She bought the cab company. Put him out of business overnight. That was a shrewd move she made. Mom was a mom, just like any other mom. She just wasn't home too much because she had other things to do. She married Eddie Murphy, who owned a pawnshop there in Vallejo. He used to play piano for Doris Day. I went to Hogan High School out there while I was there.

Did you know what she did while you were in high school?
No, I did not know, just thought she was on a business trip. I was in the military when I found out. Her sister told me. Other than that, I wouldn't have known. I thought she was out buying stock for the pawnshop. Never did question it.

How did she get started in the business? Did she ever talk to you about that?
Oh yeah, she'd go out with somebody and they'd beat the thunder out of her and take advantage of her. So she figured, well, if I'm going to have a boyfriend, he's going to pay. So that's how she got started.

Do you know why she ended up in Wallace?
She was in Vallejo and she was looking for another place. She went to Vegas for about a year and a half. She heard about Wallace up there being wide open and the last red light on I-90. So she went up there and she bought the place. Went to work, got in with chief of police, made payoffs and everything run smooth. Oasis and Arment, and maybe another place. Know one of them was Arment, because there was a bar and she used to let her dogs out

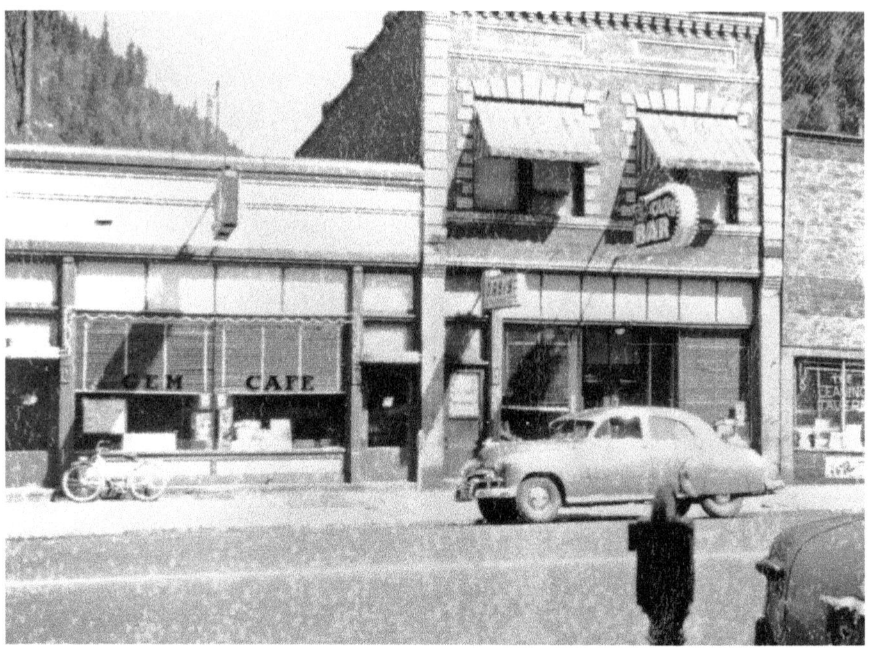

Gem Cafe and Oasis on Cedar Street. *Historic Wallace Preservation Society.*

on this roof [of the Gem Cafe]. She could just walk out across the roof and go to the Arment. So she could run both places from one place. If they had trouble over there she could run over and take care of it right across the roof. She bought the Oasis first, and then she bought these other ones.

Do you know how she recruited women or found women to come work for her?
I think it was all word of mouth. Cause she had them out of Montana, Idaho, Washington, Oregon. [There were also a lot of them from California.] She was pretty well known. A couple of them came up to visit after Mom passed. Don't know where they all are now, a bunch of them scattered with the wind. Both of them married, one lives in a state on the East Coast, is actually a welder. The other lady married, is a housewife. Her husband has a contract for a state prison system, furnishes concessions.

What was her name to you?
Ginger, that's what she went by everywhere. Even though her real name was Darlene, nobody called her by that name. Everybody knew her as Ginger. She stayed married to Eddie and worked in Vegas first and then went up to

Wallace. She married another fellow by the name of MacMillan. She wound up with him for probably seven or eight years. So she did get her divorce from Eddie Murphy.

What was she like as a person?
Very good, very stern, very direct about everything. Well, she had to be. She had to keep everything under control, including me.

We sold the home over in Coeur d'Alene this year. Used to go there and stay for six months of the year and then come back to Alabama. That was Ginger's old home.

Did she just move there after she left Wallace or did she live there part of the time while she was in Wallace?
She bought that house and just come over maybe once a month and stay two or three days and then go back over to Wallace. She stayed in Wallace because she had to keep her hands in everything.

Do you know how much money the houses brought in?
I guess it must have been all right because I never heard of her missing a meal. I know she must have been making pretty good money because she bought the high school football uniforms and bought a car for the police. After the mining [disaster] up there [in 1972], she put all the ladies up. She just closed down the house, opened all the bedrooms up and told the girls to take off the month and let all the ladies in whose husbands were trapped down in the [Sunshine] mine up there. She sent food to all the workers who were fighting the fire and working in the mine. So she had to be banking a little bit of money to be able to do that.

What did she look like?
There's a picture of her there in the museum.

Is that what she looked like?
Yeah, sure was.

[At this point, Norval passed the phone over to Edith.]

They called her Ginger because her hair was just a beautiful light cinnamon color. She was just a tall, lanky, beautiful woman. Her wit and her personality made her more beautiful. Minds make people more beautiful, is what I should say. When I look at her pictures, I found her to be quite striking and beautiful as a young woman. She sure had a good mind, I'll tell you.

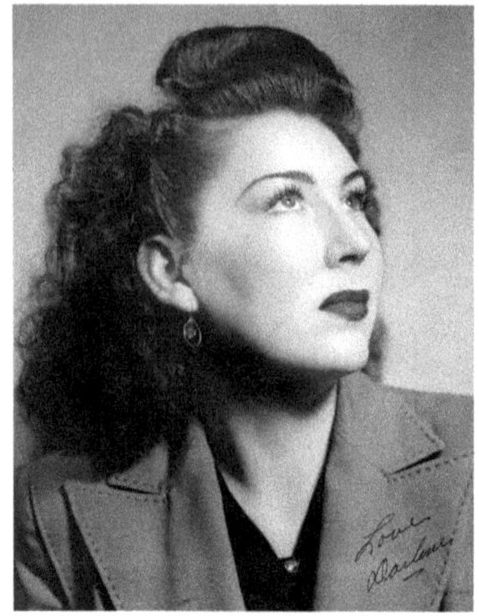

Ginger, 1970s. *Oasis Bordello Museum display.*

[Edith passed the phone back to Norval.]

Did you know why she shut down the Oasis and the Arment?
The feds came in and really gave her a once over. She had to go down to Boise two or three times. She always paid her taxes, and she kept a record on everything, and they didn't find anything else wrong with her. And, too, that venereal disease was coming into play. And she said, by gosh I can't fight everything. So she just closed up.

Are you talking about AIDS?
Yeah, yeah, you know when it was just getting started, she had all these ladies working for her. She said, "I've got to shut the doors. I can't put up with that." She always had sent her ladies over to the doctor to get their monthly clearance and she just said, "AIDS is going around; it's running rampant from what I hear, I'm just shutting down." I don't know if any of the girls ever showed up with any AIDS. I don't think they did, that I heard of. I think she just did it because it was coming in and there was no cure for it and they said you could get it for saliva or tears or whatever and she said, "By gosh that is too much for me now."

Do you know why there were so many belongings left?
Hey, she just grabbed what she could carry and out of there she come, said, "That is it."

I heard the same was true for the Arment, that there was a lot of stuff left up there.
Yeah, she just told her girls, "Hey, I'm closing, get your stuff and get out." Of course they didn't come with a whole lot of stuff to begin with. And that was it. Whatever was left was left. She just washed her hands of it. But that's why all that stuff was left in there.

Do you know how much money she was paying to operate? Was she paying for police protection? Was it extortion or a reciprocal arrangement? Do you know what the system was?
I don't know how all that come about. That was all a quiet ordeal that was taking place. I just heard that it had to be paid and that was it. I don't know how it was done or how much.

Did she ever tell you any stories about things that happened up there?
No, she was a closed-mouthed lady. If the place would burn down, she wouldn't tell you nothing about it. She just didn't talk about it. When she got out of there and come over to the house, it [was] all about how pretty the place was and, "Leave me alone, I've got to rest."

Do you know what kind of childhood she had?
Well, I guess she had a pretty nice childhood. She was raised on a ranch in Colorado. When I was born, she packed up and her and her sister went to Oregon, to work in a café up there. I don't know what happened from there because I was just a baby. Heck, I didn't have anything to do with that. Her mom and dad raised me.

[Norval passed the phone to Edith, who continued the rest of the interview.]

Heather, I'm prompting him a little bit, because where he was raised, of course, it was the same ranch his mother was raised on, it was just all flatlands in Colorado, and there was just nothing as far as the eye could see. When I met my husband, he told me, "You need to see where I grew up because the only thing I had to play with was tumbleweed and prairie dogs." I mean, it was just flatland and no trees just as far as the eye could see. I think she was fifteen when Norval was born. She just spread her wings and went to Oregon.... Whatever lumber they used to build that house had to be hauled there because there weren't trees to cut down and mill to build a house. Her daddy homesteaded that land; it was a section of land that they homesteaded when Colorado was giving away land. If you would homestead and go and fence and make whatever required improvements, then you could gain ownership.

At one time Mom was a call girl in Vegas. I don't know if anybody's ever given you that tidbit of information or not.... I remember a few things that she told me. She got in really good with the police there and so if there was going to be a raid or a bust they would just casually come to her and say, "Ginger, tonight would be a good night to go play Keno." She was pretty well respected.... In Vegas she was good friends with Sammy Davis and all the Rat Pack guys; she knew Frank Sinatra and Bennie Goodman, and she knew all their wives and all their kids' names, and she was a $25,000-a-night gal back then.

Twenty thousand dollars a night, is that what you said?
Twenty-five. And I got that tidbit of information from actually her accountant after Mom was totally retired, and she asked me if Mom had ever told me the story and, of course, Mother had never confided in me about that. But Mother was very tight-lipped about any of her past because she did know a lot of very wealthy and famous people and did hobnob with them a lot in Vegas.

I had heard that she was in good with the police in Vegas, which was why she ended up leaving because they told her it was not going to be a good place for her to work anymore.
Mother was very well respected, and they did watch out for her; 1961 was when she was in Vegas.

Did you get the impression that she was happy with her life choices? Did she ever feel guilty about anything? Did she have an ethical code of some sort?
She had some real ethical codes as far as when she operated her houses. She never allowed her girls out on the street, if it was their day off, no no no, you get out of town. It would be cause to be excommunicated if you didn't do what Mom said. She had some real hardline rules, and she did rule with an iron fist. And absolutely no drugs. She would not have any girl who smoked any marijuana or did any kind of pills. It was absolutely forbidden. Later, two of the girls came to visit quite a bit, and I really think they came because they thought there'd be some inheritance there. They said they would probably be dead if it wasn't for Mother. Because she just laid down the rules, and she made them follow them, and it really made them more aware of their surroundings and made them think and instilled some worth in them.

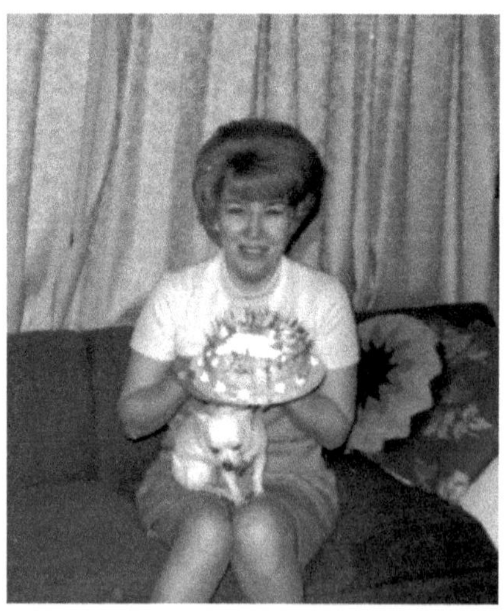

Ginger, 1980. *Richard Caron Collection.*

Instilled what?
Some worth, some self-worth. They said they'd have been drug addicts or dead or both.

So Ginger was responsible for helping them have self-respect, is what you're saying?
Absolutely. Absolutely. You find that interesting?

Yeah, I do.
Well, if you're gonna give it away, why not sell it and get something for it, you know? Basically, she would take girls that were, you know, they could have been drunks or drug addicts and been with a different guy every night, but she instilled in them pride and value and how to handle themselves. Yeah, she was profiting from it. They were both profiting from it. But it was—it is what it is.

Very pragmatic.
Yeah. She was very good to her girls.... They would call from all over the country, just checking in on her. They all had a good deal of respect for her.... All the way up to the time of her death, she had girls calling and checking in on her, and I thought it was a very admirable thing.

So it's kind of like they were family?
Mmm hmm.

Did they call her "Mom"?
They did.

What do you guys think, personally, about her profession?
Well, you know, Mother said a very wise thing to me about Wallace. She said, "You know, as long as I had a house in town, men weren't beating their wives and raping their daughters. And some of the sickest sons a bitches that ever walked the street were your judges and your attorneys." And those were her words.

Did she ever tell you any stories about what went on up there?
That's one thing I can say about Mom, is she never shared names. Never, you know, it's a small town. And of course me being an outsider. I met Norval in Michigan and he lived in Oklahoma and we came to Alabama and got married because I went to school in Auburn and I wanted to come

back to Alabama. So, I was kind of an outsider, and maybe that's why she would, you know, talk a little bit, but she never ever named any names.

And I remember the one story. I was kind of prodding Norval to say something. You know history is history, but you asked him why did she close the house? Or why was there so much clothing left? I believe she got a phone call telling her that the FeeBees [FBI agents] were coming and she needed to get out, so she just grabbed what she could and got out. Later in life, she developed agoraphobia, so she never wanted to go out in public because she would get very sick. I remember she had to go to Boise, and it was very upsetting to her that she had to go. She just toughened up and went because she had to do what she had to do. But that is why there was so much stuff left in the house.

She had to go to Boise, was that to testify [in the corruption case against the sheriff]*?*
It was. [But it may have been Moscow.]

What am I not thinking about to ask you that might be relevant or that people might be interested in?
I would suspect that most people told you she was really a very generous person. At least I would hope that they would have. She did a lot for people who didn't have things. Boy Scout uniforms, Girl Scout uniforms, baseball uniforms and she gave money away at Halloween. One of the neighbors said, "She was the madam! We loved to hit the house. They gave five-dollar bills away!" So I thought that was a pretty interesting story that Mom did that and I didn't know.

She was highly organized. She was a very detailed individual. In fact, when we were selling the house, I came across, she made notes to the nines. She just organized everything, detailed all around. But she never wrote any names down as far as people coming to the houses, never let her girls keep any books. She was strict with the girls, didn't allow them to be out on the street during their days off, they had to be out of town.

Do you know how long the women worked there on average? Did they stay there for quite some time or were they transient?
I would assume that the girls stayed a long time. I met three of them that through her lifetime continued to stay in contact with her. There were some girls if they passed through, they were gone because she would not tolerate any drugs at all, would not put up with it. She was not a drinker; she had no kind of vices, which I think is pretty admirable for a madam.

After she became a madam in Wallace, did she ever continue to see men professionally? Or did she retire from that?
I would think not, considering her standards, but let me ask my husband if I can tell this. He says I can. When she and MacMillan split, she went down to the house—and she called him Mac—he cleaned her out; he cleaned out every safe deposit box. He stole every dime she had and left her flat-ass broke. And for five years, she never stepped out of the house again in Wallace. She worked every day to get back what she had lost.

People have told me that she didn't really leave the Oasis, that she didn't leave her bedroom and lived in her pajamas and just kinda stayed up there.
He nearly destroyed her. He nearly destroyed her. She was pretty broke after that. And that may have been what made her a recluse, I don't know. Pretty sad story. And pajamas? That gal had pajamas. I would say when she passed she had five hundred pair of beautiful pajamas. And people would send her pajamas as gifts. Beautiful pajamas. And when she went shopping and found something she liked, she would order one in every color.

What kind of pajamas did she prefer?
Silk. Silk. In fact, that really was almost always what I ever saw Mother in. The only time I ever saw her dressed was if I had to take her to the doctor.

And I doubt you really heard anything on the negative aspect because she really genuinely cared about people. But she had no problem telling you how the cow eats the cabbage either. But she was only fifteen when Norval was born and that's the only child she ever had.

You know, you asked about how I felt about her profession. I mean, it really does just make a difference [in people's lives]. And only a madam could put it in such an honest raw perspective of men not beating their wives and raping their daughters. Because it happens more than people realize....

Anonymous 2: Ginger's Attorney

Ginger's attorney spoke with me about getting to know her during the aftermath of the FBI raid. We were talking in a local bar in the Arment building. The bar was called the Silver Corner, on Sixth and Cedar, located directly beneath one of the houses that Ginger managed. The upstairs was called the Arment Rooms for most of the town's history, up until 1977, when Dolores relocated the Lux Rooms there. The attorney first went to see her at her house in Coeur d'Alene.

I spent about half an hour/hour with her and she said, "You need a retainer." And I said, "Ginger, I don't need a retainer; I'll just bill you in a month."

But she wouldn't hear of it and walks down this hallway and goes into a room. She unlocks it and I heard her lock it again, then she unlocks it, comes out and locked it again and she handed me four $100 bills. She says, "When that's over, come back, and I'll give you more."

And I'm like, "Nobody's ever given me cash like that before." And she had to testify in a grand jury trial in Moscow.... She told us stories, "Oh my God, I didn't need to know this, this is too much information, Ginger," but I learned more about that business. And I don't know where you'd ever learn that otherwise, to get into the business....

But she said she worked on the Strip in Las Vegas...and I think she started real young, around fifteen. She paid off all the cops and she knew them and she worked a particular territory and one day got tipped off by one of the cops that they were going to crack down on the girls working in Vegas. And they told her, "You need to get out of here, or they're going to arrest you."

So she got on a bus, and she took off. And somehow she knew to come to Wallace. And I'm not quite sure how she knew to come here, but she got here, and she went to the Exxon station where the Red Light Garage is, and she says to the guy, "I understand this is kind of a hooker town, and who's the queenie?"

And he was surprised she knew that, and he goes, "Dolores Arnold" [and she asked him where the house was and he told her] so she goes right up to the door.

She said, "I'd like to run a brothel."

And Dolores told her, "The Oasis is available, that building, you could probably rent it easily. But here's the rules, you gotta do this and this and this, that's all my territory."

Just phenomenal to me. And then she told me about the condition the miners were in when they came up there. They were just filthy. And she would tell them, "Go home and shower and come back and we'll be available." Just some of that stuff, oh those poor girls, I don't know how they did it.

[Ginger came into town] maybe '62, '64, something like that. And I have to say from talking to Ginger they were very particular with the girls. And this payoff thing that they talked about [whispering, almost inaudibly], well, they *had* to. Because if one of those girls gets beat up by these [again, whispering] *asshole* guys—I mean, I'd see them every day as a public defender, they want to kill women. And so she'd just call up the cops and they'd be right there and take them away. But their lifestyle,

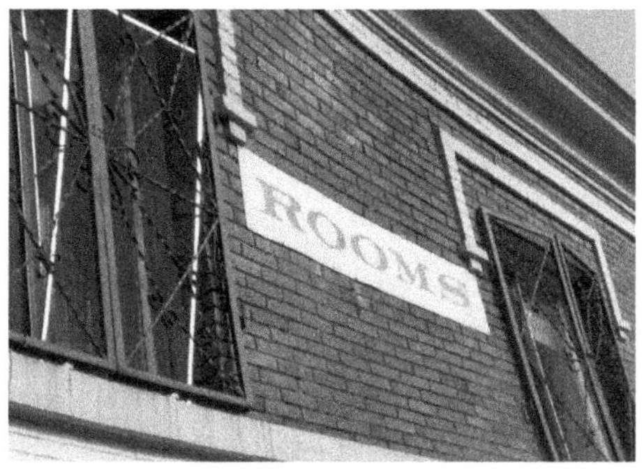

The Arment's sign in 2010. It was covered up during a recent remodel. *Photo by Heather Branstetter.*

I just, I mean, I bet she had a million bucks when she retired, but how she earned that? I just can't imagine.

[Ginger's attorney didn't think she continued to see men while she was in Wallace, however. I asked if Ginger seemed to have mixed feelings about being a brothel manager.]

No. Most of the madams in Wallace felt like they were the mother hens. And that's that weird thinking I don't get. I mean, if you were her *real* mother hen, you would get her out of that crap. But no, she felt she had *arrived* when she got to Wallace, and I think that's why she stayed here. And she had great connections here. When I was representing her, I mean, she had people in high regard that respected her, and I think she deserved it.... I had a lot of respect for her. I mean she was a businesswoman, odd business, for me, but then, I always tell everybody, "I charge by the hour, too, so what the heck...." So, I kind of have forgiven a lot of that. Not that I needed to forgive it, but maybe I understand it more because we're all just trying to make a living.

I don't want to glorify prostitution in Wallace, but I love Wallace. My spirit is in Wallace, and we work so hard to keep it alive, which is just amazing to me all the time. And I'm not proud of the brothels, but I'm proud that we have that history and we kept it for a long time.... But we have great history in this town and it needs to be preserved.

"James Arnuff," Bragging About Various Experiences in the Houses

I was only about fifteen at the time. As soon as we were in the room, the robe came open, and I could see everything, nipples, camel toe, and of course being fifteen, I got excited, and as I was installing the stereo, she reached down and caressed me.

Then the maid came in—she's kind of like the sergeant of arms—and she says, "What's up, are you done?"

"Yeah, I'm done. Just got to plug it in and see if it works." So then the woman closed up her robe. She reached into her dresser and pulled out a bunch of bills and gave me a tip.

I was walking down the stairs and trying to count the money, and she said, "Well, thanks for everything. If I need you again, I'll call you."

I said, "OK."

About that time another guy was coming up the stairs, and he looked at me counting my money and said, "They pay *you*?"

And I looked at him and said, "Of course." That was my first experience up there....

Did you develop any personal relationships with any of the women?
One.

Do you remember her name?
Raime. I don't think that was her real name.... She kinda fell in love with me. I was eighteen at the time—actually I was seventeen. And she was probably twenty-three, twenty-four. And the relationship we had was if I put in ten, she'd put in ten. If I put in twenty, she'd put in twenty. She'd match my price. And she bought me gifts all the time.... And at one time she wanted to give me her grandfather's antique watch. I refused it.

Why?
Because I had no feelings for her except for sexually.

How did things end with you guys?
She left town, moved on.

How long did it last?
About a year and a half.

What did you know about her?
Not much. She had no kids. That's about all I know.

Did you know how she got started in the profession?
Nope. Didn't ask. Didn't care.

Do you know where she came from?
Nope.

Why did she like you/love you?
Eleven and seven-eighths inches.... She officially measured me. Now all it does is get me closer to the toilet.

Did you get the feeling that she enjoyed sex with you, then?
Yes, she did. And most of the girls up there, I got the feeling, they didn't like it like that.

They did not?
They did *not*. They were there for a job. But she enjoyed sex.

Did you think that what they were making was worth the services they provided or should they have been paid more? Did you have a feeling about all that?
In my opinion, they did what they did for fairly cheap.... At that time it was ten bucks for a quickie. Which was about a dollar a minute, and well, back in the '70s I guess that was pretty fair wages, but I don't know what the cut was, how much the house took.

Were you a miner?
Yeah.

Do you remember what you were making at the time?
In 1971, I was making thirty-five dollars a day.

So as far as what you were making versus what they were, they were outdoing you.
Oh yeah.

And you felt like that was fair.
Well, yeah. About up to the end, 1985, I guess, I was making close to $500 a day.

And in '85, what were the women making in the houses, do you know?
Twenty dollars for a quickie.

[Bartender interrupts] *Hey how do you know so much about the cathouses?*
How do you think?

[Bartender] *I used to tell the guys where they were.*
That's the way we used to get our beers in high school. Would hang out in front of the Lucky Horseshoe bar [603 Cedar]. Sooner or later, a guy would

come out from out of town, "Hey kids, where the cathouses at?" Well, we'll tell you if you'll buy us a case of beer. And sure enough, nine times out of ten, we'd get a case of beer out of it....

In junior high, used to hang around the Wallace corner [Sixth and Cedar], and a couple times tourists would come up, "Hey, what are good places to stay in town?"

And at that time, all the cathouses had neon signs, the Arment Rooms, you know, we'd say, "This place over here has air conditioning."

And Ma and Pa and the kids would go up there. About five minutes later, they'd come back down, and the dad would give us a dirty look, really dirty look, and the kids would be tugging on mom's skirt, asking questions. And they'd get in the car and leave, so we weren't very good for business, but we got a kick out of it....

Want to hear the story about how I got officially measured? It was Christmas. Stopped by up there and Raime goes, "This is all paid for, don't worry about it." And in come three—like I said, it was Christmas vacation—three college girls. Beautiful. Well, she had them put on different color lipstick. And then they had a high mark contest.

A high mark contest?

Who could go up the farthest, yeah. Different color lipstick. And they all put in a buck, just for the hell of it. And after that when I got good and excited, she pulled out a "dick-a-pult." I don't know what it was. It was a little contraption that was lined with a fur type of cloth, and she put that on my dick and I'm excited. Then she had the girls with their different color lipstick kiss my body to see where this fur would land. And I told Raime, "I'll put in a buck. Kiss my forehead just for luck." And they weren't allowed to jerk me off or anything. They just had to kiss me, rub their boobs on me, whatever....

Needless to say, it hit me right there [points to his chest]. I won. So then they got me hard again. And Raime says to the girls, "You're outta here. It's my turn." And she screwed me then....

Want one more cathouse story?

Yes.

OK. This was the first time. You know the movie *Barbarella*, Jane Fonda? I'd just watched the movie *Barbarella* at the Wilma Theater here in Wallace. At the time, that was a pretty risqué movie. I came out of it, and I was horny as hell. I don't know if I was sixteen or seventeen. Came out, walked to the car—it was 1970, because I had a car. Walking to my car, and I was horny as hell. And I had ten bucks in my pocket. Passed the U&I, and I stopped there. OK, I'll give it a try.

Walked up the steps, pushed the doorbell. Maid: "Hey how are you? Come on in."

I was surprised, thought they'd turn me away because I was definitely underage. Anyway, these gals come walking in and there was a petite gal, very beautiful. Blond hair, short blond hair, named Crystal. And we go back into the room. And that's when you gave her the money, and she'd give it to the maid. I gave her ten bucks, and she looks at me and says, "Are you a virgin?" Well, yeah, I am. And she goes, "OK."

So she goes and takes the money back and comes back in. The procedure was, they held this wash bin down here, and they'd wash you off.... Then she tells me to lay on the bed, and she goes down on me and she gave me a full blowjob. All the way.

And I go, "Oh, I didn't want to go like this."

And she goes, "Don't worry. I talked to the maid. You get the virgin special."

What's the virgin special?
Well, I got a full blowjob. Then she got me up again, and she climbed on top of me and she gave me the best ride of my life. The whole thing took about twenty minutes when it only should have taken ten.

The best ride of your life?
Well, it was the first ride, so it was the best.

[Bartender] *So that's where you lost your virginity, up in some whorehouse?*
Yep, so did five other people I know about in town.... After our session, with the gal, I go, "How come I got special treatment?"

She goes, "Why do you think people call us hookers? Now you're hooked."

And I was.[271]

"Santa Claus," Used to Do Repairs in the Houses

When I was fifty, no, fifty-nine/sixty, I was in Sweets, having a drink. I don't know why, this guy says, "You know anything about the houses?" This was just before they all closed.

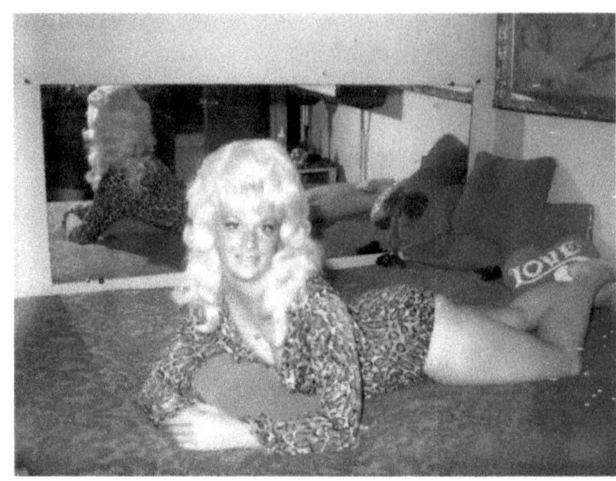

"Sonja," 1970s. *Richard Caron Collection.*

I said, "Yeah, I know all about them." Well this guy run a big farm deal in Washington. He had two teenage boys, and he brought them over for their first go around—that's what we used to call it.

He says, "Where do you think we should go?"

Depends on what they want, how much money they brought. And I explained to him, I said, "Now, you only give them exactly what you want them to spend. Because trust me, them girls"—and by that time, I'd known a lot of them for years, personally—I said, "If you don't, and you send them up there with fifty dollars, they're going to lose fifty. You send them up with five hundred, they're going to lose three hundred of that, at least."

"Oh not my boys, they're smarter than that."

I said, "Hey, trust me, these girls are professionals. They'll talk them into anything."

So, about three hours later they come back to town, and I see that same guy sitting at the bar and he's all madder than hell. I said, "What happened?"

He said, "Them boys went up there and they spent three times what they were supposed to." I said, "I warned you. Them girls, they're not here for the fun of it, they're professionals. You know, it's an occupation for them. Some of them have kids to raise and everything else. That's just the way life is."

But these girls, they were, they were professionals.[272]

Lee Martin, Tanya and the U&I Rooms

Lee Martin ran the U&I Rooms in the later years. She was nicknamed "Mama Lee" because of the way she was said to look out for people. Several people talked about how she had a daughter or granddaughter, and a teacher said she once received a phone call from Lee because the madam was concerned the girl was reading a book that glorified prostitution.[273] She was known for enabling the girls who worked in the house to have more freedom to integrate into the town than the madams in the earlier years. In the 1980s, Tanya took over more of the operations at the U&I. She was known for being kind, and one man described her as "ambitious, genuine and nice."[274]

Former Miner Bill Mooney, Wife Karen Mooney, Anonymous 10 and Anonymous 31

B. Mooney: Lee had a husband we called Magoo. She would turn an occasional trick, and the husband didn't like that so they broke up. We threw a party in Lee's apartment one day, and she was so upset. We took advantage of her kindness.

Anonymous 31: Visited the girls because you got lonely.

B. Mooney: Once we were stuck in Colorado, had been tramp mining and landed in jail with Ronnie Stack for a month after getting into a bar brawl. Jimmy Tear-em-up Taylor spent all our money in the meantime. We dug through the car once we got out and only came up with a dime. We called all the people we thought might send money but couldn't get enough to make it back to Wallace. Called Lee, and she sent $500 right away.

Anonymous 31: Lee gave me $1,000 so I could get on my feet when I first moved here. She told me I didn't have to pay it back but should just instead make sure I came up to visit once a week.

B. Mooney: Some girls stayed for years.

Anonymous 31: Casey was here fifteen years.

B. Mooney: Lee liked for the girls to have a social life. That was part of her business model, kept the girls here. Sunny was here a long time, died of asthma. If the houses didn't provide a social life, then the girls quit on them. But that could also get out of control, get away from them, because the girls were easier to control if they were more isolated from people around town....

One guy had a heart attack up here, and they took him out the back, out of concern for his family, so it wasn't said he died in a whorehouse. [Others have told a version of this story along with the one-liner, "They said he came and then he went."][275]...

Anonymous 10: Poor gals came into town with no shoes, and they left with diamonds.... Canadians would come down here and stay at the Samuels Hotel, run across the street to the hook shops, spend all their money and have to pawn their watches to get back to Canada. Then they'd come back the next month with another wad of cash to spend.

Do you know what Dolores said her biggest problem was? She used to say, "The biggest problem is the high school girls giving it away for free. Only jewel they got and they're *giving* it away."

K. Mooney: When I used to work at the bank we had to drill into one of the girls' safe deposit box. Inside was a hypodermic needle, so that shows it wasn't as glamorous as some people make it out to be.[276]

Kristi Gnaedinger, Maid at the U&I Rooms

When I first started was just a maid, cleaning the rooms, making dinner for the girls, doing the laundry....I ran the errands for the girls. Kept their rooms straightened. Changed the sheets on their beds, besides having to keep their working rooms clean. Did the dishes. Groceries were delivered. They did their own banking.... Just a week into it, everything kind of fell apart, and Lee had to work. I made $7 a day, plus a dollar from each girl for errands once a week, so another $7. The guys paid for their drinks, and I got to keep all my tips. So that's where I made my money. After about a week when things fell apart, I started answering the door at night, not every night, but eventually that, too. I answered the door till one or two in the morning, and then Lee would take over the last few hours, because it was quieter. I was paid in cash, doing great, bringing home $125, $150 bucks a week, so I thought I was living high.

I went up there and started working the same day I interviewed. The interview was strange. I was so apprehensive. The very first night I worked, I was doing laundry and had left something in the sink so I flooded the bathroom. I worried I'd get fired on my first night....

We opened pretty early in the afternoon, and one girl would get up early. Most would sleep until two because things didn't really get hopping until after dinner. They worked every day when they were there, and they had to pay the house half their money.

I made the drinks. I learned how to float the drinks. You didn't want the guys to get too drunk because then they couldn't perform. So I'd put alcohol on the very top so they got the flavor of it when they took their first drink. Try to sober them up.

[At the U&I,] the girls would sleep up there in the rooms together. After I wasn't working anymore, they changed it up there and made it so each girl's working room was their bedroom. Originally, they had to share one bedroom in the front of the house, and Lee had the bedroom in the very front of the building, and she had to share a bathroom with the girls, too. Wasn't really a well set-up place up there. Eventually, they put in a second bathroom as well.

I was reading that article about the Oasis, which said that the girls rotated in and out every few months, but most of the girls at the U&I worked there for months and months at a time. Maybe on average of a year at a time. And Tanya was there for years and years. Wendy was there for at least a year. Lydia was there for at least a year. Marsha was there for two or three years, and Sunny was in and out for five or six years. She'd go away for a while, but she always came back. Maybe they were more stable there than some of the places. There were always a few who didn't make it and they didn't last very long if they weren't making money. They'd disappear. [The turnover rates seem to depend on the era and the house.]...

I was stuck in the hospital feeling sorry for myself. She [Lee] told them she was a relative, so they let her in and she came and saw me. When I had ankle surgery. That was the other thing I forgot about. I had to have a ligament replaced in my ankle in September, so I had a walking cast and worked a couple weeks on crutches. She sent me a really nice gift when I was in the hospital at Sacred Heart.

In London, I had this purple tee-shirt that said "Enjoy Wallace" with a logo like Coca-Cola, and this guy got belligerent about me wearing this shirt because he thought it was degrading. But he'd heard about Wallace even over in London. The clientele was from all over—truckers, kids from the college, that was the big thing, you had to come up from the college. Even Spokane, Eastern, Gonzaga—they'd come from all over, the Catholic boys. Also from Missoula, the frat boys. And then there was this circuit of guys that would come from Canada, from Montreal every few months.

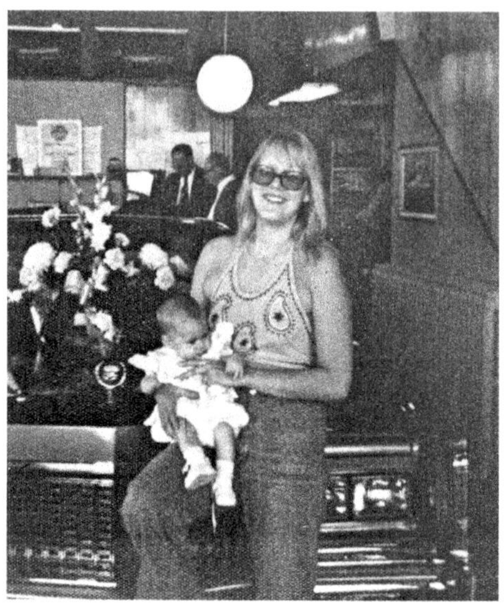

Sunny, in 1975, holding Gnaedinger's daughter and leaning on a car at Dave Smith's in Kellogg. *Kristi Gnaedinger Collection.*

The relationships between the women in the houses was similar to any workplace where women worked together. They got along pretty well, but they got into spats, especially because they were stuck there. There was petty—somebody would get mad at somebody for stupid things. But at the U&I when I was working there they had to share bedrooms, because the rooms they were set up in were just for work. They were not for sleeping, but just for working. So you had two or three women sharing spaces, so they got into spats. They would rotate in and out. But mostly they got along.... Most of the girls were between nineteen and twenty-five years old, except for Lee, who was in her forties, and there was another woman who was really old, and she looked like she was forty-five, because she had some years on her.

We always had dinner together every night. I made the dinner, but it was Lee who had absolutely no spices. They weren't allowed to have any spices—no garlic—the girls weren't supposed to smell like garlic or have farts or anything. She had seven different meals that the girls would have, on this rotating schedule. They were boring. I'd try to spice them up and was told I couldn't do that, because you didn't want those girls farting. I did the laundry, the cooking. I vacuumed and mopped the stairs every day. I hated mopping. After I did that job I hated vacuuming for years. Every day, I'd have to vacuum the place. Never got tired of the laundry, but I hated the vacuum. I answered the doors.

When Lee was around everyone stuck to their schedule. When I was around, sometimes those guys would get a little crazy, loose. You're supposed to knock on their door and get them to come out when their time was up, when their timer went off. And when I was running the place the guys knew it was looser up there, and they'd come up and party and drink all the booze. And then at the end of the week I would say, "OK, you guys, you've used up this booze. Now you've got to give me some money for it."

There was a guy that liked to be spanked, and he came every three or four months.

And then—this is one of the best ones—when I first started working there I was in the kitchen making dinner, standing there, and I turned around, and there was this guy standing there probably about six-foot-five, and he had a wig on, and he was dressed up like a woman, and he goes, "Honey, I got loose, you have to tie me back up." And I was like, "Lee, Lee…" This guy would come up, and they'd tie him up and do mean things to him and leave him in the room. And charge him for the privilege.

The best times were when Lee would leave town and all my friends would come up and we'd party. Drink up all the booze and pay up at the end. If Lee knew about it, she never let on.

There was one time when they had this double-headed dildo, I don't remember what happened, but we were playing around and I was running down the hall, chasing one of the girls with the dildo, and one of the guys saw me do it and they thought I was a little AC/DC [slang for someone who is bisexual, or "goes both ways," like alternating current/direct current]. It was just a joke, because we were playing with it because it was so ugly. "I'm gonna get you, I'm gonna get you with this dildo."

Of course the guys were supposed to stay in the rooms unless they were brought out by one of the girls. They would always call out, "On the floor!" And then everybody else had to be kept in the rooms so two guys wouldn't run into each other in the hallway. Usually, it was the girl who was taking the guy out of the room that would yell, "On the floor," but that particular time somebody must have forgot to yell it out. We were just playing….

Some of my girlfriends were jealous because they knew the guys were up there partying, and they wanted to come up there, but they weren't allowed. I had to learn how to keep my mouth shut, too. Because you'd see people in there that you knew, and "I know your girlfriend," and you have to keep your mouth shut. It wasn't just single men. There were married men, every type of men, boyfriends. But you had to keep your mouth shut. Of course there was the story about Hank Day who would go up to the Lux once a week to visit Dolores. But I don't know if that's true. When I was a kid everybody used to talk about Hank Day visiting Dolores at the whorehouses. And the story was that his wife drove him.

Would get bored sometimes. In the winter it would be slow at night sometimes, so we'd start playing cards, telling jokes, being stupid. We played a lot of gin rummy, cribbage, read a lot of magazines. That's when *Playgirl* first started. We'd thumb through catalogues and look at lingerie. This guy would come into town, kind of like a Fredrick's of Hollywood–type bus converted to a store. So they'd go down to buy their negligees. Most girls wore swimsuits but would buy negligee when they went home to their pimps. That was the first time I had a negligee, because Lee bought it for me.

Most of them had pimps, and they'd come in and make all this money, and they'd go home on their days off and the pimps would take their money and beat them up and you'd try to talk to them and say that you don't need this guy. He's just using you, but they didn't get it. That was probably due to an inferiority complex and broken homes, so they thought they needed this guy, but they'd take all their money and they'd get nothing. Sometimes, they'd come back with black eyes. You'd think, why are you doing this to yourself? And there occasionally were a couple of underage girls. They would lie about their age, and the madams were pretty careful to make sure they were legal age, but sometimes they probably weren't.

There were women using drugs. Speed, mostly. There was one girl who was a really sad case, and she ended up a heroin addict. The other thing that was sad was the abuse they took from their pimps. I was the only one who ever got beat up at the business, as far as I knew, but they would get beat up by their pimps, wanting to show ownership over them. You've got to be a pretty ghastly person to be a pimp. Using these women for money. Get a job. You shouldn't have to live off somebody else. Like that meth commercial on TV, where the guy sells his girlfriend to get drugs. How degrading that you would actually use another human being to make money. It's like a form of slavery. But they had low self-esteem and felt that they had to have these guys. They don't love you—they are using you. But they couldn't see that they were being used. They were used to being abused. A couple of them alluded to sexual abuse when they were kids. One girl had been sexually abused by her father.

There had been a couple of instances where she [Lee] had a boyfriend who tried to beat me up. Lee had this guy who she was seeing in Oregon somewhere, she had this boyfriend on the side [in Wallace] and they'd had an argument. This was in October. I'd been working there for three or four months and she'd left me in charge of the operation. I'm nineteen and running this place, and this guy got really drunk. And he came up and wanted the key to the boxes where they kept the money, and I wouldn't give it to him. So I was walking down the hall with towels for the girls, and he grabbed me by the back of the head and started pulling me and kicking me. And I was pregnant. I threw him the keys and went running out the door to the sheriff's office.

Then they had to stand around and have a debate about whether they would go in and get this guy, because it was illegal, but they couldn't have this guy beating up women. So they finally went in and got him and took him to the outside of town and told him to get out of there or they would arrest him. Scared him enough that he left.... Then later in February or March of the following year, Lee had set him up with a house here in town. Lee ended up getting pneumonia and ended up in the hospital. So he came up there, and he smashed up the car windows in her car. I saw him walking up the stairs, and I was out the back door as fast as I could. And this time, I didn't go to the sheriff. I just went to some friends in town and told them. They went up there, brought him down and beat the holy crap out of the guy. He left town then. For good. Years later, I owned a suntan salon in Seattle, and he came into the suntan salon. He didn't recognize me, but I recognized him. I hoped he didn't recognize me, because he got beat up really good. Sometimes you have to take matters into your own hands.

When that boyfriend of hers [Lee's] beat me up, I had a walking cast in addition to being pregnant and having a handful of stuff. And he came up behind me and beat me up. He was a slimeball. But the girls always treated me well. I really enjoyed working with them up there.

Tanya, According to Gnaedinger

Tanya is such a nice person, such an easygoing person. Kind and considerate. But when she first came she was quiet. Her husband had abused her. So she left her children and the husband and ended up with this pimp in Seattle. He had a whole bunch of girls. He sent her over to Wallace, and over time, she liked it and blossomed and realized she didn't need the guy and got rid of him. She worked for Lee for years, and when Lee decided to retire Tanya took over running the place [from 1985 to 1991]. Now her kids live there in California where she does, and she's a grandma, and most people probably don't have a clue what she did, because she's just a typical grandmother....

Tanya was a skinny little bean-pole, tall and skinny. Lee was the madam then, and Tanya just came on as a girl from Seattle, pretty sure her pimp was in Seattle. She had a pimp at the time but got smart and got rid of him. Didn't take her long to figure out she didn't need a guy.

When Tanya first got there, she'd be lucky if she made fifty bucks a night—it was sad. Then eventually the guys figured out that she really enjoyed her job, and then she was making more money than the rest of them. Tanya was different. She liked working. Most of them, they did their time, whatever they paid for, and it was easy to get them out of the rooms.... A couple of times, I'd have trouble getting Tanya to come out. They were having a great old time. It's like, "Your time is up." One time, I had to go in there and grab some guy by the foot and yank him off the bed. "I'm not looking, I'm not looking, but your time is up."

We've kept in touch over the years. I'd been up to see her at the U&I just before they closed down for good. I know that the Oasis says that they were the last one to close, but I really think the U&I was the last one. Because they were open right up until just before the raid. And the Oasis closed down a couple of years before the raid. And I know that I had been up to visit her just before the raid.

A Story from John Hansen

They were filming *Heaven's Gate* [in] 1979. And they had a façade all around my grocery store, where the depot is now. And the caterers set up their tables in that parking lot next to the Oasis Bordello. So when it came time to feed the crew, [Kris] Kristofferson would go over there to eat, and all the hookers would be throwing pictures and matchbooks and notes and telling him to come up and all that, out their window. If I'm not mistaken, the Oasis was on one side and the Luxette was on the other side. And the Arment. And the Oasis, the girls would throw matchbooks, roses, notes. And the gal that starred with Kristofferson [Isabelle Huppert] was up there for a week, learning how to be a hooker for that movie.

I met Kristofferson, but I never met the lady. I'm sure he probably went up there, but it was different hours, I don't know. And of course there were quite a few, production and carpenters, I'm sure that they were busy all the time up there. They did well, I'm sure.[277]

A Few Stories from the Silver Corner Bar

Anonymous 27: Did Magnuson tell you about how he set up his office when they remodeled the courthouse? His office was the one down at the end of the hall and then all the other doors were leading up to it so he could see them as he looked out. He said, "It's set up like a whorehouse, because that seems like a pretty efficient system." He was down at the end. The prosecutor's office, because Dick was the prosecutor [at the time]. Yeah, I was in the "Madam's Office" there for a while. That's what he'd told me when I went into the prosecutor's office, that's what he told me about how he set up the office.

Posnick [bartender and owner at the time]: Wallace was fun. It was a fun place to be. All the kids who went down to [University of] Idaho, they were always the most popular kids, because everybody wanted to come home with them on weekends. I remember used to be that guys would take their girls to the prom, and they'd take them to a cheap restaurant, because they were saving their money to go up to the whorehouse after they took the girls home....

Vern Carlson [used to tell a story] about a guy that came out of the rooms after doing his thing, and he had his head down like he was a little embarrassed, and Dolores put her arm around him and says, "So how was it, so-and-so?"

And he goes, "She didn't have any hair down there..."

And Dolores says, she goes, "You don't see any grass growing on a racetrack, do you?"

Anonymous 11: A couple of guys married them.

Posnick: That's right.... I'd have girls come into the bar, they'd come in here and ask where they were supposed to go, where's the Oasis Rooms or whatever. But when they went to the, like the doctor's office, they were pretty wild. You could see them. They stood out.

Anonymous 11: The highlight of a teenage boy's life.

Posnick: No, that wasn't the highlight. When the bars closed, everyone would say, let's go up to the whorehouses, window-shop. Half the time you didn't want to, you weren't going to do anything, you just wanted to look. Look around.

Anonymous 11: But you couldn't stay up there for hours.

Posnick: They'd always try and hustle you up, "You guys got any money, wanna go into a room?" And you know, we'd say, "Oh we're shopping. We're looking." You'd go up and bullshit them, you'd laugh and giggle, and your buddies would laugh and joke around, maybe, you know, one guy would have enough money so you'd go.... We'd close the bar and say, hey, let's go up, we're going to go up to the whorehouses. You'd go up there two to three hours, bullshit, have a drink, you know. For a while there, you couldn't drink unless you were going to go into the rooms. Then Mama Lee started the drinking, so there was nights she sold a lot of booze up there. Awful lot, probably more than some of the bars.

I remember when they were doing some carpentry work up there [at the U&I], couple three months job. And at the end of the job, they [the carpenters] owed *them* [the women] money.

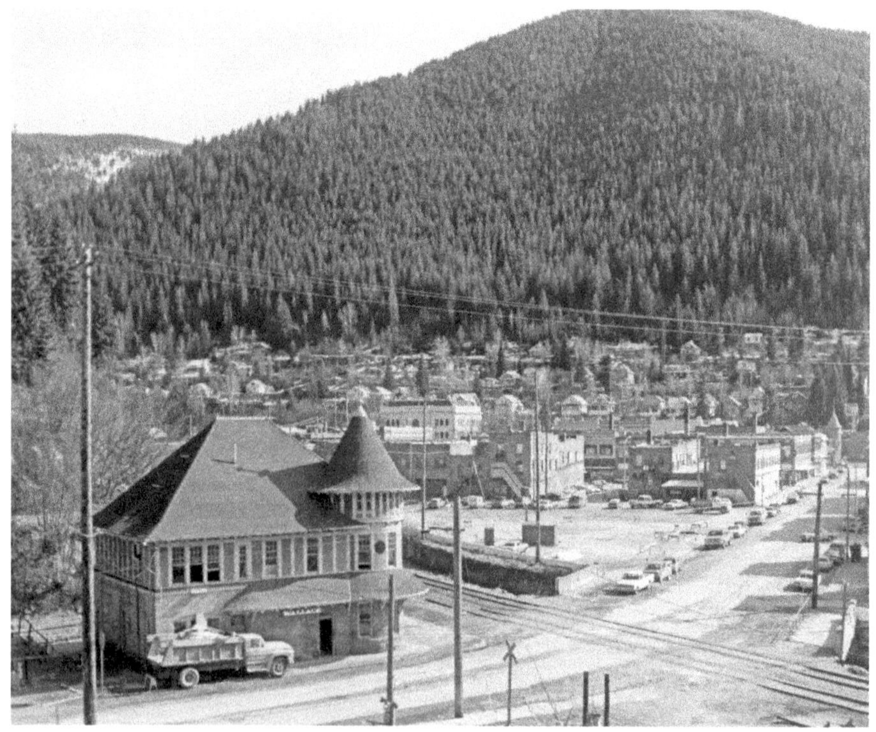

Looking south along Sixth Street from above the depot, before it was moved across the river to its current location. *Historic Wallace Preservation Society.*

Anonymous 11: [Like they were] pounding nails for free.

Posnick: They did, they owed *them* money....

I had a buddy one time, and we were playing golf, and I got a hole in one at the golf course, and it was Tuesday night men's night, so we had dinner and drank a bunch, we come back here, and he wanted to go to the whorehouses, but I said, "I'm going home. I'm going home." I'd already put the money away. And they didn't take checks, you know. There weren't any debit cards back then. But since I paid rent to the place, I just gave him a check from here and signed it. So he went up there and the next day he says, "Don't you *ever* leave me in a whorehouse again with a blank check." He goes, "Because that's like letting Colonel Sanders baby-sit your chicken."[278]

Anonymous 28, Miner Born and Raised in Wallace

I mean, everybody in town knew what was going on. And like I said, they were providing a service—they helped buy band uniforms, they kept Wallace going forward. They contributed to the community. They weren't strutting their shit up and down the street. So local mothers didn't really have nothing to say. Hell, half the local women knew their hubbies were going to get laid at the houses, but what could they say? Could they admit it back in those days in public? Hey, I ain't giving it to my old man the way he likes it, so he's going to the houses. You know. Or I'm getting a little older now, and he likes younger girls.

It was the best-known secret in the fucking state, if you know what I'm trying to say. Hell, the police knew what was happening. You went up there, you started to get a little rowdy or something? Fuck, cops arrested you right now, threw you downstairs and to fucking jail you went. Them girls were providing a service. They did not, in any way, reflect badly on this area. They provided a service.

They provided specialty services too. I can tell you for a fact back in 1977, there were special services to be had.

What kind of specialty services?
Are you seeing how kinky I am or what's your point in this?

Well, that's what they say, that if you want something—
You can pay for it. We're talking about, the girls would take a guy, strip him down, put him in a bubble bath, scrub him out and then have him. You know, good guys coming out of work from the mine. Had an old partner who ended up married one of those girls. He just loved the way she gave him those bubble baths....

And he married her. Did they stay in town here?
They're still here.

Who can I talk to about that?
Boy, that would be a tough one. You don't want to walk up to one of those girls and say, hey old pro, let me ask you a couple of questions, you know? How do you do that discreetly? I mean, we all know. I know three of them and all three of them, they're definitely good women, they raised good kids and take great care of them. I don't think their kids know. So how do you tell someone to go and say, hey you old pro, let me ask you a question. You know what I mean? That's just wrong.

I would have to promise them that it would be—
No, it's just wrong to point you in that direction. Do you know what I'm trying to say?

But I feel like their stories need to be told because people are telling stories about them. I feel like their perspective needs to be shared, you know?
But don't their privacy—

Absolutely, I wouldn't name them—
Need to be respected?

I wouldn't name them by name or anything.
No, no, I mean, for someone to point you in that direction. Doesn't their privacy need to be respected?

...Most of the town didn't know which girls were which, because when they walked through town they dressed down. They treated themselves very well out in public. And if you happened to be on the street and see one that you happened to know, nobody ever pointed them out and said, yeah, I know that hooker.... It was a fact of life that was the best-known secret ever kept in this area.[279]

Different Perspectives

Most of my research participants accepted sex work in the Silver Valley as a part of life, and they expressed support for its existence. Many even said they wished we still had the brothels around. But, in addition to the discussion with Shewmaker featured in the fourth chapter, I had a couple of conversations with people who offered insight to extend the narrative further.

"Yours Is a Historical Perspective. Mine Is Very Much Personal."

I deleted the names, locations and some parts of this conversation out of respect for my informant and her family. Ellipses and brackets indicate editing for clarity and privacy.

We moved [away from Wallace] because my stepmom, who was a prostitute up there, was treated horribly by pretty much everybody in town [after she married my dad].

Why did they treat her horribly?
Because she was a prostitute.

And that was it?
Yeah. If she was any girl on the street they wouldn't have cared, but my dad's family treated her horribly.... I don't care what people say. They did not treat her good. They didn't treat [my stepmom] good.... Was it an accepted part? Yeah, OK, I mean you could say it was an accepted part of Wallace society, but it wasn't accepted like, "Come over for tea"; it wasn't like that at all. And the reason that [my stepmom] left, the reason that Dad and [she] left was because my grandpa and grandma and that whole side of the family treated her horrible because she was a whore. And my stepmom was abused horribly as a kid. And I don't mean just emotionally, like physically. Think of the worst possible scenario for a kid. That was what my stepmom went through.... Not everybody is trying to pay off college loans.

Did [she] *tell you what she went through?*
That's why I am so adamant that this not like somebody paying for fucking college. You know what I mean? It's just so much, old school. If we're going to seriously talk about old school prostitution, it's nothing like—it wasn't

even fucking close to a real lifestyle at all. Have you heard that, ever? That that's not really, whatever people think of prostitution now, isn't the same as prostitution then?

There weren't many options for women, right? Back then?
There weren't?

No.
There weren't or there were?

I don't think there were, no.
For some there were. [My stepmom's sister] turned her on to prostitution at the age of sixteen. [Her sister] and her mother. She didn't *decide* to go into prostitution. She was *forced* to go into prostitution by her mom and her sister....

How did [her sister] *get into it? Was it her mom?*
I don't know how [she] got into it.... I never heard or even asked how [she] got into it. I can only imagine, they lived a hard fucking life; like, whatever I went through as a kid was fucking nothing compared to what [my stepmom] and [her sister] went through when they were kids. And I mean, physical abuse, like all kinds of crazy shit.

Sexual abuse?
I never heard about sexual abuse. Never heard about sexual abuse with regard to [my stepmom]. I don't know about [her sister], and [they] had different dads, so I'm not sure about that.... They grew up in [a city]; they were like [city] street people. And [my stepmom's] mom was batshit crazy. They were all fucking crazy.

Did [your stepmom and her sister] *have the same mom?*
Yeah. And there's more kids. They weren't like the only kids. Two of them did stints in prison. They were just fucked up, a fucked up group of people. But I don't know how [her sister] got into prostitution.... I know [my stepmom] had a pimp for a long time and he brought her over here and [her sister] brought her over here.

How far apart were they?
I don't know exactly, but [her sister was] quite a bit older than her, maybe like eight to ten years older than [my stepmom].

It's hard for me to imagine turning out my younger sister, you know.
And your *daughter*. I mean, it wasn't just [her sister]. It was their mom, too. It's fucking disgusting. And [my stepmom] was horribly abused physically by her dad.... Back in those days when a kid got in trouble or whatever, they would send them to Catholic school, not just Catholic, but like reform school, that's what [my stepmom] got sent to. Her dad was an abusive, alcoholic piece of shit that beat the hell out of her and she ended up in Catholic reform school, like *she* did something wrong. It's not the same now, I mean, shit's different now, but it's kinda why I feel so strongly about the whole industry. It's not just some good girls working their way through college, it's... I don't believe that if you have innate self-respect that you do that for any reason. As bad as my life ever was, there was not a part of me that was ever like, "Aww fuck it, I don't have anything else. Might as well just..."

You'll never get that self-respect back.... *Yours* is a historical perspective. *Mine* is very much personal. And it's way more emotional. Way more, it affects a whole family. It's not just—everybody knew she was a whore. Everybody [in Wallace] knew she was a whore. And you can either live with the stigma, as stupid as that sounds in these days. It is what it is.... Because there was shame involved. It's not historic; it was shame. Because everybody made her feel bad for what she was. My dad's family. And the truth is, she was just an abused lost woman. And then when she was old enough to make her own decisions, her family couldn't accept who she had been.

What did she do afterward?
She married my dad and became a housewife. You know what I mean? She made dinner and started fresh. That's why we moved. Everybody in Wallace knew who she was, but nobody [where we moved] knew who she was.

So people didn't accept her in the community regardless of how accepted people say it was.
Regardless of not just that, but regardless of how she went on to live her life. When she was with my dad, she wasn't a prostitute anymore. It wouldn't have mattered. It wouldn't have mattered what she did. OK, maybe twenty years down the road it would have changed the minds of people, but you can be here for like a month and hear people go, "ba ba ba ba ba, ba ba ba ba ba." If you're living right, it's OK. If you're not, it's depressing. There's a lot of hurt there.... It's hard to grow up with that and break those walls down and be open. It's hard.... The thing is, everybody made mistakes. Back in those days, everybody did. And when you live in a small town, and your dad marries a prostitute, and your mom marries a guy who—my stepdad—ugh,

all of my stepdad's guy friends beat their wives. Including my stepdad. Every single fucking one of them. It was just a different time and it was a different mindset and not every man was like, "You don't hit your wives." It was *most* men in my life growing up, where, "Oh, yeah, yes, you do. If she pushes you enough, you fucking smack the shit out of her."[280]

Lori Bunde, Wallace High School Class of 1978

Some older women thought it was disgusting. I never heard a man complain about it. People didn't sit around and talk about it though. I don't remember my mom making any comments either. A few of my friends' parents divorced because of it. The guys, they didn't necessarily want sex, so they would just go up there and visit and sit around and chat. Because you could go up there and drink after hours. They could go up and have another drink. I was always curious, wanted to go up there, but you couldn't unless you were selling something. The maid would answer the door, and you could kinda look around and see some of the girls in there drinking coffee.

The girls would wear high heels and short little mink coats. They always looked classy. They looked like movie stars. We would be in awe watching them walk down the street. It was a treat to see one of them out and about. Pretty classy. Always looked perfect, beautiful nails. There was a couple that overdid the makeup, but there were a few times they would come in [to the print shop where I worked] without makeup on.

At least half of them had husbands and kids, maybe up to 70 percent. They missed out on a lot of their kids' lives. And it was like they lived two lives, one a secret life and one just a regular mom. It was just the money, the money was great.

They would say, "Honey you're so beautiful, you should do this. You might like it." Those girls were all beautiful. I don't remember ever seeing an ugly one. Teeth were perfect, lips, they were gorgeous. Looked like movie stars.

There was a couple of them, if they didn't get in to Western Union they would start panicking because their families were depending on the money. One girl came back into town with a black eye. She'd kept it a secret, and he beat her. She came back into town to get her stuff and move away....

Never heard any of them complain about nothing. Sometimes they would stay there and chat so they could stay out a little longer. There were a few of the girls who didn't really like it, but the money was too good to pass up. And once they were in it, was hard to get out, try a regular job but couldn't make anywhere near the same kinda money.[281]

8

End of an Era

What allowed it to continue was that Shoshone County was the wealthiest county in the state. With money comes influence.... We lost influence when the mining was devastated.

—Mayor Dick Vester, 2010

While the brothels in Wallace certainly served an economic need, money alone does not explain the high degree of acceptance that the town's residents express when discussing the presence of commercial sex. And even though the madams' donations to the city served a persuasive function that complemented the public image they cultivated, it would be a mistake to interpret their monetary contributions as bribery or extortion. City leaders understood they would lose their jobs if they did not serve the collective will of the community.[282] Thus, the sheriff and city council members chose not to override local preferences to impose the written laws of the state and federal government. Why did the brothels finally close down, then? One man argued, "What really demised the cathouses" was the departure of madams like Dolores and Loma and their "old time supervision" management style: "A bunch of young broads took these places over, and they went to shit."[283]

Most Wallace residents deny the credibility of any narrative that attributes the closure of the houses to the 1991 FBI raid. I didn't bring it up as a suggestion during any of the oral history interviews and yet my research participants often brought it up as a wrong-headed idea that needed to be dismissed. Mayor Vester told me, "A lot of people think the FBI raid caused the houses to go away, but probably it was more likely the general

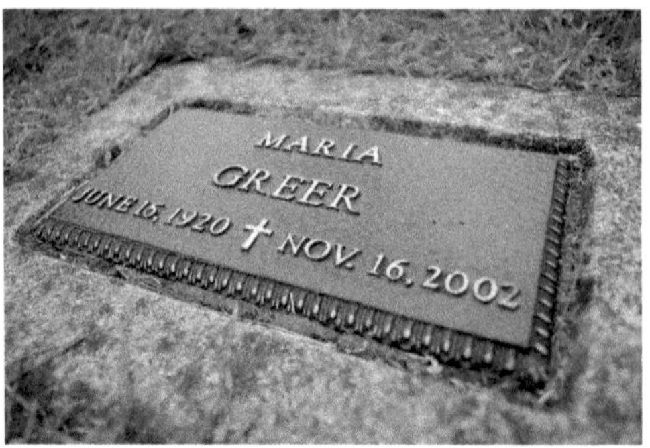

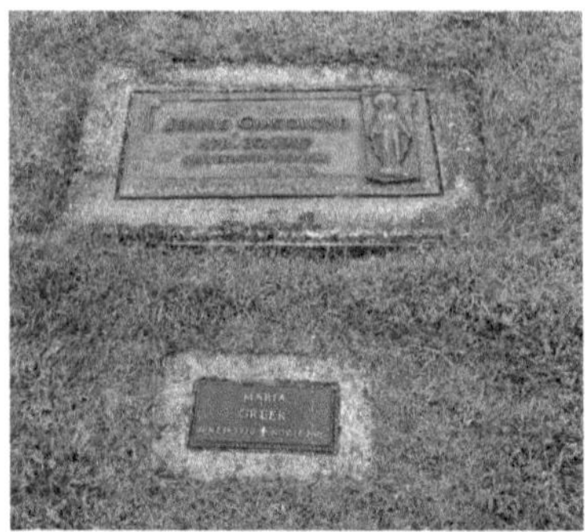

Dolores's grave in Tacoma, Washington, near the grave of her mother, Jennie. *Photos by Heather Branstetter.*

bad economy and AIDS." Gnaedinger, who was still good friends with the women at the U&I when it closed, affirms this interpretation, as does former police officer and local museum manager Butch Jacobson, who echoed, "The FBI did not close them down—it was the AIDS scare," adding, "my own personal opinion: I wish we still had them around." That's as close as it gets to an official story around town. The last brothel, the U&I Rooms, stayed open until just a few weeks prior to the raid, but people say the real reason the century of brothels ended was a result of AIDS and the lousy economy.

It does seem likely that federal intervention affected the timing of the houses' closure, however. Local historian and former Wallace District Mining Museum director John Amonson agreed with the majority opinion that a dwindling demand for services had contributed to the end of decriminalized prostitution in Wallace, but Amonson also named "the influence of the FBI's investigation" as the "final blow" that "brought what was probably a tapering off of that industry to a more abrupt halt."[284] Another research informant told me that "one of the FBI agents had went up there [to the U&I] and evidently in a 'moment of weakness' he told Tanya, 'better get out of town, something's coming down.' And that's why they left, just overnight."[285] In a move that many people would later describe as "overkill," the FBI sent agents over the Fourth of July Pass and raided almost every bar in Shoshone County from Cataldo to Mullan. They even accidentally raided one or two bars in neighboring Kootenai County as well. Amonson summarized the local attitude as he told a story about how one of the regional newspapers reported the incident. An article

> *talking about the* [outsider] *cop who was scared of the people here and left Wallace speeding "out of control with paranoia" and "perceived danger" was just overblown and sensationalized. When you're working underground you have* real *danger. There's enough serious crime in this country that when you have 150 FBI agents staying in Post Falls and coming to raid almost harmless crimes, it seems like a waste of money and resources. Busting into the bar with guns drawn was overkill. Things were just done differently around here.*[286]

In the valley, June 23, 1991, is now referred to as "Black Sunday" as a result. Federal officials focused on gambling and racketeering rather than prostitution and did "not so much [target] the machines as the local authorities who had allowed them to flourish."[287] Bar owners and bartenders say that the agents were also looking to make a large drug bust, but they never found anything related to that.[288] Money may have been part of the motivation as well: during the raid, FBI agents took more than a half a million dollars in cash from the bars and "seized all the video poker machines."[289] Locally, we know that an informal "phone tree" gave bars on the east end of the valley enough advance warning they were able to sneak out some of the machines as the agents moved from west to east along the I-90 corridor. The government kept the money and other confiscated property unless the bar owners or operators could prove in court that the earnings weren't the result of illegal activity.

About a month later, in a *New York Times* article titled "Gambling Raid Angers Mining Town," Egan wrote:

> *It wasn't exactly a surprise when, on the morning of June 23, Federal agents from all over the West raided virtually every bar here in Shoshone County and found more than 200 video poker machines.... What is so perplexing to residents of the panhandle of north Idaho, and to outsiders as well, is why the Federal Bureau of Investigation used such a show of force.... Not since the late 19th century, when Federal troops were sent here to battle union organizers, have so many Government agents moved so heavily against one community in the region.*[290]

This narrative, repeated on the streets of Wallace and in the newspapers, was difficult for the FBI to counter. It was a clear case of big government versus a small town trying to get by in a changing economy. The federal agents didn't care enough to look into the Silver Valley interest until a few disgruntled sheriff's deputies complained about corruption.

As a result of the raid, the U.S. Justice Department tried Sheriff Frank Crnkovich on allegations that he violated the RICO (Racketeer Influenced and Corrupt Organizations) Act. The two trials following the FBI raid revealed the extent to which Shoshone County's sheriffs learned to respond to the community's wishes. After bragging that he had never lost a case, the prosecutor for the well-funded U.S. Office of Public Integrity tried the sheriff twice in a federal court and failed to make the case both times. Because the jury was not persuaded by the government's attempt to turn the sheriff into a scapegoat responsible for one hundred years of gambling and prostitution, the first case resulted in a mistrial and the second ended in the sheriff's acquittal.

When I asked Crnkovich's defense lawyer, Sam Eismann, what his main argument was, he said:

> *They* [the prosecution] *had all this fancy gear. So the jury could listen to all the* [surveillance] *tapes, high-tech stuff. So in my argument I stood up, and I said, "Well, I'm sorry I don't have all this high-tech equipment, I can't afford it, I guess the government can. But what this case is really about is," and I wrote on the board that "Frank's a* scapegoat.*" And it stayed there during the whole argument, you know, and a couple of jurors after the trial said, "That guy was nothing but a scapegoat." So if you can put out a little keyword like that in some trials it helps.*

A few others were prosecuted along with the sheriff. Terry Douglas, who began working for Prendergast Amusement in 1978, put his own case into perspective this way: "Now, I bought the [electronic gambling] business March 14, 1989. Three-fourteen-eighty-nine. And then on six-twenty-three-ninety-one, twenty-seven months later, the feds tried to blame me for a hundred years of gambling in Shoshone County."[291] Douglas was sentenced to house arrest. Merrill Field, who also ran a machine business, did not want to revisit the incident and talked with me reluctantly. "They were not after prostitution—they were after me and my machines.... That cost me $200,000," he claimed. Field said most of that money was from vending machines and jukeboxes, though, not gambling machines. Again, he added bitterly, "I don't really want to think about it. Lost two hundred grand."[292] Even if the federal government was not interested in the prostitution angle, the investigation and prosecution needed to include the houses in the case because a successful conviction

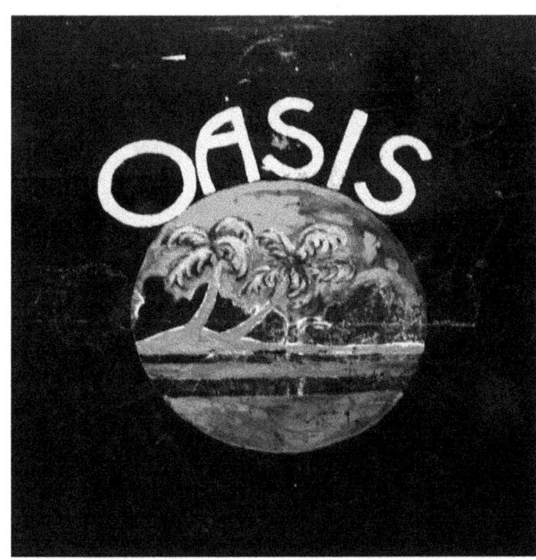

Oasis door in the 1980s. *Oasis Bordello Museum; photo by Heather Branstetter.*

under the RICO Act required evidence of more than one kind of corruption.[293]

When I interviewed Eismann in 2010, he told me that the investigation began sometime between 1987 and 1989, after five sheriff's deputies took records from the Shoshone County Sheriff's Office and brought them to the FBI's office in Coeur d'Alene, Idaho, or Spokane, Washington. Eismann explained that the FBI conducted a two-year investigation prior to the raid. He mentioned that the FBI "bought a tavern" and "bought a whorehouse up there.... And they had that all [set up] with [the ability to record] videotape and were catching pay-offs and stuff.... And there were some people on there that shouldn't have been, like law enforcement people.... A couple guys rolled over and said there was graft and corruption and payoffs." Eismann further told me that "a few days before the trial, they [the U.S. Justice Department attorneys] brought in like sixty or seventy audio tapes and probably forty or fifty video tapes, and I had to review all those at the last minute to see what was on them." Eismann recalled listening to these tapes, especially "some of the phone calls on the day of the raid. Like one person would call somebody: 'Oh, the FBI's in town.' And the other person would say, 'Well, don't say anything, this might be taped,' and then he'd still blab on, you know, it was really something." The FBI has not yet sent the files I requested through a Freedom of Information Act submission almost two years ago, so this part of the history is still rather open-ended.

Even though Crnkovich was not convicted, the whole episode

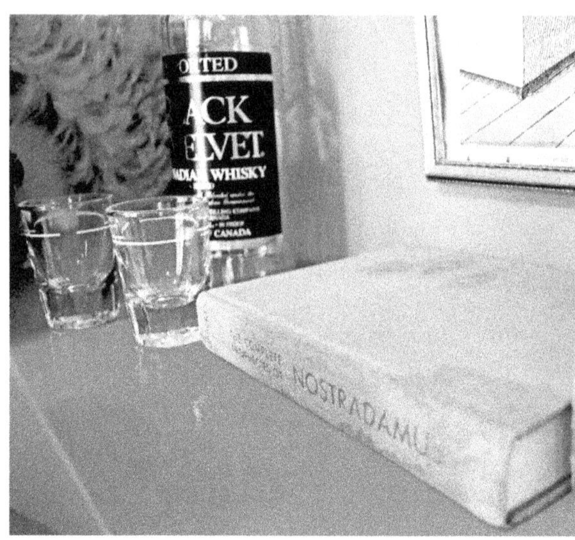

Black Velvet and Nostradamus. *Oasis Bordello Museum display; photo by Heather Branstetter.*

> *broke his spirit. You go through one of these graft and corruption cases, for some reason, it doesn't matter if you're found not guilty. It haunts them the rest of their lives. It's just amazing to me. It just totally changes them. I think you go into a phase where you just want to be undercover because you've been through this whole public spectacle, and I bet you think everybody's staring at you and talking about you, all this stuff, you know, even though you're not guilty.*[294]

Eismann explained that he'd told one of the prosecuting attorneys:

> *What you really ought to do is get up there and get to know these folks. Get to know why they do what they do. Get to know the history of the community. Get to know why they have to have poker machines in their bars to survive. You know I said, "It's a different world up there, and maybe that will help you understand this, and maybe we can get this case dismissed."*
>
> *"I don't need to do that," the justice department's lawyer responded, "I've tried these cases* [before] *and I've never lost one."*

Apparently the trials didn't examine the women who worked in the brothels in too much depth, but they did talk about the houses as a part of the community's willingness to accept illegal activity:

We went into what the gals did—the community accepted them up there. They served a purpose, I think, in the old mining days. And they gave band uniforms. They bought the police department a new police car. But it wasn't the result of any graft, it was just being good to the community, really, for allowing them to be there. The madams did good public relations. I think something like that probably was necessary in the old days, you know, it kept the local gals safe. That's what some of the old-timers told me.[295]

Ginger's attorney echoed Eismann's feelings about the work and the attitude of the town:

That was probably the highlight of my career. Oh, it was awesome. Ginger takes the stand, and I can't be in there because I'm representing her. She says, "Well, Mister Butler," who was just an asshole federal prosecutor. But he was easy; we creamed him. We made creamed corn out of him. Anyway, she goes, "I don't remember ever saying that, in fact, you know, I really don't remember much about that whole thing." And then Merrill [Field] *took the stand and said, "I am sorry, I think I have the flu. So I'm not going to be very helpful to you because I don't feel good and I'm not sure I can remember everything." He left the stand never testifying to anything. And of course it was dismissed. It truly was the top of my career. I never met people that were so smart that had created a web, which they did here, to protect themselves and never stopped. You can charge me, send me to jail but this is my family and I'm protecting my family. It was awesome.*

And they didn't lie. They just didn't cooperate. Butler came back to me and said, "I hate you." And I said, "I know you do...but it's Wallace, Idaho; you should have called me before you ever came to town. I could have probably helped you with some of what you wanted, but you don't walk into Wallace and arrest the people that you arrested and destroy the businesses you destroyed trying to get the poker machines and think you're going to get anywhere. You can do that maybe in Coeur d'Alene, maybe you can do that in Washington, D.C., but you met your match in Wallace, Idaho."[296]

Regardless of whether or not there was money exchanged, the graft allegation was not confirmed, and the interpretation that aligns best with the locals' understanding is this: yes, the madams and the gambling contributed a lot of money to the community, in both official and unofficial ways, but it didn't amount to corruption. One man who used to be a miner and then an accountant told me that many people in the valley felt entitled to the privilege of gambling and prostitution because they had been here for 120 years and "our tax revenues built the state." Unfortunately, he added, "We never had the population to get the money back" because the "state is very controlling" and the politicians in charge in the southern part of Idaho "don't like to give up any power to the counties."[297] This interpretation aligns with a historic feeling that Boise stole the capital from northern Idaho along with the tax revenues that never returned to the Silver Valley. It also fits alongside the narrative that both state and federal government have bullied the isolated valley. Many people confirm the existence of a "golden fund" for the city that came from illegal activity, but it was a consensual agreement—there was neither extortion nor secrecy about it. The perspective that "at least it is honest and out in the open" is nearly identical to the argument made in response to the "north Idaho whiskey rebellion" raid of 1929. It was the way things had always been done, and it was the expectation of the community that it would continue as long as there was money in it. And so it did, for more than a century.

Notes

Introduction

1. S. Hansen, personal interview, 2010.
2. Hart and Nelson, *Mining Town*, 135.
3. Egan, "Gambling Raid Angers Mining Town," A18.
4. Goldman, *Gold Diggers and Silver Miners*, 155.
5. Magnuson, personal interview, 2014.
6. Anonymous 28, personal interview, 2016.

Chapter 1

7. Powell, "Beyond Molly B'Damn," 90.
8. Wallace City Council Minute Books, 30–36.
9. Hart and Nelson, *Mining Town*, 132.
10. Magnuson, *Coeur d'Alene Diary*, 216–41.
11. Grover, *Debaters and Dynamiters*, 33.
12. Ibid., 1–2.
13. Ibid., 35–37.
14. Clemets, quoted in Barton, "Appendix B: Informant Transcriptions," 325, emphasis added.
15. Amonson, personal interview, 2010.
16. Kottkey, quoted in Barton, "Appendix B: Informant Transcriptions," 152.
17. Laite, "Historical Perspectives," 742.
18. Murphy, *Mining Cultures*, 77.
19. Powell, "Beyond Molly B'Damn," 109.
20. Butler, *Daughters of Joy, Sisters of Misery*, 100.

21. Ibid., 101.
22. Caron, personal interview, 2014.
23. Murphy, *Mining Cultures*, 77.
24. Powell, "Beyond Molly B'Damn," 40.
25. Ibid.
26. Laite, "Historical Perspectives," 753.
27. Rosen, *Lost Sisterhood*, 139.
28. Magnuson, personal interview, 2010.
29. Ibid., 2014; Harman, personal interview, 2014.
30. Magnuson, personal interview, 2014.
31. Wallace City Council Minute Books, 7.
32. Powell, "Beyond Molly B'Damn," 57.
33. Ibid.
34. *Idaho Press*, March 18, 1905.
35. Powell, "Beyond Molly B'Damn," 57.
36. City of Wallace Police Record Journal, April 1893–June 1908, quoted in Powell, "Beyond Molly B'Damn," 43.
37. Powell, "Beyond Molly B'Damn," 137.
38. Sanborn-Perris Map, 1901 and Wallace City Council Minute Books, March 1897–October 14, 1901, May 27, 1901.
39. Powell, "Beyond Molly B'Damn," 52.
40. Ibid., 138.
41. Ibid., 99–100.
42. *Idaho State Tribune*, October 5, 1904, quoted in Powell, "Beyond Molly B'Damn," 45–46.
43. Harman, personal interview, 2014.
44. *Idaho Press*, March 4, 1909, quoted in Powell, "Beyond Molly B'Damn," 46.
45. *Times*, May 5, 1907, quoted in Powell, "Beyond Molly B'Damn," 46.
46. *Spokesman Review*, August 1909, quoted in Hart and Nelson, *Mining Town*, 138.
47. Powell, "Beyond Molly B'Damn," 156.
48. City of Wallace Council Proceedings Journal, March 1897–October 14, 1901, November 26, 1900, quoted in Powell, "Beyond Molly B'Damn," 104.
49. Powell, "Beyond Molly B'Damn," 104.
50. *Spokesman-Review*, "Mayor Connor Praised," May 4, 1903.
51. Hart and Nelson, *Mining Town*, 136–38.
52. *Spokesman-Review*, "Is Found Guilty of Gambling" and "Wallace Notes," May 10, 1903.
53. *Spokesman-Review*, "To Shut Off Red Lights," May 19, 1903.
54. Powell, "Beyond Molly B'Damn," 104.
55. Ibid.
56. Henderson, "Low-Key Brothels Survive Lousy Wallace Economy," B2.
57. Goldman, *Gold Diggers and Silver Miners*, 161, emphasis in original.
58. Roizen, personal interview, 2010.
59. Cunningham and Shah, "Decriminalizing Indoor Prostitution."

60. Bisschop, Kastoryano and van der Klaauw, "Street Prostitution Zones and Crime."
61. Kottkey, quoted in Barton, "Appendix B: Informant Transcripts," 151–53.
62. Houchin, personal interview, 2014.
63. Murphy, *Mining Cultures*, 78.
64. Petrik, *No Step Backward*, 58.
65. Powell, "Beyond Molly B'Damn," 104.
66. City of Wallace Council Minute Book, October 28, 1901–September 10, 1906, April 24, 1905, quoted in Powell, "Beyond Molly B'Damn," 104–5.
67. Anonymous 23, personal interview, 2010; Gordon, "Child's-Eye View," WDMM; Magnuson, personal interview, 2010; Rice, phone interview, 2010. Magnuson added that a gate or fence like this would not have been the sort of thing to appear on these maps.
68. Powell, "Beyond Molly B'Damn," 158.
69. Ibid., 155–58.
70. Ibid., 155.

Chapter 2

71. *Congregationalist and Christian World*, August 22, 1908, quoted in the *Idaho Press*, 3 September 1908, reprint of W.M. Proctor, "Random Portraits, Brave Work in the Coeur d'Alenes." Also appears in Powell "Beyond Molly B'Damn," 144, and Smith, "It Will All Come Out in the Courtroom," 53–54.
72. "White-Slave Traffic Act," H.R. 12315, 61st Cong., 36 Stat. 825, 1910.
73. Abbott, *Sin in the Second City*, 207, 291.
74. Powell, "Beyond Molly B'Damn," 142.
75. Ibid., 143.
76. Ibid., 151.
77. Smith, "It Will All Come Out in the Courtroom," 54–55.
78. Wegars, "Inmates of Body House," 45.
79. *Daily Idaho Press*, October 31, 1908.
80. Powell, "Beyond Molly B'Damn," 151.
81. *Daily Idaho Press*, January 18, 1908; December 6, 1909.
82. *Wallace Press-Times*, December 30, 1915, 6.
83. Rosen, *Lost Sisterhood*, 116.
84. Ibid., 129–30.
85. Ibid., 125–27. Rosen notes that Jane Addams conducted a study of prostitution especially concerned with the vulnerability of immigrant women.
86. *Idaho Press*, December 6, 1906, quoted in Powell, "Beyond Molly B'Damn," 48.
87. Shoshone County Courthouse District Court Records, Index to Register of Criminal Actions, Proceedings Book B, 497.
88. Ibid., 495 and 496.
89. Powell, "Beyond Molly B'Damn," 152.

90. *Wallace Press-Times*, December 4, 1915, 1.
91. Ibid., December 5, 1915, 6.
92. Shoshone County Courthouse District Court Record No. 655.
93. Ibid.
94. Ibid.
95. Ibid.
96. Magnuson, personal interview, 2014.
97. Shoshone County Courthouse District Court Records, Nos. 598–602.
98. Powell, "Beyond Molly B'Damn," 108.
99. Ibid., 109.
100. Wallace City Council Minute Book, 14.
101. Ibid., 30–36.
102. Ibid., 207.
103. "Keeping Fit to Fight," Potlatch Forests Papers.
104. Hart and Nelson, *Mining Town*, 138.
105. Quoted in Brandt, *No Magic Bullet*, 72.
106. "Next Steps," Potlatch Forests Papers.
107. War Department Commission on Training Camp Activities poster, "Military" folder, Potlatch Forests Papers.
108. "Prostitution" folder, historic file, WDMM.
109. Wallace City Council Minute Book, 165.
110. Quoted in Brandt, *No Magic Bullet*, 76.
111. Amonson, personal interview, 2010.
112. Gordon, "Child's-Eye View," WDMM.

Chapter 3

113. Murphy, *Mining Cultures*, 43.
114. Ibid.
115. Ibid., 61.
116. Barton, "Final Report," 63.
117. Laite, "Historical Perspectives," 753.
118. Smith, "It Will All Come Out in the Courtroom," 37.
119. Magnuson, personal interview, 2014.
120. Ibid.
121. *Wallace Press-Times*, January 12, 1916, 1.
122. Ibid. See also *Wallace Press-Times*, January 16, 1916, and *Mullan Progress*, April 28, 1916.
123. Smith, "It Will All Come Out in the Courtroom," 66–67.
124. *Wallace Press-Times*, November 5, 1917, 1.
125. Wallace City Council Minute Book, 30–31.
126. Magnuson, personal interview, 2014.

127. Smith, "It Will All Come Out in the Courtroom," 97–99. Prohibition had starved the county's communities of money. Clemets echoes this sentiment: "Things, just in general, just began to fall apart, you know. Just like any other place would be if you took all the revenue away from the city" (quoted in Barton, "Appendix B: Informant Transcriptions," 291).
128. Smith, "It Will All Come Out in the Courtroom," 170–71.
129. Shoshone County Courthouse District Court Records No. 1144, dismissed October 2, 1922, by District Judge Albert H. Featherstone and Prosecutor John L. Fitzgerald.
130. Barton, "Final Report," 65.
131. Clemets, quoted in Barton, "Appendix B: Informant Transcriptions," 322–23.
132. Hargrove, quoted in Smith, "It Will All Come Out in the Courtroom," 95.
133. Smith, "It Will All Come Out in the Courtroom," 110–16.
134. Quoted in ibid., 180.
135. Quoted in ibid., 181.
136. *Wallace Press-Times*, November 14, 1929, 1.
137. Quoted in Smith, "It Will All Come Out in the Courtroom," 183.
138. Smith, "It Will All Come Out in the Courtroom," 169.
139. Ibid., 167, 180.
140. Quoted in ibid., 244.
141. Quoted in ibid., 241.
142. Quoted in ibid., 242.
143. Quoted in ibid., 244.
144. Quoted in ibid., 196.
145. Smith, "It Will All Come Out in the Courtroom," 214.
146. Quoted in Smith, "It Will All Come Out in the Courtroom," 160, 166–67.
147. Quoted in Barton, "Appendix B: Informant Transcriptions," 320.
148. Kottkey, quoted in Barton, "Appendix B: Informant Transcriptions," 134.
149. Quoted in ibid., 323–24.
150. Gordon, "Child's-Eye View," WDMM Papers.
151. Ibid.
152. Murphy, quoted in Caron, WDMM.
153. Wallace City Council Minute Books, 1931–39, 423.
154. Ibid., 501.
155. Quoted in Barton, "Appendix B: Informant Transcriptions," 39.

Chapter 4

156. "Tommy 2Ts," personal interview, January 4, 2016.
157. Anonymous 1, personal interview, 2016; Anonymous 10, personal interview, 2014; Anonymous 22, personal interview, 2016; S. Hansen, personal interview, 2010.

158. Benson, email correspondence, 2016.
159. Vester, personal interview, 2010.
160. Kearney, personal interview, 2015; Salyer, personal interview, 2015.
161. Anonymous 27, personal interview, 2010.
162. Morrison, personal interview, 2010.
163. Stuebner, "Wallace Defends Prostitution."
164. Miles, "Community Attitudes Toward Prostitution," 40–42.
165. Ibid., 15.
166. Hart and Nelson, *Mining Town,* 135.
167. Ibid.
168. Magnuson, personal interview, 2014.
169. Shewmaker, personal interview, 2016.
170. Ibid.
171. Ibid., Facebook correspondence, 2016.
172. Anonymous 2, personal interview, 2016.
173. Henderson, "Low-Key Brothels Survive Lousy Wallace Economy," B2.
174. Stuebner, "Wallace Defends Prostitution."
175. Richards, "Once-Wild Wallace Quiets Down," D1.
176. Truean, personal interview, 2014.
177. Gnaedinger, personal interview, 2010; Houchin, personal interview, 2014; Michael, personal interview, 2014.
178. Anonymous 5, personal interview, 2014.
179. Hart and Nelson, *Mining Town*, 150.
180. Shoshone County Sheriff's Office (SCSO) files, WDMM.
181. Houchin, personal interview, 2014; Anonymous 26, personal interview, 2016.
182. B. Mooney, personal interview, 2014.
183. Gnaedinger, personal interview, 2010.
184. Ibid.
185. S. Hansen, personal interview, 2010.
186. Greer, personal interview, 2015.
187. Ibid.
188. Ibid.
189. Morrison, personal interview, 2010.
190. Ibid.
191. Gnaedinger, personal interview, 2010.
192. Johnson, personal interview, 2015. Johnson obtained this information secondhand after he began managing a hotel located in the building that had been the Lux from 1977 to 1986.
193. "Larry," personal interview, 2014.
194. Anonymous 5, personal interview, 2014; Anonymous 31, personal interview, 2014; B. Mooney, personal interview, 2014.
195. Douglas, personal interview, 2010.
196. Stewart, personal interview, 2010.
197. Higgins, personal interview, 2010.

198. Anonymous 1, personal interview, 2016.
199. U.S. census data, 1920 and 1930.
200. Pederson, quoted in Caron, WDMM.
201. Barnard-Stockbridge Collection; Mogenson, personal interview, 2014; Pederson, quoted in Caron, WDMM; Truean, personal interview, 2014.
202. Morrison, personal interview, 2010.
203. Ibid.
204. Roizen, personal interview, 2010.
205. Mayfield, phone interview, 2014; Gordon, "Child's-Eye View," WDMM.
206. Magnuson, personal interview, 2014.
207. Feiler, phone interview, 2010.
208. Ibid.
209. Magnuson, personal interview, 2014.
210. Gnaedinger, personal interview, 2010.
211. Anonymous 2, personal interview, 2016.
212. Anonymous 1, personal interview, 2016.
213. Anonymous 23, personal interview, 2010.
214. Anonymous 25, personal interview, 2014; Posnick, personal interview, 2010.
215. Caron, WDMM.
216. "Tommy 2Ts," personal interview, 4 January 2016.
217. Anonymous 1, personal interview, 2016.
218. Anonymous 23, personal interview, 2010; Houchin, personal interview, 2014; Michael, personal interview, 2014.
219. Eismann, personal interview, 2010.
220. Morrison, personal interview, 2010.
221. *New York Times*, "5 Brothels Shut in an Idaho Town," 17. Note: the article lists the number of miners who died as ninety-two, but it was actually ninety-one.
222. Henderson, "Low-Key Brothels Survive Lousy Wallace Economy," B2.
223. Ibid.
224. Ibid.
225. Jacobson, phone interview, 2014.
226. Schonhanes, personal interview, 2014.
227. Morrison, personal interview, 2010.
228. Magnuson, personal interview, 2014. Magnuson was also the deputy prosecutor in this case.
229. Ibid.
230. Anonymous 18, personal interview, 2016.

Chapter 5

231. *State of Idaho v. Russell Ralsten*, 1957, 1–24.
232. Magnuson, personal interview, 2014.
233. Ibid.
234. Letter from Gary C. Randall, May 18, 1972, Oasis Museum Papers.

235. Anonymous 31, personal interview, 2014.
236. SCSO file 515, WDMM.
237. SCSO files 968 and 1125, WDMM.
238. SCSO files 1082, 957 and 958, WDMM.
239. SCSO file 838, WDMM.
240. SCSO file 682, WDMM.
241. Ibid.
242. Magnuson, personal interview, 2010 and 2014.
243. State of Idaho Penal Code, 18-5601, 18-5606 and 18-5608.
244. State of Idaho Penal Code, 18-5613 and 18-5614.
245. SCSO file 1047, WDMM.
246. SCSO file 1094, WDMM.
247. Escobedo, *From Coveralls to Zoot Suits*, 44.
248. Escobedo, "Zoot Suit Riots."
249. Escobedo, *From Coveralls to Zoot Suits*, 182.
250. "Grand Coulee Dam Facts," Grand Coulee Dam Visitor's Guide.
251. *Missoulian*, September 26, 1971, 16.
252. Ibid., October 1, 1971, 11.
253. Ibid., October 6, 1971, 9.
254. Marconi, personal interview, 2016.
255. Goluboff, *Vagrant Nation*.
256. Solove, "HIPAA Turns 10," 22–28.
257. Albert, *Brothel*, 105.
258. Berkenkotter, *Patient Tales*, 34.
259. Ibid.

Chapter 6

260. Magnuson, personal interview, 2014.
261. Ibid., 2010.
262. Anonymous 1, personal interview, 2016.
263. Garr, personal interview, 2014.
264. Anonymous 15, personal interview, 2016.
265. Magnuson, personal interview, 2014.
266. Anonymous 1, personal interview, 2016; Parsons, personal interview, May 2016.
267. Parsons, personal interview, June 2016.
268. Anonymous 22, personal interview, 2016.
269. Greer, personal interview, 2015.
270. *New York Times*, "5 Brothels Shut in an Idaho Town," 17.

Chapter 7

271. "Arnuff," personal interview, 2015.
272. "Claus," personal interview, 2015.
273. Schaeffer, phone interview, 2014.
274. Roberts, personal interview, 2014.
275. Anonymous 4, personal interview, 2015; Anonymous 12, personal interview, 2015; "Frosty," personal interview, 2015.
276. Anonymous 10, personal interview, 2014; Anonymous 31, personal interview, 2014; B. Mooney, personal interview, 2014.
277. J. Hansen, personal interview, 2010.
278. Posnick, personal interview, 2010; Anonymous 11, personal interview, 2010; Anonymous 27, personal interview, 2010.
279. Anonymous 28, personal interview, 2016.
280. Anonymous 26, personal interview, 2015.
281. Bunde, personal interview, 2016.

Chapter 8

282. Eismann, personal interview, 2010.
283. Anonymous 1, personal interview, 2016.
284. Amonson, personal interview, 2010.
285. S. Hansen, personal interview, 2010.
286. Amonson, personal interview, 2010.
287. Egan, "Gambling Raid Angers Mining Town," A18.
288. Polla, personal interview, 2015; Posnick, personal interview, 2010.
289. Egan, "Gambling Raid Angers Mining Town," A18.
290. Ibid.
291. Douglas, personal interview, 2010.
292. Field, phone interview, 2014.
293. "An Act Relating to the Control of Organized Crime in the United States," 18 U.S.C. § 1961, 1970.
294. Eismann, personal interview, 2010.
295. Ibid.
296. Anonymous 2, personal interview, 2016.
297. Austin, personal interview, 2015.

Bibliography

Personal Interviews and Correspondence

Aiken, Katherine G. Personal interview. July 30, 2010. Coeur d'Alene, Idaho.
Amonson, John. Personal interview. August 3, 2010. Wallace, Idaho.
Austin, John. Personal interview. June 25, 2015. Medimont, Idaho.
Benson, Jim. Email correspondence. March 22, 2015.
Breidenbach, Susan. Personal interview. November 14, 2015. Olympia, Washington.
Breidt, Cheri. Facebook correspondence. January 6, 2016.
Bunde, Lori. Personal interview. April 3, 2016. Wallace, Idaho.
Carlson, Bill. Personal interview. August 5, 2010. Wallace, Idaho.
Caron, Dick. Personal interview. July 16, 2010. Wallace, Idaho.
———. Personal interview. July 28, 2010. Wallace, Idaho.
———. Personal interview. June 11, 2014. Wallace, Idaho.
Clark, Dan. Personal interview. May 24, 2015. Wallace, Idaho.
Covi, Joann. Personal interview. July 31, 2015. Wallace, Idaho.
Douglas, Terry. Personal interview. August 17, 2010. Kellogg, Idaho.
Eismann, Sam. Personal interview. July 22, 2010. Coeur d'Alene, Idaho.
Feiler, Mike. Phone interview. August 16, 2010.
Field, Merrill. Phone interview. July 31, 2014.
Garr, Penny. Phone interview. August 1, 2014.
Gnaedinger, Kristi. Personal interview. July 28, 2010. Wallace, Idaho.
———. Personal interview. August 6, 2014. Wallace, Idaho.
Greer, Dee. Personal interview. November 11, 2015. Osburn, Idaho.
Hansen, John. Personal interview. July 19, 2010. Silverton, Idaho.
———. Personal interview. July 20, 2014. Beaver Creek, Idaho.
Hansen, Sue. Personal interview. July 19, 2010. Silverton, Idaho.
———. Personal interview. July 20, 2014. Beaver Creek, Idaho.
Harman, Tom. Personal interview. July 9, 2014. Silverton, Idaho.

Higgins, Rod. Personal interview. July 8, 2010. Wallace, Idaho.
Houchin, Patti. Personal interview. August 13, 2014. Wallace, Idaho.
Howell, Eric. Personal interview. October 6, 2015. Kellogg, Idaho.
Jacobson, Butch. Phone interview. July 17, 2014.
Johnson, Tim. Personal interview. August 5, 2015. Wallace, Idaho.
Kearney, Janet. Personal interview. June 10, 2015. Wallace, Idaho.
———. Personal interview. June 12, 2015. Wallace, Idaho.
Kearney, Tim. Personal interview. June 10, 2015. Wallace, Idaho.
———. Personal interview. June 12, 2015. Wallace, Idaho.
Lavigne, Mike. Personal interview. May 6, 2016. Wallace, Idaho.
Magnuson, Richard. Personal interview. August 5, 2010. Wallace, Idaho.
———. Personal interview. July 30, 2014. Wallace, Idaho.
Marconi, Hugh. Personal interview. August 3, 2016. Wallace, Idaho.
Mayfield, Michelle. Phone interview. July 30, 2014.
McNair, Virginia. Facebook correspondence. January 7, 2016.
McNeill, Maggie. Personal interview. July 26, 2015. Sandpoint, Idaho.
Michael, Penny. Personal interview. August 13, 2014. Wallace, Idaho.
Mogensen, Lynn. Personal interview. June 27, 2014. Wallace, Idaho.
Mooney, Bill. Personal interview. July 18, 2014. Wallace, Idaho.
Mooney, Karen. Personal interview. July 18, 2014. Wallace, Idaho.
Morrison, Gary. Personal interview. July 7, 2010. Post Falls, Idaho.
Parsons, Sonny. Personal interview. May 6, 2016. Wallace, Idaho.
———. Personal interview. June 17, 2016. Wallace, Idaho.
Pellissier, Maurice. Personal interview. July 11, 2014. Wallace, Idaho.
Pennington, Edith. Phone interview. July 20, 2016.
Pennington, Norval. Phone interview. July 20, 2016.
Polla, Tammy. Personal interview. June 26, 2015. Mullan, Idaho.
Posnick, John. Personal interview. August 5, 2010. Wallace, Idaho.
Rice, Justin. Phone interview. July 16, 2010.
Roberts, Chuck. Personal interview. July 30, 2014. Wallace, Idaho.
Roizen, Ron. Personal interview. July 21, 2010. Wallace, Idaho.
Salyer, Max. Personal interview. June 10, 2015. Wallace, Idaho.
———. Personal interview. June 12, 2015. Wallace, Idaho.
Sanborn, Chase. Personal interview. July 30, 2015. Wallace, Idaho.
Schaeffer, Patty. Phone interview. August 5, 2014. Idaho.
Schonhanes, Tammy. Personal interview. August 12, 2014. Wallace, Idaho.
Shewmaker, Holly. Facebook correspondence. January 22, 2016.
———. Personal interview. February 8, 2016. Wallace, Idaho.
Stewart, Julie Austin. Personal interview. June 18, 2010. Wallace, Idaho.
Stroud, Patrick. Email correspondence. January 6, 2016.
———. Phone interview. January 6, 2016.
Thatcher, Randy. Email correspondence. January 21, 2016.
Truean, Eva. Personal interview. June 9, 2014. Wallace, Idaho.
Vester, Dick. Personal interview. August 6, 2010. Wallace, Idaho.
Yanzick, Bumper. Facebook correspondence. January 10, 2016.

Young, Cathy. Facebook correspondence. January 6, 2016.
Zent, Rick. Personal interview. March 22, 2016. Wallace, Idaho.

Anonymous Personal Interviews and Correspondence

Anonymous 1. Personal interview. May 6, 2016. Wallace, Idaho.
Anonymous 2. Personal interview. January 4, 2016. Wallace, Idaho.
Anonymous 3. Personal interview. July 30, 2014. Wallace, Idaho.
Anonymous 4. Personal interview. December 20, 2015. Wallace, Idaho.
Anonymous 5. Personal interview. August 12, 2014. Wallace, Idaho.
Anonymous 6. Personal interview. May 6, 2016. Wallace, Idaho.
Anonymous 7. Personal interview. August 2, 2015. Wallace, Idaho.
Anonymous 8. Personal interview. July 19, 2010. Anonymous Town.
———. Personal interview. July 20, 2014. Anonymous Town.
———. Personal interview. August 2, 2015. Wallace, Idaho.
Anonymous 9. Personal interview. July 19, 2010. Anonymous Town.
Anonymous 10. Personal interview. July 18, 2014. Wallace, Idaho.
Anonymous 11. Personal interview. August 5, 2010. Wallace, Idaho.
Anonymous 12. Personal interview. December 20, 2015. Wallace, Idaho.
———. Personal interview. January 4, 2016. Wallace, Idaho.
Anonymous 13. Personal interview. January 4, 2016. Wallace, Idaho.
Anonymous 14. Personal interview. July 1, 2015. Anonymous Town.
———. Phone interview. June 28, 2015.
Anonymous 15. Personal interview. January 28, 2016. Anonymous Town.
Anonymous 16. Personal interview. July 31, 2015. Wallace, Idaho.
Anonymous 17. Personal interview. July 31, 2015. Wallace, Idaho.
Anonymous 18. Personal interview. July 19, 2014. Anonymous Town.
———. Personal interview. June 25, 2016. Wallace, Idaho.
Anonymous 19. Personal interview. April 2, 2016. Wallace, Idaho.
Anonymous 20. Personal interview. January 4, 2016. Wallace, Idaho.
Anonymous 21. Personal interview. February 28, 2016. Wallace, Idaho.
Anonymous 22. Personal interview. February 28, 2016. Wallace, Idaho.
Anonymous 23. Personal interview. July 7, 2010. Wallace, Idaho.
Anonymous 24. Personal interview. January 4, 2016. Wallace, Idaho.
Anonymous 25. Personal interview. July 18, 2014. Wallace, Idaho.
Anonymous 26. Personal interview. July 30, 2015. Wallace, Idaho.
Anonymous 27. Personal interview. August 5, 2010. Wallace, Idaho.
Anonymous 28. Personal interview. February 20, 2016. Wallace, Idaho.
———. Personal interview. May 6, 2016. Wallace, Idaho.
Anonymous 29. Personal interview. July 31, 2015. Wallace, Idaho.
Anonymous 30. Email correspondence. January 12, 2016.
———. Email correspondence. January 26, 2016.
Anonymous 31. Personal interview. July 18, 2014. Wallace, Idaho.
"Arnuff, James." Personal interview. November 4, 2015. Wallace, Idaho.
"Bobby." Personal interview. August 12, 2014. Wallace, Idaho.

"Claus, Santa." Personal interview. December 1, 2015. Wallace, Idaho.
"Frosty." Personal interview. December 20, 2015. Wallace, Idaho.
"Larry." Personal interview. August 12, 2014. Wallace, Idaho.
"Squirley." Personal interview. November 4, 2015. Wallace, Idaho.
"Tommy 2Ts." Personal interview. January 4, 2016. Wallace, Idaho.
———. Personal interview. August 4, 2016. Wallace, Idaho.

Kellogg Museum Archival Collection

Sanborn Map Company. *Wallace, Shoshone County, Idaho* [map]. Scale not given. New York: Sanborn Map Company, 1927 and 1948.

North Idaho College Special Collections

Barton, David. "Appendix B: Informant Transcriptions." Idaho Panhandle National Forests Oral History Study, 1980. Conducted and compiled by Barton, 1980.
———. "Final Report." Idaho Panhandle National Forests Oral History Study. Conducted and compiled by Barton, 1980.

Oasis Museum Papers

Oasis Rooms Letters and Business Records.

University of Idaho Library Special Collections and Archives

Barnard-Stockbridge Ledgers and Papers, MG 362.
Barnard-Stockbridge Photograph Collection, PG 8.
Potlach Forests Papers, MG 96.
Wegars, Priscilla. "'Inmates of Body House': Prostitution in Moscow, Idaho, 1885–1910." A version also appeared in *Idaho Yesterdays* 33 (Spring 1989): 25–37.

Wallace District Mining Museum (WDMM) Archival Collection

Branstetter, Heather. Brothel Project files.

Caron, Dick. Prostitution file.
Gordon, Mary White. "A Child's-Eye View." Autobiographical written narrative.
Prostitution folder. Historic file.
Sanborn-Perris Map Co., Limited. *Wallace, Shoshone County, Idaho* [map]. Scale 50 feet to an inch. New York: Sanborn-Perris Map Co., Limited, 1891, 1892, 1896, 1901, 1905, 1908.
Shoshone County folder. Historic file.
Shoshone County Sheriff's Office (SCSO) records.

Government Records

"An Act Relating to the Control of Organized Crime in the United States." 84 Stat. 941, 1970. Enacted as Pub. Law 91-451.
Shoshone County Courthouse District Court Records, Wallace, ID.
State of Idaho. Penal Code Title 18, Chapter 56, Nos. 18-5601, 18-5606, 18-5608, 18-5613, 18-5614.
State of Idaho v. Russell Ralsten. Probate Court of Shoshone County. Preliminary Hearing, July 11, 1957. Reprint in Jerry Keane's personal collection.
United States Department of Commerce, Census Bureau. "Fifteenth Census of the United States—1920." Washington, D.C.: National Archives and Records Administration, n.d.
———. "Fourteenth Census of the United States—1930." Washington, D.C.: National Archives and Records Administration, n.d.
Wallace City Council Minute Books, City Hall, Wallace, ID.
"White-Slave Traffic Act." H.R. 12315, 61st Cong., 36 Stat. 825, June 25, 1910. Enacted as Pub. Law 277.

Theses and Unpublished Scholarship

Bisschop, Paul, Stephen Kastoryano and Bas van der Klaauw. "Street Prostitution Zones and Crime." Discussion Paper 9038, Institute of Labor Economics, Bonn, Germany, 2015.
Cunningham, Scott, and Manisha Shah. "Decriminalizing Indoor Prostitution: Implications for Sexual Violence and Public Health." Working Paper 20281, National Bureau of Economic Research, Cambridge, MA, 2014.
Miles, Robert. "Community Attitudes Toward Prostitution." Master's thesis, Washington State University, 1977.
Powell, Cynthia S. "Beyond Molly B'Damn: Prostitution in the Coeur d'Alenes, 1880–1911." Master's thesis, Central Washington University, 1994.
Smith, Donna Krulitz. "'It Will All Come Out in the Courtroom': Prohibition in Shoshone County, Idaho." Master's thesis, University of Idaho, 2004.

Published Sources

Abbott, Karen. *Sin in the Second City: Madams, Ministers, Playboys, and the Battle for America's Soul*. New York: Random House, 2007.

Aiken, Katherine G. *Idaho's Bunker Hill: The Rise and Fall of a Great Mining Company, 1885–1981*. Norman: University of Oklahoma Press, 2005.

Albert, Alexa. *Brothel: Mustang Ranch and Its Women*. New York: Random House, 2001.

Berkenkotter, Carol. *Patient Tales: Case Histories and the Uses of Narrative in Psychiatry*. Columbia: University of South Carolina Press, 2008.

Brandt, Allan M. *No Magic Bullet: A Social History of Venereal Disease in the United States Since 1880*. New York: Oxford University Press, 1985.

Butler, Anne M. *Daughters of Joy, Sisters of Misery: Prostitutes in the American West, 1865–90*. Urbana-Champaign: University of Illinois Press, 1987.

Egan, Timothy. "Gambling Raid Angers Mining Town." *New York Times*, August 20, 1991, A18.

Escobedo, Elizabeth R. *From Coveralls to Zoot Suits: The Lives of Mexican American Women on the World War II Home Front*. Chapel Hill: University of North Carolina Press, 2013.

———. "Zoot Suit Riots." *PBS American Experience Documentary*.

Fahey, John. *The Days of the Hercules*. Moscow: University of Idaho Press, 1978.

Goldman, Marion S. *Gold Diggers and Silver Miners: Prostitution and Social Life on the Comstock Lode*. Ann Arbor: University of Michigan Press, 1981.

Goluboff, Risa. *Vagrant Nation: Police Power, Constitutional Change, and the Making of the 1960s*. New York: Oxford University Press, 2016.

"Grand Coulee Dam Facts." *Grand Coulee Dam Visitor's Guide*. http://www.gcdvisitor.com/grand-coulee-dam-facts.

Grover, David H. *Debaters and Dynamiters: The Story of the Haywood Trial*. Caldwell, ID: Caxton Press, 2006. Originally published Corvallis: Oregon State University Press, 1964.

Hart, Patricia, and Ivar Nelson. *Mining Town: The Photographic Record of T.N. Barnard and Nellie Stockbridge from the Coeur d'Alenes*. Seattle: University of Washington Press, 1984.

Henderson, Paul. "Low-Key Brothels Survive Lousy Wallace Economy." *Seattle Times*, November 8, 1982, B2.

Holbrook, Stewart. *The Rocky Mountain Revolution*. New York: Henry Holt and Company, 1956.

Laite, Julia Ann. "Historical Perspectives on Industrial Development, Mining, and Prostitution." *The Historical Journal* 52, no. 3 (2009): 739–61.

MacKell, Jan. *Brothels, Bordellos, and Bad Girls: Prostitution in Colorado, 1860–1930*. Albuquerque: University of New Mexico Press, 2004.

———. *Red-Light Women of the Rocky Mountains*. Albuquerque: University of New Mexico Press, 2009.

Magnuson, Richard C. *Coeur d'Alene Diary: The First Ten Years of Hardrock Mining in North Idaho*. Portland, OR: Binford and Mort, 1968.

Murphy, Mary. *Mining Cultures: Men, Women, and Leisure in Butte, 1914–41*. Urbana-Champaign: University of Illinois Press, 1997.

New York Times. "5 Brothels Shut in an Idaho Town." November 5, 1973, special edition, 17.

Petrik, Paula. *No Step Backward: Women and Family on the Rocky Mountain Mining Frontier, Helena, Montana, 1865–1900*. Helena: Montana Historical Society Press, 1987.

Richards, Bill. "Once-Wild Wallace Quiets Down—Last Red Light on I-90 Is Removed." *Seattle Post-Intelligencer*, September 16, 1991, D1.

Rosen, Ruth. *The Lost Sisterhood: Prostitution in America, 1900–1918*. Baltimore: Johns Hopkins University Press, 1982.

Solove, Daniel J. "HIPAA Turns 10: Analyzing the Past, Present and Future Impact." *Journal of AHIMA* 84, no. 4 (April 2013): 22–28.

Stoll, William T. *Silver Strike: The True Story of Silver Mining in the Coeur d'Alenes*. Moscow: University of Idaho Press, 1991. Originally published by Little, Brown, and Company, 1932.

Stuebner, Steven. "Wallace Defends Prostitution—'A Mining Town Needs Brothels.'" *Idaho Statesman*, n.d. [between 1987 and 1991], 1A and back page. Clipping in author's collection.

Newspapers

Coeur d'Alene Miner
Coeur d'Alene Press
Daily Idaho Press
Idaho Press
Idaho Statesman
Kellogg Evening News
Missoulian
Mullan Mirror
Mullan Progress
New York Times
North Idaho Press
Seattle Post-Intelligencer
Silver Valley Trader
Spokesman-Review
Times
Wallace Miner
Wallace Press-Times

Index

K

L

M

N

O

R

S

T

U

W

About the Author

"Congratulations, Dr. Branstetter," my University of North Carolina PhD committee said when its members welcomed me back into the defense room after debating my qualifications. At that point, I didn't even know if I still wanted to be a professor. I have come to believe the force of inertia, like nostalgia, is powerful in ways we often underestimate. Inertia kept me in the Southeast for three more years, even as I continued to work on the brothel project during the summers.

I was born and raised in the Silver Valley, and in 2015, I finally quit my professor career to move back to Wallace and finish this book, which I started in 2010. Throughout this writing, my grandma Jo's inner strength and moral compass inspired me. Her lifelong partner, my grandpa Ken, was the Wallace Depot's station agent for about a quarter of a century. He passed away in September 2016, but I keep them both in my heart and am grateful for their guidance and choice to raise their family in Wallace, because growing up in the Silver Valley taught me to keep my mind open, my heart judgment-free and my spirit independent. I hope this work serves my local community by helping to preserve its rich history and collective memory.

www.ingramcontent.com/pod-product-compliance
Lightning Source LLC
LaVergne TN
LVHW052339100826
845147LV00021B/1122

* 9 7 8 1 4 6 7 1 3 6 5 6 3 *